WILL ROGERS
IN HOLLYWOOD

WILL ROGERS IN HOLLYWOOD

By Bryan B. Sterling
and Frances N. Sterling

Foreword by James Blake Rogers

A Lou Reda Book
CROWN PUBLISHERS, INC. ★ NEW YORK

In remembrance of
P a u l a M c S p a d d e n L o v e
curator, 1938–1973
and

R o b e r t W i l l a r d L o v e
manager, 1938–1975
Will Rogers Memorial
Claremore, Oklahoma

Our project began in Claremore,
and, with their usual dedication and infectious enthusiasm,
Bob and Paula urged us on.
They did not live to see us complete our research,
yet their own devotion to Will Rogers has remained the beacon
that lights the path for all of us who follow their lead.

Frances and Bryan Sterling

Published by Crown Publishers, Inc., One Park Avenue, New York, New York 10016, and simultaneously in Canada by General Publishing Company Limited

Manufactured in the United States of America

Library of Congress Cataloging in Publication Data
Main entry under title:
Will Rogers in Hollywood
Includes index.
1. Rogers, Will, 1879–1935. 2. Moving-picture actors and actresses—United States—Biography.
3. Comedians—United States—Biography. I. Sterling, Bryan B. II. Sterling, Frances N.
PN2287.R74A36   1984   791.43′028′0924
[B]   83-15298
ISBN 0-517-55264-7

Book design by Deborah Waxberg

10 9 8 7 6 5 4 3 2 1
First Edition

CREDITS

Twentieth Century-Fox Film Corporation

Ambassador Bill. Copyright 1931, Twentieth Century-Fox Film Corporation. All rights reserved. *Business and Pleasure.* Copyright 1931, Twentieth Century-Fox Film Corporation. All rights reserved. *A Connecticut Yankee.* Copyright 1931, Twentieth Century-Fox Film Corporation. All rights reserved. *The County Chairman.* Copyright 1935, Twentieth Century-Fox Film Corporation. All rights reserved. *David Harum.* Copyright 1934, Twentieth Century-Fox Film Corporation. All rights reserved. *Doctor Bull.* Copyright 1933, Twentieth Century-Fox Film Corporation. All rights reserved. *Doubting Thomas.* Copyright 1935, Twentieth Century-Fox Film Corporation. All rihts reserved. *Down to Earth.* Copyright 1932, Twentieth Century-Fox Film Corporation. All rights reserved. *Handy Andy.* Copyright 1934, Twentieth Century-Fox Film Corporation. All rights reserved. *Happy Days.* Copyright 1929, Twentieth Century-Fox Film Corporation. All rights reserved. *In Old Kentucky.* Copyright 1935, Twentieth Century-Fox Film Corporation. All rights reserved. *Life Begins at Forty.* Copyright 1935, Twentieth Century-Fox Film Corporation. All rights reserved. *Lightnin'.* Copyright 1930, Twentieth Century-Fox Film Corporation. All rights reserved. *Mr. Skitch.* Copyright 1933, Twentieth Century-Fox Film Corporation. All rights reserved. *So This Is London.* Copyright 1930, Twentieth Century-Fox Film Corporation. All rights reserved. *State Fair.* Copyright 1933, Twentieth Century-Fox Film Corporation. All rights reserved. *Steamboat Round the Bend.* Copyright 1935, Twentieth Century-Fox Film Corporation. All rights reserved. *They Had to See Paris.* Copyright 1929, Twentieth Century-Fox Film Corporation. All rights reserved. *Too Busy to Work.* Copyright 1932, Twentieth Century-Fox Film Corporation. All rights reserved. *Young as You Feel.* Copyright 1931, Twentieth Century-Fox Film Corporation. All rights reserved. *Stand Up and Cheer.* Copyright 1934, Twentieth Century-Fox Film Corporation. All rights reserved.

Photographs obtained through the courtesy of the Academy of Motion Picture Arts and Sciences, the National Air and Space Museum, Smithsonian Institution, the National Archives, and the Penguin Collection are properly identified in the captions.

Credit for permission to print a manuscript by Clarence G. Badger: Unpublished manuscript by Clarence G. Badger, courtesy of the International Museum of Photography at George Eastman House and its film curator, George C. Pratt.

CONTENTS

ACKNOWLEDGMENTS

We thank the many individuals and organizations who gave their time and knowledge, and who assisted us in the preparation of this book:

Artist

Charles Banks Wilson

Authors

Ben Lucien Burman (*Steamboat Round the Bend*, 1935)
Homer Croy (*They Had to See Paris*, 1929; *Down to Earth*, 1932; *Our Will Rogers*, 1953)

Director of Photography

Hal Mohr, A.S.C. (*David Harum*, 1933; *State Fair*, 1933; *The County Chairman*, 1935)

Directors

David Butler (*A Connecticut Yankee*, 1931; *Business and Pleasure*, 1931; *Down to Earth*, 1932; *Doubting Thomas*, 1935)
John Ford (*Doctor Bull*, 1933; *Judge Priest*, 1934; *Steamboat Round the Bend*, 1935)
Henry King (*Lightnin'*, 1930; *State Fair*, 1933)
George Marshall (*Life Begins at Forty*, 1935; *In Old Kentucky*, 1935)

Film Historians

William K. Everson
Paul Killiam

Motion-Picture and Stage Performers

Lew Ayres (*State Fair*, 1933)
Hermione Baddeley (*Charles Cochran Revue*, London, 1926)
Tom Brown (*Judge Priest*, 1934)
Harry Carey, Jr. (friend of the family)
Olive Carey (friend of the family)
Charles Collins (friend of the family)
Dorothy Stone Collins (*Three Cheers*, 1928–29, friend)
Viola Dana (silent-picture star)
Andy Devine (*Doctor Bull*, 1933)
Fifi Dorsay (*They Had to See Paris*, 1929; *Young as You Feel*, 1931)
Janet Gaynor (*State Fair*, 1933)

Sterling Holloway (*Life Begins at Forty*, 1935; *Doubting Thomas*, 1935)
Rochelle Hudson (*Doctor Bull*, 1933; *Mr. Skitch*, 1933; *Judge Priest*, 1934; *Life Begins at Forty*, 1935)
Maria Jeritza (friend)
Myrna Loy (*A Connecticut Yankee*, 1931)
Frank Luther (DeReszke Singer)
Joel McCrea (*Lightnin'*, 1930; *Business and Pleasure*, 1931)
Maureen O'Sullivan (*So This Is London*, 1930; *A Connecticut Yankee*, 1931)
Irene Rich (*Water, Water Everywhere*, 1919; *Strange Boarder*, 1920; *Jes' Call Me Jim*, 1920; *Boys Will Be Boys*, 1921; *The Ropin' Fool*, 1922; *Fruits of Faith*, 1922; *They Had to See Paris*, 1929; *So This Is London*, 1930; *Down to Earth*, 1932)
Virginia Sale (friend)
Anne Shirley (*Steamboat Round the Bend*, 1935)
Anne Shoemaker (*Ah, Wilderness!*, 1934)
Kent Taylor (*David Harum*, 1934; *The County Chairman*, 1935)
Regis Toomey (friend)
Peggy Wood (*Almost a Husband*, 1919; *Handy Andy*, 1934)
Evelyn Venable (Mohr) (*David Harum*, 1934; *The County Chairman*, 1935)
Keenan Wynn (friend of Mary Rogers)

Motion Picture and Television Country House & Hospital

Bill Campbell, director of public relations
John Pavlick, director

Private Contributors

Carol Baker
Lyman Brewster, Alaskan pioneer
William A. Kelly, executive vice-president, Elberton Granite Association, Inc.
Richard Allen Sanders, foremost authority on early Lockheed aircraft
Louise Walden, Kelly Monument Co.

Producer

Hal E. Roach, Sr. (producer and friend)

Publications

American Classic Screen
American Film Institute Catalogues

American Magazine
Catalogue of Copyright Entries
Coronet Magazine
Dramatic Mirror
Exhibitor's Trade Review
Film Daily
Film Daily Year Book
Filmgoers' Annual
Film Index
Filmlovers' Annual
Film Play Journal
Film Spectator
Houston Chronicle
Journal of Popular Film
Kansas City Star
Liberty Magazine
Life Magazine
Literary Digest
London Daily Mail
London Times
Los Angeles Times
Motion Picture Almanac
Motion Picture Classic
Motion Picture Daily
Motion Picture News Booking Guide
Motion Picture Herald
Motion Picture Journal
Motion Picture News
Motion Picture Performers
Motion Picture Weekly
Motion Picture World
New Republic
Newsweek
New York American
New York Evening Post
New York Journal
New York Mirror
New York Sun
New York Times
New York World Telegram
Photoplay Magazine
Reader's Digest
The Reel Journal
Rob Wagner's Script
Saturday Evening Post
Saturday Review of Literature
Theatre
Time
The Tulsa World
Variety
Wid's Year Book

FOREWORD

When I learned that Bryan and Fran Sterling were doing this book on Dad's movies I was very pleased, for I have believed that such a book is long overdue. For some strange reasons most of the people who have written about his life seem to treat his movie career as a sort of sideline and often infer that he looked at it in the same way.

No matter how much Dad joked and kidded about his various activities, I can't think of anything he did, be it roping, playing polo, writing, acting, or his talks and radio programs, that he didn't go at whole hog. I can remember many nights coming home well after midnight and seeing the light on in Mother and Dad's bedroom. He would be reading a book or story or script that might make a good picture, and generally he would have an early morning call for the picture he was working on at the time.

It would be difficult to say how he looked at himself professionally, but one thing is certain, to him his work was very serious business. He always had a lot of jokes about his acting ability, or lack of it; I have never talked to anyone, however, who ever worked with him who didn't have the highest regard for his acting talent.

It is a shame that many of his silent films, made between 1918 and 1927, have been lost. The few that remain show an amazng versatility of roles from the dramatic to pure slapstick. *The Ropin' Fool,* which he produced and made to show off his trick roping, was not successful in 1922, but today it is one of the most popular of his silents.

It has always been a mystery, and I might add a rather sore point, to me that Twentieth Century-Fox has been reluctant to re-release his sound films. As Leonard Maltin says in his book *The Great Movie Comedians*, "Although Will Rogers' humor was frequently topical, it endures today, in his writings and speeches as well as in his films, because he touched on the very heart of things. Because human nature has not changed, Rogers' wit has remained fresh. His films are a delight because they are a living vehicle for his ideas and ideals; they deserve to be shown again and again to remind us that in a world filled with trouble and hatred, there is still room for such a good man."

This is why I wish to thank Bryan and Fran for putting out this book. The movies were a big part of Dad's life and Will Rogers was a very big part of the movies. Like Mr. Maltin, I wish all of you could see some of them.

James Blake Rogers

ABOUT THIS BOOK

In this book we have compiled the information we collected. We have spent literally years trying to find certain missing data, checking and then rechecking. We spent uncounted weeks in various government offices in Washington, D.C., and surrounding Maryland and Virginia, where old files are stored. We hunched over records—some dusty, some moldy—and interviewed dozens of people who could furnish us with firsthand information. In Los Angeles, we stooped over long-forgotten fan and trade magazines and, after hours, sometimes extracted only a single kernel of additional knowledge. We sat in front of dim microfilm readers, staring at pages of newspapers long out of circulation, until our eyes tried to convince us that the lines of type converged at the edge of the page. We stood—and occasionally sat—for days, checking index cards, reading statistics, comparing summaries, matching names, weighing conflicting information, pitting one authority against another, tracing original documents, contrasting different interpretations, reading reports and accounts, studying reviews and news items, and, finally, categorizing all that information into usable form.

There is some information in other summaries that we chose not to list, primarily because we found conflicting data, and we could not go back to original sources no longer extant to verify them. Therefore, rather than repeat uncorroborated or suspect information, we omitted it completely. Take for example the running time of films. On one particular film, we came across three reputable sources—all claiming to have seen the film—reporting the length of it as 64 minutes, 84 minutes, and 104 minutes respectively. Rather than go with the most renowned of the reviewers, we omitted the information, or rather misinformation. We thought it wiser simply to say, in effect, "We don't know," than to perpetuate wrong data. When a copyright was renewed, we stated so; when we could find no indication of a renewal, we made no mention of it—we did not wish to state the obvious.

Periodically the project would be put aside for a more pressing one. Months would pass without a single fact being added. Then came another research trip to Washington or California, and once again we had to visit all the same, now-familiar, centers, because new material had been added, private collections had become public in the meantime, and the search began anew. Unfortunately some facts may never be determined at this late stage.

If this description of our research gives the impression that it was an unbearable chore, do not believe it. True, it is concentrated work, but exciting. Like a detective, one follows a trail —mile after mile, hour after hour—and then, without warning, you find another clue, a serendipity, a rare gem whose existence you did not even suspect. Director Clarence Badger's personal account was such a treasure. The news item that Will

Rogers appeared as an "extra" in a Mabel Normand film—as a lark and perhaps as a studio-concocted publicity stunt—was such a lucky strike. The fact that major studios, supposedly efficient in the ways of protecting their property, would overlook the need to renew their copyrights, was such a find; the discovery that the production of Jes' Call Me Jim was held up because four-year-old Jimmy Rogers had the measles, was perhaps not of earthshaking importance, but it was an interesting discovery. (We knew that Will, Jr., the older son, did not catch measles until he was twenty-three years old—as Will Rogers commented: "He was a mighty big old boy to be measeling.")

And then there is information that we believe to be true, but that we omitted here. It is generally believed that Will Rogers wrote most of the titles (that is, dialogue and descriptions) for the Goldwyn films. Reviewers suspected it, audiences believed it, but no proof could be located. We cannot claim it, even though we, too, believe it. Another fact we do not list is whether a film is lost; several Will Rogers films thought to be lost forever, were found—hale and almost hearty. Since the early nitrate films will hypo—that is, disintegrate—it was feared that most of the early films would be lost. The fact that producers could not foresee any future interest in films already shown added to the negligence with which these films were handled. Boxes of Will Rogers' films were stored at one time in concrete "bunkers," set into the hillside behind Will's ranch house. While the danger of fire made such precaution necessary, it was hardly a scientific form of storage. After Will's California ranch was turned over to the state, the films were "stored" in a reputable Los Angeles warehouse, subject to the constant changes of temperature and humidity. Years went by, and no one even inspected them. Finally they were sent to the Will Rogers Memorial in Claremore, Oklahoma, for safekeeping. There they lay for a period in a vault, before Paula M. Love, the curator, and Robert W. Love, the manager, asked us to see whether we could find some benevolent source to assist in the preservation of these priceless films. The Loves had made inquiries where the conversion from the perishable and dangerous nitrate film to safety film could be done, and how much this would cost. There are very few places that are equipped even to handle nitrate film, and the cost, so they learned, would be astronomical. Unless a benefactor could be found, the Loves would simply have to sit by while those films would deteriorate right in the cans.

We made contact with several organizations, public and private, and government agencies, both state and federal, but the prospects were not good. At last we were successful. We found the best possible "angel," the Museum of Modern Art, in New York City. Eileen Bowser, the curator of its film divi-

sion (and film is, of course, modern art), proved to be the savior of the entire *Will Rogers* collection: the family-owned films, clips, trims, and outtakes, as well as the films still in storage at Twentieth Century-Fox. These films were inspected and graded as to immediate need for transfer to safety film. Those found to be in danger were processed at once; the balance is inspected regularly and transferred on a "need" basis. Negatives have been made, as well as fine-grain masters. Whatever footage is available today will be preserved; not another frame will be lost. Unfortunately this process was begun far too late. A large number of the silent films are missing at this time. Yet "missing" films do turn up.

In the family's collection of Will's films was "found" a copy of Judge Priest, at one time thought to be among the "lost" films. Another such lost film, A Connecticut Yankee, was "discovered" in Twentieth Century-Fox's own vaults in Australia. Eileen Bowser discovered one "positively lost" Will Rogers two-reeler, Jus' Passin' Through, made for Hal Roach. She found the film in vaults in Czechoslovakia—and since this was a silent film, naturally, the titles are in Czech. It will be translated so that we can learn just what it was that Will wrote.

You can now see why we would refrain from flatly stating that any film was "no longer extant." The fact that no copy may be in any public collection does not make it lost. There are a substantial number of private film collectors, each guarding the secret of his list of films like the number to a Swiss bank account. We personally know of such a collector who has a copy of a lost Goldwyn film, yet he will swear before the Supreme Court that he never even heard of it. That is just one such collector, and there are over a hundred across the country.

Perhaps we should have stated that certain films did no longer exist and let the readers prove us wrong, and in the process we could learn of the location of films we, too, think lost.

We also learned in the course of this research that the long-believed myth that Will Rogers was unsuccessful in his silent films—handed down from writer to writer like a treasured legacy—was just that, a myth. Nothing could be farther from fact. Artistically and critically, those silent films were acclaimed. One Glorious Day was chosen the foremost motion picture of 1922 by the National Board of Review—tantamount to today's Academy Award as best picture of the year. While we offer in these pages just a few reviews with limited quotations, we could have flooded these pages with praises. Since the vast majority of the reviews were complimentary, they were repetitive. Rogers' acting talent—thought to be nonexistent—is praised again and again. There were long lines forming to see some of Will Rogers' pictures, and once the theater was filled, moviegoers would patiently wait for the "next showing," a good hour and a half later.

In an interview with Mr. Lew Ayres, we discussed Will Rogers' acting ability. Said Mr. Ayres: "He [Will Rogers] was far ahead of his time. Not only as a human being, but as an actor, too. . . . I wish today I had just his talent as a performer. I consider him a fine actor, though apparently he would never admit it."

Why Mr. Goldwyn did not negotiate a new contract with Will Rogers we do not know. Many reasons have been advanced and suggest themselves, but the lack of artistic acclaim is not one of them. Yes, there were some adverse reviews, and we quote them, but they were the small minority and usually based on a personal dislike of Rogers' type of humor.

Herewith we present what we found.

CHRONOLOGY

1879   November 4, William Penn Adair Rogers born on his father's ranch, near Oologah, I.T. (Indian Territory), now Oklahoma.

1887   [–92] Attends schools (Drumgoole, near Chelsea, I.T.; Presbyterian Mission School, Tahlequah, I.T.; Harrell Institute, Muskogee, I.T.).

1890   Mary America Rogers (mother) dies.

1892   Willie Halsell College, Vinita, I.T. (attended approximately four years).

1896   Scarritt College Institute, Neosho, Missouri.

1897   [–98] Kemper Military School, Boonville, Missouri.

1898   Begins work as cowboy on the Ewing Ranch, Higgins, Texas.

1899   [–1902] Manages Rogers Ranch, attends roping contests and rodeos.

1902   Leaves for South America, via England; works for about five months with gauchos, then leaves for South Africa.

1903   South Africa, joins Texas Jack's Wild West Show, billed as the Cherokee Kid. Leaves to tour Australia and New Zealand with Wirth Brothers Circus.

1904   With Col. Zach Mulhall Show at St. Louis, Missouri (world's fair). A few vaudeville bookings in Chicago.

1905   With Mulhall Show at New York's Madison Square Garden, as part of horse fair. First New York vaudeville appearances. Vaudeville career begins, lasts to 1915, including three trips to Europe and Broadway musicals.

1908   November 25, marries Betty Blake, at Rogers, Arkansas.

1911   Clement Vann Rogers (father) dies. Birth of first son, Will, Jr., in New York City.

1912   [–13] Specialty act in Broadway show The Wall Street Girl, starring Blanche Ring.

1913   Birth of only daughter, Mary Amelia, at Rogers, Arkansas.

1914   London, England, in show Merry-Go-Round. Vaudeville in America.

1915   First airplane flight at Atlantic City, New Jersey. Appears in musical Hands Up, Ned Wayburn's Town Topics, and Ziegfeld's Midnight Frolic. Birth of second son, James Blake, in New York City.

1916   [–25] Ziegfeld Follies, with several intervals for motion pictures in California.

1918 Birth of third son, Fred. While working in *Follies* makes first motion picture (studio at Ft. Lee, New Jersey), *Laughing Bill Hyde.*

1919 Published *The Cowboy Philosopher on the Peace Conference* and *The Cowboy Philosopher on Prohibition.* Moves to California to begin motion-picture career with Goldwyn Studios.

1920 Fred Rogers, aged twenty months, dies during diphtheria epidemic.

1922 First radio broadcast (Pittsburgh, Pennsylvania). Produces and stars in his own motion pictures. Begins series of syndicated weekly articles (McNaught Syndicate), which continue to 1935.

1923 [–24] Stars in two-reel comedies for Hal Roach. Publishes *Illiterate Digest.*

1925 [–28] Travels all over America on lecture tours. [–27] Writes daily article "Worst Story I've Heard Today."

1926 London, England, appears for four weeks in the *Charles Cochran Revue.* Writes *Letters of a Self-Made Diplomat to His President.* Benefit for Florida hurricane victims. Made honorary mayor of Beverly Hills. Trip to Russia. [–35] Begins series of "Daily Telegrams," syndicated to over four hundred newspapers.

1927 First civilian to fly from coast to coast with mail pilots. Publishes *There's Not a Bathing Suit in Russia.* Made "ambassador-at-large of U.S." by National Press Club, Washington, D.C. Visits Mexico with Charles A. Lindbergh, as guest of Ambassador Dwight Morrow. Own benefit tour for Mississippi flood victims. Suffers serious gallstone attack, requiring surgery.

1928 [–29] Forgoes fully booked lecture tour and substitutes for friend Fred Stone in musical comedy *Three Cheers,* with Dorothy Stone.

1929 First sound film for Fox Film Corporation, *They Had to See Paris,* with Irene Rich. Publishes *Ether and Me,* account of gallstone operation. [–35] Twenty-one films for Fox.

1930 Radio broadcasts for E.R. Squibb & Sons.

1931 To London to observe Disarmament Conference. Self-financed benefit tour for drought victims in Southwest. Appears on national radio broadcast on unemployment, with President Hoover, Calvin Coolidge, Al Smith, and others. To Managua, Nicaragua, for self-financed benefit for earthquake and fire victims. [–32] To the Orient.

1932 Central and South American tour.

1933 [–35] Radio broadcasts for Gulf Oil.

1934 Trip around the world. Stars in Eugene O'Neill's stage play *Ah, Wilderness!* in San Francisco and Los Angeles, California.

1935 August 15, dies in plane crash with Wiley Post, famous pilot, near Barrow, Alaska.

A great tradition is that of Will Rogers. He ought to be taught in the schools because of what he embodied of the best of the Constitution and the Declaration of Independence.
He was as homely as a mud fence and yet as beautiful as a sunrise over an Oklahoma field of alfalfa.
Will Rogers was one of those individuals who we as Americans could call without embarrassment a great man.

CARL SANDBURG

An actor is a fellow that just has a little more monkey in him than a fellow that can't act.

WILL ROGERS (1879–1935)

1
SAMUEL GOLDWYN PRESENTS

THE BEGINNING

During the week of August 11, 1918, Florenz Ziegfeld, Jr., released a stern warning through the New York City newspapers. The producer of the incomparable Follies declared that he had exclusive contractual control of the professional services of every single member of the Follies cast, and that if any member attempted to appear in one of those new motion pictures without his permission, he, Ziegfeld, would obtain an injunction against the producer of any picture involved and would initiate a lawsuit for damages against any theater exhibiting such a film.

Unperturbed, Will Rogers continued to commute early each morning to the studio in Fort Lee, New Jersey, to complete filming his first motion picture, Laughing Bill Hyde. Sam Goldfish, the producer and president of Goldwyn Pictures Corporation (he would later change his name), also paid little heed to Ziegfeld's challenge.

The Ziegfeld Follies of 1918, starring Will Rogers, Marilyn Miller, Eddie Cantor, W. C. Fields, Ann Pennington, and Gus Minton, had opened on June 18. It was generally agreed that in the three years since Will Rogers had first appeared in a Ziegfeld production—the Midnight Frolic at the New Amsterdam Theatre Roof—he had become the single most important performer contributing to the success of the shows. And while it is true that Will was, as Billie Burke (Mrs. Florenz Ziegfeld) was to say, "Ziegfeld's greatest star," he never missed a performance, whether evening or matinee, during the entire filming. And as for "contractual control," all that existed between Ziegfeld and Rogers was a handshake.

At the very beginning of their business relationship, Ziegfeld had called in a secretary to draw up a contract. Rogers had looked at him. "A contract?" he had drawled. "We don't need a contract. You can trust me, and I know I can trust you." Ziegfeld, wary of such unorthodoxy, had asked Charles Dillingham, the famous producer, who happened to be in the office, to hear the simple agreement and to witness the handshake.

Why then had Ziegfeld bothered to issue the threat of retribution when he knew that he had no written contract with Will Rogers? The budding film industry had begun to lure away a number of important Broadway performers, and Ziegfeld believed that a warning in time might deter others from leaving the Follies in search of a film career. Perhaps, he thought, it was necessary to remind Will Rogers that no matter how successful his first film might be, there was still the matter of the 1918 Follies to be considered. If Ziegfeld thought for a moment that Will Rogers would forget his obligation—whether verbal or written—he did not know this man. No written contract could be more binding on Will than his word. He fully intended to live up to the spirit of his understanding with "Mr. Ziegfield." He stayed with the show through its full New York City run and then went along on the Follies' annual tour of major American cities. And when the show finally closed in the spring of 1919, Will volunteered to appear for a few more weeks in Ziegfeld's Midnight Frolic, until it was time for him to leave for California. Will was now committed to a change in his career. For the first time in thirteen years he was to leave the stage, where he had been simply himself. Now he would explore further the strange world of acting in moving pictures.

Because Laughing Bill Hyde had received popular and critical acclaim, Goldfish had offered Rogers a contract. He did not want to lose him to another studio, even

From South Africa, Texas Jack's program, August 3, 1903. Rogers—No. 13—is featured as "Lassoing Extraordinary by the Cherokee Kid."

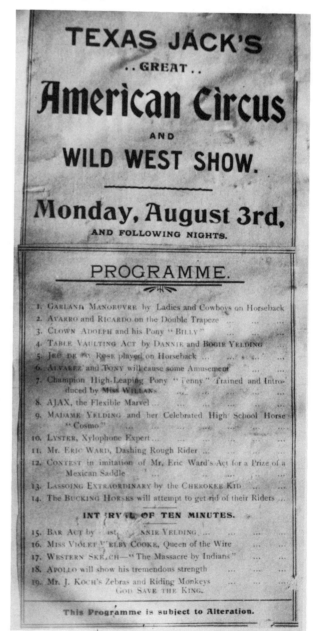

though films could not yet take advantage of Will's greatest asset, his voice. There was only one major demand in the contract: Will would have to work at the studio in California.

As in all such matters, Will had discussed the Goldfish offer with his wife, Betty. There were many questions to be considered. Should they uproot their lives for the sake of an experiment that might not work out? Should Will give up the security of starring in Ziegfeld's Follies? Should they move three thousand miles, when Will could be the star of a new musical Ziegfeld had offered to produce for him?

Now that the Rogers family had grown to three sons and one daughter the healthful climate and the wide open spaces of California were quite a lure. The huge salary, too, was tempting. Will and Betty decided to move westward.

On September 30, 1918, Will Rogers and Samuel Goldfish signed the contract. Paragraph 7 called for Will to report to the Goldwyn studio in Culver City, California, no later than the sixteenth of June 1919, to begin a one-year period of acting in films, for the sum of $2,250 per week—fifty-two weeks per year. The company had an option, to be exercised no later than three months before termination, to extend the contract for one additional year, at the new salary of $3,000 per week.

The years of living in the East would now come to an end. The family made plans. Will would go alone to the "Celluloid Coast," as he called it, rent a suitable house, and then Betty, the children, and the horses would follow. It was going to be a major move. An entirely new life-style was about to begin.

Will Rogers notified Florenz Ziegfeld that he would be closing on Saturday night, May 31, 1919. At a farewell party Ziegfeld presented Will with a gold watch. Engraved was the lesson he had learned: "To Will Rogers, in appreciation of a great fellow, whose word is his bond."

On Monday, June 2, Will Rogers was still in New York City. Having nothing special to do, he arrived at the New Amsterdam Theatre Roof in time to perform a new routine. He had not been scheduled and was received with thunderous applause. Even the usually noisy

Impersonating Broadway star Lenore Ulric, with Brandon Tynan as Belasco, in *Ziegfeld Follies* sketch, 1923.

waiters stopped and listened; way in the back, from the kitchen, the chefs stuck their heads through the open doors and laughed at Will's views on the foibles of statesmen and politicians. It was one of Rogers' greatest impromptu performances. It would be three years before Will Rogers would be back in a Ziegfeld production. But for now he was about to begin yet another career that would eventually make him the number-one box-office attraction.

LAUGHING BILL HYDE

Goldwyn Pictures Corp.,   Copyright September 30, 1918, LP 15678; b&w; silent; 6 reels (as per copyright registration); running time approximately 66 minutes. Release: September 30, 1918, Rivoli Theatre, NYC. Filmed at studio in Ft. Lee, N.J.; location shots: Boonton, N.J.

Production Staff: Director: Hobart Henley; cameraman: Arthur A. Cadwell; based on book by Rex Beach; adaptation and titles: Rex Beach.

Cast:

Will Rogers	"Laughing" Bill Hyde	Robert Conville	Denny Slevin
Anna Lehr	Ponotah	Dan Mason	Danny Dorgan
Clarence Oliver	Dr. Evan Thomas	John Sainpolis	Black Jack Burg
Joseph Herbert	Joseph Wesley Slayforth	Mabel Ballin	Alice Walker

Synopsis: Bill Hyde is in jail, serving a five-year sentence for assaulting his brother-in-law, who abused Bill's sister. Bill has been in trouble since he was ten years old, usually for "borrowing" things while their owners are away. He now breaks out of jail with his pal, who is mortally wounded in the escape. Disregarding his own safety, Bill carries the injured man to the home of Dr. Thomas, then takes a ship for the Alaskan goldfields. Robbing a stateroom, he is surprised by its occupant, Dr. Thomas. The doctor wants to reform Bill and tells him that he, too, is on his way to Alaska to make his fortune, so he can marry the girl back home. In Alaska, Bill meets Ponotah, an Indian girl, who has been cheated out of her gold mine. Resorting to dishonesty for the last time, Bill "salts" a worthless mine. This way Bill straightens everything out for Dr. Thomas, and Ponotah, who becomes his wife.

Reviews: ★ "Will Rogers turns out to be such a fine screen actor, that you would never know he was acting."

Motion Picture News, October 5, 1918

★ "The first Will Rogers picture may be set down as a success. If future ones fit his personality as snugly, we shall have another star."

Variety, September 27, 1918

★ "This is the very finest film released under the Goldwyn banner. . . . 'Laughing Bill Hyde' serves as the film debut of Will Rogers, and his performance would have been a credit to any veteran in the business."

Motion Pictures, December 1918

★ ". . . one of the most powerful and appealing pictures we have ever seen . . . ."

Board of Review

Since these films were silent, motion-picture houses provided mood music appropriate to the narrative on the screen. The musical accompaniment was usually played by a pianist who would ad-lib what seemed suitable to the action the pianist saw that moment. In the more luxurious, big-city theaters, orchestras would perform carefully prepared, complex scores. Our research has located accompanying music, suggested for the Goldwyn-produced Will Rogers films. Since these arrangements are generally unknown, and rarely seen, we are presenting several of them.

In addition to their own value as curios, these arrange-

Filming *Laughing Bill Hyde,* with director Hobart Henley (*seated*) and cameraman A. A. Cadwell, 1918. "Fellow prisoner" is Dan Mason.

In a romantic scene with Anna Lehr. (*Laughing Bill Hyde*)

ments are interesting for other reasons. They give an approximate indication of the length of those films that are no longer extant; they provide information not available elsewhere. In Laughing Bill Hyde, *for example, we learn that the character known earlier only as Alice is named Alice Walker (see music cue number 4); or that*

Ponotah is introduced into the story, since "Ponotah ran the camp laundry" (see music cue number 11).

We are also given some insight into "T," Titles, the legend that passed for conversation, and we learn about "S," Scenes, when an abrupt change was indicated.

Music: *Laughing Bill Hyde* (Goldwyn—Will Rogers) Specially selected and compiled by M. Winkler

The timing is based on a speed limit of 14 minutes per reel (1,000 ft.).

Theme: "My Paradise" (moderato ballad) by J. S. Zamecnik (used by permission of Sam Fox through Belwin, Inc., 701 Seventh Avenue, New York City)

1 Theme (1 minute and 45 seconds), until—T: "Laughing Bill Hyde."

2 "Sinister Theme" (dramatic), by Vely (3 minutes and 50 seconds), until—T: "Before Bill lay the open———"

3 "Heavy Mysterioso," by Levy (2 minutes and 30 seconds), until—T: "Evan Thomas, the village doctor."

4 "Bleeding Heart" (dramatic pathetic), by Levy (4 minutes and 40 seconds), until—T: "Alice Walker, the doctor's———"

5 "Summer Nights" (moderato), by Roberts (1 minute and 45 seconds), until—T: "Traveling by blind baggage."

6 "Rêve d'Amour" (melodious allegretto), by Zamecnik (2 minutes and 25 seconds) until—T: "Laughing Bill Hyde had———"

7 Theme (2 minutes and 30 seconds), until—T: "Joseph Wesley Slayforth."

8 "Ecstasy" (melody allegro), by Zamecnik (3 minutes and 30 seconds), until—T: "The Aurora is mine."

9 "Dramatic Recitative," by Levy (1 minute), until—T: "There was great excitement."

10 "Turbulence" (allegro agitato), by Borch (55 seconds), until—T: "Those were great days."

11 "May Dreams" (moderato serenade), by Borch (1 minute and 50 seconds), until—T: "Ponotah ran the camp laundry."

12 "Dramatic Agitato" (to action pp. or ff.), by Hough (1 minute and 25 seconds), until—T: "No, if I wanted to kill him."

13 Continue pp. and slow (40 seconds), until—T: "The Aurora claim where———"

14 "Return to Me Soon" (allegro), by Cregh (2 minutes and 35 seconds), until—T: "Dry panning a Mexican trick."

15 "Dramatic Tension No. 9," by Andino (2 minutes and 25 seconds), until—T: "My father was the teacher."

16 Continue ff. (35 seconds), until—T: "Set a thief to———"

17 Continue pp. (45 seconds), until—T: "Laughing Bill had almost———"

18 "Golden Youth" (valse lento), by Rosey (1 minute and 20 seconds), until—S: Near mining camp.

19 "Phyllis" (valse novelette), by Deppen (1 minute and 25 seconds), until—T: "Dr. Thomas did have———"

20 Continue pp. (45 seconds), until—T: "Burg and Slevin ventured———"

21 Theme (4 minutes), until—S: Near landing.

22 "Perpetual Motion" (allegro agitato), by Borch (1 minute and 35 seconds), until—T: "Doc, here's a customer."

23 "Sparklers" (allegretto 6/8), by Miles (1 minute and 15 seconds), until—S: Interior of saloon.

24 "Savannah" (one-step), by Rosey (1 minute and 55 seconds), until—T: "Better walk around."

25 "Sorrow Theme," by Roberts (1 minute and 35 seconds), until—S: The fight in bedroom.

26 Continue ff. with ad-lib timpani rolls (30 seconds), until—T: "He darn near killed him."

27 Theme ff. (1 minute and 25 seconds), until—T: "Week by week."

28 "Pizzicato Mysterioso," by Minot (2 minutes and 30 seconds), until—T: "Bill was not accustomed."

29 "Impish Elves" (winsome intermezzo), by Borch (4 minutes and 40 seconds), until—T: "Burg and Slevin decided———"

30 "Gruesome Mysterioso," by Borch (2 minutes and 20 seconds), until—T: "Your double crossin'."

31 Continue ff. (40 seconds), until—T: "The sale."

32 "Frills and Furbelows" (rondo rococo), by Crespi (2 minutes and 55 seconds), until—T: "Here's some news, kid."

33 Theme ff. (2 minutes and 45 seconds). The end.

$500 REWARD

FOR THE ARREST AND DELIVERY OF

LAUGHING BILL HYDE

CHARGED WITH BEING A

NOTORIOUS BURGLAR AND CONFIDENCE MAN

DESCRIPTION Wm. Hyde, White: born in Key West, Fla.; age, 38 years: occupation, machinist: Prominent scars and marks: Front view mole near center of neck, on left of chest, and right of knee. Has a constant tendency to laugh when in danger.

A REWARD OF $500.00 will be paid for his apprehension and delivery.

MONTANA STATE PRISON
BUTTE, MONT.

Will is wanted. (*Laughing Bill Hyde*)

Will Rogers Said

Now about this movie business and how I got my start. The way I figure things, a fellow has to be a success before he goes lecturing and crowing about himself. Out in Hollywood, they say you're not a success unless you owe fifty thousand dollars to somebody, have five cars, can develop temperament without notice or reason at all, and have been mixed up in four divorce cases and two breach-of-promise cases. Well, as a success in Hollywood, I'm a rank failure, and I guess I am too old to be taught new tricks, and besides I'm pretty well off domestically speaking and ain't yearning for a change. I hold only two distinctions in the movie business: ugliest fellow in 'em, and I still have the same wife I started out with.

Now about how I actually got started. Well, one day Mrs. Beach, Rex Beach's wife, drove out to our place—we'd rented Fred Stone's home out on Long Island—and asked me would I consider going into pictures. I told her I didn't know anything about the blamed thing. I thought pictures were made up of just three people: Mary Pickford, Charlie Chaplin, and Douglas Fairbanks.

She said: "That's all right, you can learn. I want you to play Rex's 'Laughing' Bill Hyde." Mrs. Beach

had seen my little act in the *Follies*, so she decided that I was the one to do naturally this crook.

She left the book with me to read, which I did, and I liked the story, so I asked my wife, you know, should I try it and she said: "Yes, the money'd come in kind of handy."

So it was Mrs. Rex Beach that really was the one who helped me get started by selling the idea to Sam Goldwyn that he ought to star me in the movies. Anyway, Sam signed me up, and I starred in a series of six-reel comedies for him during 1920 and 1921.

I was playing that summer in the *Follies*. We made *Laughing Bill Hyde* while I was working in the show. It was made at the old Fort Lee studios in New Jersey, just across the river from New York City. They used to make an awful lot of pictures there.

Anyhow, I took a flyer. Now, I had been on the stage a few years, but I never yet had any of that makeup junk on my face. I was told I would photograph black if I didn't make up. I asked to make it a blackface part; then I could play it straight.

Well, they had to put a hitch on my upper lip to get me to smear paint all over my contour. Even that could not disguise this old, homely pan of mine. They said the day of the pretty actor is gone. You are so ugly, you are a novelty.

We then went into, what they call, the studio. It's a big, glassed-in place like those up in the Bronx Park, where they stable those big South American palm trees.

It was a bad day outside, and it had hazed all those companies under cover. You couldn't move around without stepping on a five- or six-thousand-dollar-a-week star. And moving cameras were thicker around there than Army Commission hunters in Washington. I got lost from my director and started to take a near cut across when some guy bawled me out. It sounded like a Teddy Roosevelt speech. I was only between Mabel Normand and three cameras, and them all cranking on her most particular scene in a picture called *A Perfect 36*.

Confrontation between Anna Lehr and John Sainpolis. (*Laughing Bill Hyde*)

So I had really gone into movies quicker than I had figured on. Imagine me, a principal in *A Perfect 36*. When they all got through cussing me, a fellow said: "What company are you working for?" I told him, Goldwyn! He said: "It's all Goldwyn! I mean, who is your director?"

Miss Normand was looking at me and I couldn't think of that guy's name to save my life. This bird says: "He must be in Madge Kennedy's company, they are taking a Bowery lodging house scene!" I got pretty sore at that and walked away.

Now you wouldn't think a fellow could pull the same bonehead thing twice, but leave it to an old country boy to horn in wrong. I was feeling my way around among scenery and sets, trying to locate my man, when a big burly nabbed me by the coattail and yanked me back, and said: "You poor boob! I saved your life. That's Miss Geraldine Farrar taking close-ups for *The Hell Cat*." I heard what she did to Caruso one time, and I thanked him. I watched her awhile in hopes she would sing, but I tell you what she did have, she had an orchestra playing appropriate music in all her scenes.

This man said he would show me where I belonged, so we passed through an Irish farmhouse of Tom Moore's, stopped to see Mae Marsh's propaganda picture of choking the kaiser, passed through the Metropolitan Opera House and Cheyenne Joe's saloon, on the way to my gang. By the time I got there they thought I had given up the picture and gone home. It was now ten-thirty, and I thought I was late. We took the first scene at exactly three-forty-five in the afternoon.

The director says, "Now, Will, we are going to take the scene where your old pal dies. You have broken out of jail, and he gets hurt and you are bringing him into the doctor's office at night to get him treated, and he dies. It's the dramatic scene of the whole opera."

I says, "But I haven't got out of jail yet!"

He says, "No, you won't for a couple of weeks yet. Besides, the jail is not built yet."

That's the first time I learned that they just hop around any old way. Once we took a scene that was the start of a fellow and I fighting outdoors, and then a lot of rainy weather come, and a week later he knocked me down in the same fight.

They get me confused taking scenes here and there. One day I escaped from prison, and three days later I'm back behind bars doing a scene that takes place before the other one. I only hope they know how to put the thing together.

I thought I'd kid our director, Hobart Henley, the other day, and I said to him, "They aren't really going to release this thing, are they?" Henley looked aghast. "Are you kidding, Will?"

"Do I look as if I was kidding?" says I.

"Of course they're going to release it! What did you think they'd do with it?"

"Oh, I don't know—throw it away?"

You see, I've been working four weeks in a studio now, and naturally, I know all about the business from A to Z. Already I have decided to do away with close-ups. I just hate 'em. I ain't never going to get used to standing quivering all over with a camera three inches from my nose. Don't you think it is distracting when you see a picture, for the camera to suddenly switch from a whole scene to the hero's beaded eyelashes, magnified so that they look like Zeppelins? The other day we were on location and near us another company was working. They were taking long shots. So I told Henley: "I am going over to work for them; they got the right idea."

And another thing. I've been trying to find out why they call it *Laughing Bill Hyde*. So far I've had a doleful career, with jail escapes, death of pals, funerals, and so on. I said to Henley yesterday: "Say, Hen, when am I going to laugh?"

You know I met a theatrical manager once who told me: "Will, if you are going to try the movies, sign up for one picture, get all you can for it, and then never answer the telephones after it appears. That's what I am going to do when *Laughing Bill Hyde* comes out. Say, I went down in the projection room once to see the first pieces of the picture. Whew! Never again! They keep asking me to come down, but I know better. As far as I can see, the first scene I've done is one in which I grab a man. You can see the man in the film and just see my hand appear as it seizes his shirt. That's my best piece of acting.

The director said: "I am not going to tell you how to act."

I said to him: "Why, these correspondence schools do that."

He instructed me as follows: "Now, thought photographs. If you are thinking a thing, the camera will show it!"

So I told him I would try and keep my thoughts as clean as possible. He said: "Now we will rehearse the scene, and then take it. Now carry your old pal in. Ha! Wait a minute, you wouldn't carry him in that way, would you? You will hurt him worse than he is even supposed to be in the story!"

I told him to change the story around and let me be hurt and him do the carrying, that the other fellow was the biggest. But those guys are set in their ways and won't change anything.

Then we took it, him ballyhooing at me through a megaphone just what to do. He says: "That's fine, very good!" Then I heard him say to the cameraman, "Mark that N.G."

The next take I was really getting along fine on it, I was drama-ing all over the place, holding this pal, a-pleading with the doctor to do something for him. My mind was more on my art than on the load I had, and I dropped him.

Well, I want to tell you folks, somebody could have bought my moving-picture future pretty cheap right then. The director kept impressing on me that my only pal was dying. Well, he didn't have anything on me. I was almost dying. He looked and he saw I had tears in my eyes, and he says: "That's great!" He thought I was crying about my pal, but I was crying about getting into the darn thing.

Now I wear two different kinds of shirts in *Laughing Bill Hyde,* and no matter what scene they take, I always happen to have the wrong shirt on. I shift shirts on an average eight times a day. The way I change those shirts they are never going to last until the end of the picture.

Anyhow, I never knew whether I'd ruined the picture or not, until some day Rex Beach sent me a whole bunch of newspaper clippings and they all said nice things, so I decided I had better see that picture, but it was a good story, anyone coulda done it.

Oh, yes, one time I went to the barber and got a haircut right in the middle of the picture and like to spoiled it; I didn't know what I was doing—and here I was going in one door with long hair and coming out with a haircut. They all like to had a fit. I think yet it was the best picture I ever made, for I hadn't learned to try and act. There ain't nothing worse than an actor when we act.

Interview with Dorothy Stone Collins, May 25, 1970

S: Your father was the famous Fred Stone. Didn't Will Rogers' film career practically start in your home?

DSC: Oh, yes. Daddy's brother-in-law, our uncle by marriage, Rex Beach, wrote stories like Jack London. Now he was going to form a film production company with some other authors, like Rupert Hughes. There were about seven authors, and they were called the "eminent authors." They joined with Sam Goldwyn to make fine movies of their stories. And Rex's first story was called *Laughing Bill Hyde.* And one day, my aunt Greta, Rex's wife, said, "There is only one person to play *Laughing Bill Hyde,* and that's Will Rogers!" And I remember it, because it was in our home in Amityville, and Rex said, "That's the most marvelous idea!" So later, when Daddy and Will came riding in, they told Will about it. But Will just pulled away, "I'm not an actor. I'm just a roper. I can't do it!"

But they finally talked him into it. And after that film, which was made in Fort Lee, New Jersey, he went to Hollywood.

Reminiscences, by Clarence G. Badger

We discovered the existence of this manuscript in the late 1960s. Clarence Badger, having moved to Sidney, Australia, wrote his reminiscences of Will Rogers in 1957 and then sent them to his friend George Pratt at the George Eastman House, in Rochester, New York.

We considered the recollections of a man who had directed Will Rogers in fifteen films of major importance and hoped to obtain a copy. Our request was denied.

Before our next visit to Rochester, we made an appointment by telephone, asking that we be permitted to at least read the important first-person account and to make notes for this book. Upon our arrival, we were surprised to be handed a complete Xerox copy of the manuscript, including Mr. Badger's covering letter. There was just one restriction: No part of the recollection was to be reprinted in any form. We asked whether we could share this information with the curator and manager of the Will Rogers Memorial at Claremore, Oklahoma (Paula and Robert Love)—naturally with the same stipulation—and that permission was granted.

As we had agreed, these reminiscences have been kept from the public until now. We are most grateful to George Pratt and the George Eastman House for granting us permission to now print Mr. Badger's retrospection of his association with Will Rogers.

Among the many fond memories of my early film days I have preserved against time, the most treasured is that of my association with Will Rogers. Years long, it's beginning was singularly built on a fortuitous circumstance; which, I might say, was the why and wherefore of how I became his director.

One day—it was in the early autumn of 1919—our studio lot was rocked by the exciting news that Florenz Ziegfeld's star entertainer, the Oklahoman cowboy philosopher and America's foremost humorist, had been signed up by our chief, Mr. Samuel Goldwyn, and, furthermore, would be amongst us in Hollywood within the next few weeks.

I was a member of Mr. Goldwyn's directorial staff at the time,—had been since his Fort Lee days—and was now carrying on in his recently-acquired Culver City studio, diligently turning out light comedy features starring Madge Kennedy, a young and talented New York stage actress.

Although I had never met Will Rogers personally, I had seen him many times at the Ziegfeld Follies and had become so intrigued by his cleverness with a rope, rare wit and personality, that now, hearing this news of his film ambitions, I would gladly have given my eye teeth to be his director. However, this was not to be, it seemed. I was bound by deep-rooted routine to the Madge Kennedy series, and, besides,—as I soon found out—Victor Schertzinger, another Goldwyn director, had already been awarded the assignment. Be all that as it may, however, there was a pig in the poke yet to be reckoned with: a fateful tangle of dates.

The humorist's contract—as I was given to understand—was to start operating the day he reported at the studio. Not expecting him for another two or three weeks, Mr. Goldwyn was upset no end one morning by a telegram from the humorist announcing he was well on his way and would be reporting in a couple of days' time, "rearin' to go." The chief had reason to be upset. Victor, the humorist's appointed director, could not possibly "go" by that time; busy as he then was with a far-from-finished production.

Mr. Goldwyn was faced with a headachey problem. Nagging visions of his new, high-salaried star hanging around doing nothing, beset him. Then, while desperately scanning through the production schedules, he discovered that I had just finished another picture, recalling, at the same time, that my star, Miss Kennedy, keen for a month's holiday in New York, was already enroute aboard an East-bound train.

The chief's decision was quick. I was to take on the humorist. But there was a catch. I was to direct *only* his first picture. Mr. Goldwyn made that clear. After I had finished it, Victor was to carry on with Will Rogers. And me? I was to carry on with Madge Kennedy.

A shooting script of this, the humorist's first picture,—entitled: *Almost a Husband*—was thrust into my hand. Immediate preparations were ordered. Cameras must start grinding just as soon as possible after Will Rogers reported. To play opposite him, Mr. Goldwyn rushed out from New York Peggy Wood, a well-known actress. So, as far as cast was concerned, I was to have the last word, it seemed.

My first meeting with Will came a few days later —memory of which still sparkles. Hurrying across the studio grounds to my office, located on the second floor of one of the studio buildings and reached by means of an outside, open-air stairway, I suddenly saw him. His back was to me, but easily recognizable as Will's. He was perched slouchingly on the guard railing that ran around the high landing at the top of that same stairway that led to my office. A few of his cowboy friends, as I imagined them to be, were idling about up there with him. While still a fair distance away I saw one of them casually nudge Will and as casually flick his head in my direction. This informative gesture on Will's behalf, subtly as it was executed, none the less disclosed to me Will's awareness of how I was to fit into his present sphere of things; proven when he slowly twisted around on the rail and from under his Western-type hat shot me a seemingly indifferent quick look. But I was not fooled by it's indifference. It was a look of appraisement. And, upon reaching the stairway's base,—well, I can still see, still feel, Will's follow-up barrage of appraising,

analytical glances streaming down at me from under the brim of his Stetson as I hurried up to greet him.

It was easy to guess Will's thoughts during those moments. So much was at stake for him. Vital was the ability and understanding of his director. Vital to have one who would harmonize in appreciation of his unique talents, and present their entertaining qualities to their fullest value on the screen; particularly so in this, his first film effort.

As we shook hands up there on that high landing, he said he hoped I did not mind; it was just that he had been waiting "for you all to show up up here 'cause of an itchin' notion we should get acquainted like."

Will Rogers never disclosed his first impression of me; heaven only knows what he thought. But still, he never did warm up immediately to new acquaintances. He had to know one for some time and quite well, before lowering his subtle barriers of reserve. Once he did, you were his friend for life.

Personally, I warmed up to Will immediately; this warmth increasing many fold after I had launched our picture into production. I found the association to be most inspiring; and, because of the inimitable humanness of his acting, a pleasure to direct. Hence, as work on the picture progressed, regret that I was not to continue on with him, grew daily greater.

Those comedies I had been producing, seemed, now, namby pamby rubbish. Another thing that gnawed at me as I faced those last days of my association with Will, was the story that Mr. Goldwyn had given Victor Schertzinger to direct as Vic's first when he took over the humorist. Written by Ben Ames Williams, it was entitled; *Jubilo;* the main character fitting Will's personality like a glove. It had one of those cleverly-wrought plots that directors dream about. Victor had been handed a box-office certainty on a silver platter.

The day I said good-bye to Will,—our picture completed—without telling anyone where I was going, I motored out into the solitudes of the Mojave desert. In my glove compartment was the script of my next Kennedy comedy. I had decided not to read it, or even glance at it, until I came across a site suitable for a few days camping; hoping against hope the while that when I did read it, the picture material and story it told would be interesting and inspiring enough to put an end to my doleful fit of dumps.

Camped at last in a picturesque old ghost town, I read the script. My heart sank. Never had I been handed such trash! The tranquillizing inspiration I had prayed for, and which would have meant so much to me,—well, it just failed to materialize; there being nothing in the concoction to rouse such a feeling, except, perhaps, the inspiration to start my camp fire with it. It was something about a smart-alecky girl advertising cosmetics by plastering the pink stuff all over the hide of an elephant. Because of the comparison, *Jubilo* began tantalizing my mind. The more

I thought of that inspiringly-wrought job, the more disgusted, the more frustrated I became with my pink elephant.

Several days later, in a most depressed state, I returned to the studio. On driving through the gate, the policeman on duty stopped me.

"Hey, Mr. Badger!" he exclaimed, poking his head through the car's open window. "Sufferin' mackerel, it's you all right! Why, the big boss' had practically the whole police force of Hollywood searchin' for you! Where in thunder've you been hiding out?"

"Mojave desert," I said listlessly. "And not exactly hiding out, either. But, why this man-hunt? Any idea?"

"Well, not exactly, Mr. Badger, but judgin' from the touchy mood Goldwyn's displayed the last few days,—sure never seen him so cantankerous—an' the all-out way he's been tryin' to locate you, Mr. Badger, looks like you're implicated in somethin' or other 'round here that's upset his digestion. You'd better scram to his office right now. Jump out. I'll have the boys park your bus."

I "scrammed," wondering how I could possibly be implicated in that "something or other" which had changed so much the boss' usual geniality. Anyway, I reckoned, it would give me a good opportunity to express to him my pent-up opinion of the pink elephant.

Samuel Goldwyn, mentally and physically always vibrating with energy, sprang to his feet as, with the pink elephant script in hand, I was ushered into his luxuriously-appointed office.

"Ha—Badger—at last!" he exclaimed as he strode around his desk and confronted me. "So—you think you're smart, eh? Hiding from me while I search everywhere high and low—"

"I'm sorry, Mr. Goldwyn," I cut in, "been out on the Mojave, that's all, trying to digest this bunch of tripe, this pink elephant your scenario department's foisted on me. Why, it's the most—"

"I'm not interested in elephants, Badger!" he interrupted caustically. "What I *am* interested in is, why you, Badger, dare to dictate to me how I shall run my business!"

"Gosh, Mr. Goldwyn, what gave you that idea? Something I'd never do. You should know that. But, look, won't you please read this script? I'll bet if you do, you'll agree that this pink elephant is—"

"Badger, I'm asking you—be quiet about that elephant!" Then, his face only inches from mine: "Dammit, what I want to know is, what's all this monkey-business going on between you and Will Rogers?"

"Monkey-business? I don't get it, Mr. Goldwyn. Why, I haven't seen Rogers, or anyone else for that matter, since finishing *Almost a Husband*, and that was over a week ago. And here I am, all ready to get going on another Kennedy comedy. But please, not

with this pink elephant. The damn thing is a—is a—"

My tongue hung fire—checked by surprise. He had turned away, was now pacing the floor; moreover, muttering to himself. What about was beyond me. In a short time, however, he was standing before me again and saying, in a seemingly sincere reconciliatory tone, "For those accusations, Badger, I apologize."

"That's a relief!" I exclaimed. "Whew! Thanks, Mr. Goldwyn. But why? The reason? The cause? I certainly have a right to know?"

"Driven to it, Badger, driven to it!" he burst out. "Drastic,—oh, yes. But a way to rid my mind of an irritatingly significant matter. Of you, I ask—forget it. In this business goes on much chicanery. One becomes always suspicious. But you are not of trickster breed. That I now know—to *my* relief."

Hmm,—I thought—doing some tricking, himself, in his game of trying to trick a suspected trickster! Suspected of what? I still did not know.

"You may go now," he went on. "Your elephant, you can leave. After your criticisms, I had better read it." Then, a mysterious sort of smile crinkling his face, "I give you now an order. Go look up Rogers. You'll probably find him on the lot somewhere trampling t'hell my best lawn."

It was easy to find Will. And sure enough, he was trampling "t'hell" the Goldwyn lawn. Semi-circled by a gathering of cowboys and studio extras, he was dexterously lassoing the "KEEP OFF THE GRASS—THIS MEANS YOU!" sign, his audience enjoying uproariously his wise-cracking comments about the general uselessness of lawns.

With one of those side-long glances—so characteristic of Will—he soon singled me out from the others watching him. Without pausing from his sign roping, he called out, "How you all, Mr. Badger? Been dustin' up Mojave way, they tell me."

"That's right, Will," I replied, approaching him,

Scott Studio photograph, New York City.

but keeping clear of his whirling lariat, "and came back with a bad case of the blues."

"Blues?" he questioned, "an' when the skies' so blue? Don't square up none, somehow."

"It's because of my next with Kennedy, Will. The story's a bunch of junk—got a pink elephant in it. Will, I just left Goldwyn. He told me to look you up. Didn't say why. But Goldwyn's like that today. You should've heard the screwy things he accused me of; and then the way he apologized. I'll tell you about it some time. Right now my real worry is my pink elephant; sure gives me a headache when I compare it with *Jubilo*. Schertzinger's a lucky guy."

He threw the lariet; neatly snared the sign. I then noticed that most of the onlookers had drifted away. I was glad,—our conversation being so personal.

"Not that I'm stickin' my nose in," Will said, "but when you all was holed in with Sammy, did he touch on that there *Jubilo?*"

"Why, no, Will."

"Well, that bein' so, an' you mentionin' it," he drawled casually as he coiled up his lariat for another throw, "reminds me. You'll find a copy of the *Jubilo* script over yonder in my dressin' room. Better get studyin' on it. Word came from Sammy, jus' 'fore you showed up here, that we gotter start her off next week."

I stared at him goggle-eyed.

"What do you mean,—*we?*" I cried. "Will Rogers—please—what are you talking about?" I implored, clutching his arm in my excitement and causing his lasso to tangle mid-air.

As he unraveled it, he said,—continuing on with the same casual drawl—"Like I mentioned, better get studyin' on it an' get her preliminaries movin', otherwise, we'll sure have Sammy on our necks, an' I ain't foolin'."

"You really mean I'm to work with you again? Direct *Jubilo?*"

"Sure seems like it. Schertzinger's takin' over your—pink elephant." Again, he threw his twirling lasso. Again, unerringly, it embraced the sign. "Yes, you an' this here cowpuncher's stringin' along together, Mr. Badger. Reckon we'll hit it off. It's all fixed with Sammy."

"Fixed, yes,—and thanks to you, Will, I'll bet!" I exclaimed. "And the reason, too, no doubt, why Goldwyn left it to you to tell me! Darn right, we'll hit it off. Oh, Will, this was grand of you!"

"Shucks, jus' one of my notions. An' now I'm thinkin' you'd better get goin' with the studyin' an' preliminaries. Come on, I'll trot along with you to the dressin' room."

As we short-cut our way across the studio lawn, I acquainted Will with details of my session with the chief. "And him not giving me a single, solitary clue as to what prompted his attitude," I wound up, "guess I'll just have to write it all off as a joke he was pulling."

Ready for his act in vaudeville.

"No joke, I'm fearin'," Will then told me. "Sammy reared up wild-bronco-like when I broached my notion to him tother mornin'; him thinkin' right off the jump some monkey-business was brewin' 'tween us; that you, Mr. Badger, had wheedled me into approachin' him about it 'cause of a hankerin' you had to keep on stringin' along as my director. So help me, even after agreein', Sammy was still bettin' you had put me up to it, an' has been itchin' ever since to get his paws on you so's he could squeeze out the facts. So you see—"

"For heaven's sake, Will," I cut in, "what was it you *said* to Sammy that started him off thinking that way? that caused him to suspect me of such knavish scheming? the both of us of—of monkey-business?"

"Well,—was jus' comin' to that. It was when I opened up on him casual and gentle-like tother mornin', sayin' to him how I reckoned that this here physiognomy of mine'd make a powerfully better showin' in my future Goldwyn Pictures if you did the steerin'."

As I had forejudged it would, *Jubilo* did well at the box-office. But, more important to Will,—a new star in a new field of entertainment—it gained for him immediate and wide-spread acclaim as a film artist of unique endowments. I saw interesting evidence of this during the months, and even years, following *Jubilo*'s release. For instance: When away on location with our company, usually in some remote corner of the country, Will and I would often spend an evening at the nearest local cinema; and, often, as ushered to our seats, would hear a pianist, organist, or other instrumentalist,—such as were employed in those days to enhance the silent screen—suddenly fill the theatre with the strains of that old darky spiritual, "In the Days of Jubilee"! The theatre management, still intrigued with the memory of Will's picture, *Jubilo,* and also recollecting it's story connec-

Clement Vann Rogers' application for a homestead for
his absent son. Will was—as the father testifies—"in
South Africa with a show." (*The National Archives*)

tion with that old camp-meeting classic, arising to
the occasion, were now complimenting him in this
manner for his unforgotten performance. In fact, until the coming of talking pictures, the strains of that
old hymn followed Will as a sort of aura, liable to become manifest whenever he entered a picture theatre.

I would like to set down here an example of Will's
whimsical humor. He gave voice to it one day while I
was "shooting" a fight scene. The scene was for a
film I was making. It was about a cowboy; gullible,
green from Arizona,—played by Will—attempting
to crash Hollywood via screen accomplishments.
Our cowboy crashed the film capital all right—in the
film's story—but not in the way he had hoped.

His "thrilling" opportunity, an "odd" job that he
had at long last secured at one of the studios, demanded that he "double" in some fight scenes for a
big-shot actor; the latter the star in a film then supposedly under production. In the fight scene mentioned—for my picture—I showed the star seated
comfortably on the side lines arrogantly watching his
"double", Will Rogers, in his stead and made-up to
resemble him, being unmercifully bashed about by a
heavy-weight bruiser. In the midst of the fight, the

going pretty tough, Will suddenly called out implor-
ingly:

"Hey! Listen! Please, Mr. Badger! Ain't there
—such a thing—as gettin' a double to double for a
double?"

Will loved to play jokes. They were usually very
clever and very subtle. Sometimes, he would aim
them my way. One occasion was when we were
"shooting" *Boys Will Be Boys* in Jackson, Amador
County, California,—a '49 day gold mining district
of the Sierra Nevadas. The good people of the community tendered us—all members of our company—a reception, which they held one evening in
their diminutive public hall. After much feasting and
square dancing, Will was called to the speaker's platform. As an expression of the community's esteem,
he was presented with a large gold nugget. Cries of
"Speech! Speech!" then filled the hall.

Now, Will had learned beforehand, somehow,
about this nugget presentation; and also that a
speech would be expected. He had learned, further,
that following him, I, too, was to be honored in a
like manner and called on for a speech. So, the opportunity wide-open, he decided to have some fun
with me —put me in a spot, as it were. After thank-
ing the gathered townspeople for their gift, he said:

"Folks, did you ever stop to think of how the
birds in this here picture business, to say nothin' of
the public generally, don't appreciate none the guys
makin' 'em? You can talk yer heads off about them
so-called big-shot stars,—like myself, for instance;
jus' ham actors when it comes to analyzin' 'em—an'
them there executive jasbos sittin' in their mahogany
offices. You can mix the whole lot of 'em together
an' they don't contribute more 'an ten percent to the
box-office takin's of these here motion pictures.

"It's the guys like that one a'sittin' right down
there, (Pointing at me.) to my way 'er reckonin',
who should be conceded tother ninety percent of the
credit when the general public starts handin' out
medals." And so, with me involved as an example,
he went on and on, magnifying to extravagant proportions and rare humor the value of film directors,—
to his audience's delight; watching me squirm and
trying telepathically to shut him up,—to his delight.

Not until invited to the platform, there also presented with a nugget—a surprise indeed—and heard
demands for a speech, did I get a picture of what
Will had really been up to. I glanced down at him.
With eager-like anticipation, chewing away on his
gum, he was grinning up at me. Then I saw him settle back in his chair. Yes, I knew why,—to revel in
my comeback! fully expecting me—as he confessed
later—to contradict his embroidered calculations of
film directors' importance,—figuring, because of the
way he had me enmeshed, contradiction was the one
and only way out. Something of a mouthful for me to
attempt, to say the least. It would only be a mum-
bling, fumbling job, being far from as clever a hu-

morist as was Will. Anyway, I thought, the audience had already had their fun with me stooging for him, so why attempt a contradiction? especially now? recalling, as I suddenly had, the extreme embarrassment golden commendation and high praise always caused Will? The answer! Yes, a way to side-step his snare! So, as a subject for the demanded speech, I pounced on Will's rich personality.

After expressing my thanks for the nugget, I delivered an eulogistic sort of oration about Will, seasoning my praises and tributes with a sprinkling of exaggerations; doing so unmercifully. There were many wild out-bursts of applause, the audience—Will, their pin-up boy, as it were—taking all I said in good faith. I finally had Will, himself, squirming.

"I kinda got tangled in my own snare," he observed after the reception. Then, grinning broadly, added: "Turned out sort 'er general all 'round admiration wrestlin' match, seemed like."

I would like to relate now how a whim of nature dishearteningly affecting an important scene of ours, magically rectified itself.

Will had three children, none, at that time, as yet a teenager. There was Will Junior, the eldest, his daughter, Mary, and little Jimmy, the youngest. Although all three appeared in one of our pictures, little Jimmy, a cute, most lovable little fellow, was given roles in several of them. One was, *Jes' Call Me Jim;* a story about a kind-hearted backwoodsman—played by Will—whose close and beloved friend—another woodsman—victim of an accident, is discovered dying by Will.

Desperate, broken-hearted, taking his friend's young son along with him—played by little Jimmy—Will goes out into the forest where he prays to God; imploring Him to spare his friend's life; the little boy murmuring added pleadings.

Now, I wanted the setting for this scene to be as divinely solemn and ethereal in character as possible. Explaining this to a location man, I sent him off to check the possibilities of some of those groves of big redwood trees to be found on the western slopes of the Sierra Nevadas. He finally found one he reported as ideal, except that there was only enough sunlight for the scene at high noon. I immediately drove up there to see for myself. The setting was indeed ideal. The sun, when at it's zenith, streaming down as it did amongst the huge trees, augmented the setting's composition with glorious, cathedral-like shafts of light. The total effect was magnificent; divinely so; but short-lived, lasting less than an hour.

I regretted not bringing Will along, little Jimmy and the camera crews. However, it was a difficult spot to reach, and, besides, Mrs. Rogers, to whom I had already mentioned the possibility of such a trip, would have had to accompany us to take care of their little son.

A few days later, all cars reaching the location,—and in time—Will and little Jimmy rehearsed and ready for the prayer scene, cameras set-up, their crews tensed, old Sol at last arriving at his right spot in the zenith, and—and—and well, now I ask you? What miserable trick of nature is this? *Where* are those magnificent divine shafts of light of a few days ago? There just were not any! Not a hint! Never had I felt so balked, so disappointed.

Time so short, the place so difficult to reach, I was forced to go ahead and accept the setting for the scene just as it now was. Not too bad, of course, with its big trees, but it lacked the divineness, the ethereal quality I had wanted so much, and had gone to such lengths to secure.

The scene filmed, Will and his wife invited us all down to a little nearby glade for "a fill 'er bacon and eggs," as Will put it. But I was in no mood to accept their thoughtful invitation. Disappointment about that scene had me down. I stayed put up there, my only companions the cameras; still set-up on their tripods, as they had been abandoned by their hungry crews.

Before long, however, the tantalizing aroma of frying bacon wafting my way, captured my attention. I could see Will and his wife down in the glade frying heaps of it and scrambling loads of eggs for their mouth-watering crowd of hungry guests, doing so on a portable gasoline stove they had brought along. Then, deciding to join them, I cast a last glance at that grove of redwoods and started down the little knoll. Suddenly, I halted, stood frozen in my tracks. My [eyes] were blinded by an unbelievable sight! Those magnificent shafts of light of a few days before, were back! Once again they were shimmering, streaming down amongst those giant columning trunks of the sequoias with returned ethereal glory!

I let out a yell that echoed from the mountain tops— or so the gang later insisted. I yelled to everybody to come back up on the run. I yelled that we were going to reshoot that prayer scene and that there were only seconds to spare. I yelled to Mrs. Rogers to please keep on with her frying, not only because those heavenly shafts of light owed their existance to the wrack arising from her sizzling bacon, but because I had suddenly got a desire for heaps and heaps of it.

After the scene had been beautifully and touchingly reenacted and magnificently reshot by the newly inspired participants, I then remembered that there had been a mist in the air that other time I had been here. Of course, nowadays a picture company would carry equipment with which to secure such an effect, regardless of nature's whims; and that would be a mist-making machine—unheard of when films were in their teens.

After the expiration of Will's Goldwyn contract, he financed and produced three films himself; in which he starred and I directed. Pending and worrying Will at the time, however, were commitments he had made with Flo Ziegfeld, and it was not long before Will lit out for New York and the Follies. But this did not spell severance of our friendship; a tie that had grown during our association at Goldwyns'— which had been for two and a half years—to an unbreakable bond of depth, warmth and understanding.

During the years that followed, when visiting New York, and Will was programmed, I would never miss taking in the Follies. Upon spotting me in the audience, as he invariably did, he would immediately suspend his act and from the footlights wave clasped hands at me—symbol of a handshake. I would, of course, acknowledge his greeting in a like manner. Then, with a subtle flip of his thumb, he would high-sign me to come back stage between acts for a "pow-wow."

On one such occasion, both reminiscing away in his dressing room, Will told me how, at the President's invitation, he recently had been a week-end guest at the White House; mentioning at the same time a couple of amusing incidents. It was during Calvin Coolidge's administration. While it seemed to Will that practically the entire White House personnel was waiting to greet him when he arrived, it was the President, himself, who stepped forward with outstretched hand. Now, Calvin Coolidge's voice— as was well-known—was extremely high-pitched and nasal. Grasping Will's hand, he said:

"Welcome to the White House, Will. Mighty glad to see you. And how is your family? Well, I trust?"

Not answering, but instead, Will, dropping his hand, glanced sharply about the White House grounds, looked under his car, toward the people grouped behind the President.

"Why, Will, what on earth's all that about?" the puzzled Chief of State inquired; still, of course, in that high-pitched voice of his.

"Hey, Mister President!" Will then burst out, "is he included in this welcoming committee? that there ventriloquist I'm hearin' hidin' out 'round here?"

Will said Coolidge eyed him sharply "for several mighty embarressin' moments," then suddenly roared with laughter. "Not that I'm meanin' Cal, particularly, 'cause he's O.K." Will divulged. "But you know, Clarence, I can always find out quick if a politician's really deservin' of the job us trustin' voters hand him jus' by the bird's reactions when I kid him a bit about somethin'—'specially 'fore people. Sure proves he's really a great guy if he's a good sport about it, an' don't act resentful like."

Will then informed me that just previous to his own visit, the Queen of Romania was a guest there at the White House, and that he was allotted to the same quarters she had occupied. "Gosh, Clarence," he chuckled, "sleepin' in that same bed where royalty'd snoozed kinda seemed out 'er place for an onery cowpuncher. I dreamed for a fact I'd been elected some kinda King an' was back in Oklahoma, ropin' longhorns with my durn crown always gettin' tangled up an' messin' with my ropin'."

Speaking of "ropin'," Will Rogers was certainly a top-notcher at it. I have seen him throw three lassos at the same time at a horse being ridden "hell-for-leather" past him; throwing one with the left hand, the other two with the right; one lasso "ropin'" the rider around the waist, the second his neck, the third lasso dropping neatly over the horse's head. I filmed him doing this for one of our pictures, using a very high speed camera, thereby making a very slow motion scene; the action being slowed down to such a degree, that every detail of Will's skillful manipulation of the three lassos could be clearly studied.

I am now "itchin',"—as Will would say—to set down here a noble action which he once undertook on behalf of a sorely distressed friend. This friend was the highly talented stage star, Fred Stone, of the famous vaudeville team of Montgomery and Stone, and, also, well-known as the original Scarecrow in the stage production, "Wizard of Oz." Their friendship —Will and Fred's—was brother-like and of years' standing.

Fred, when at the point of introducing a new show to New York, which he had been meticulously preparing for months, and in which both he and his daughter, Dorothy, were to star, was badly injured in a 'plane crash.

Will, in California and about to embark on a lucrative Chautauquan "gab an' gossip" tour at the time, on hearing the news, immediately side-tracked the tour and went "hell-for-leather" to Fred's assistance. Reaching New York, working around the clock rehearsing and familiarizing himself with Fred's role in the play, finally "figurin'" he was "up to it", Will took it on an out-of-town, break-in jaunt. Though still hospitalized, this gesture of Will's was remedial tonic to his stricken friend, bringing to him rapid mending of body and soul.

Then, on the night of October 15, 1928, Will opened the play at the Globe theatre in New York. It's name was *Three Cheers*, and Will's role in it, which he had taken over on behalf of his brother humorist, was "King Pompanola." *Three Cheers* ran for 210 performances.

An interesting incident involving me took place a few weeks after the play's New York opening, which time happened to mark the end of a year or so's world-wide run of my Paramount picture *It*. Clara Bow, who by now had become internationally famous as the It girl, being needed in New York to lend allure to a Paramount publicity drive, was sent there by her Hollywood studio officials. Now, because at that time Clara Bow and my wife were sister-like pals, Clara, upon receiving her travelling orders, persuaded my lady to accompany her.

Arrived in New York and settled down in their hotel, it was only natural that my wife should want to see Will in *Three Cheers*, being, as she was, a years-long friend of the humorist, having often accompanied us on location trips. He had a nickname for her.

It had seemingly stuck to her since their first meeting. It was, "Goofus." Her mention to Clara of her desire to see Will's show, resulted in the girls buying not two, but four tickets, they having invited two of Paramount's publicity chaps to accompany them—as escorts. But, alas, at the last moment, Clara could not go. However, my lady went—with the two male escorts.

Will, in the middle of his first act, absorbed in his fast-moving role of "King Pompanola," chanced suddenly to glimpse a familiar face in the audience. Immediately disregarding stage ethics, he ambled to the footlights. "Pardon the interruption, folks," he said, "but a mighty important matter's come up needin' a little investigatin'." His eyes then focused on my wife.

"Hey, there! You—Goofus!" he called to her. "Where's Clarence?"

But embarrassment had her tongue in knots. She just could not answer.

"Come on, Goofus," Will persisted, "speak up—you're delayin' the show. Where's Clarence?"

"Out—why—out in California," she finally blurted out, red-faced.

"California, eh? Hmm. Then what are you doin' in this here wild and woolly burg with those there two guys you're asittin' with? Listen, Goofus, when the curtain falls on this here act, please come back stage an' do a little explainin'."

The act over, an usher appeared and conducted my lady willy-nilly back stage to where Will awaited her. After her explanation of the situation, he said:

"Hmm—so you're prancin' 'round with Clara Bow, eh? Well, I'm from Missouri—you've got to make good that there one, Goofus."

"A cinch, Will Rogers," she came back. "You just fix me up with two seats for tomorrow night, and I'll bring Clara along."

She kept her promise. During a planned lull in the first act—that next night—Will ambled to the footlights again and said:

"All you men folk out there—please lend an ear. An' that includes all from teenagers to you frisky octogenarians. I'm aimin' to hand you a real treat; somethin' I'll bet has had you actin' feverish-like for quite a spell now. Boys, how would you like to meet the It gal?"

After silencing the resulting applause, Will, addressing the "It gal," said, "Come on, Clara—please—up on your pretty feet now an' give the boys an eyeful. And, gosh, Clara! Off with them there dark glasses so's they can see I ain't foolin' 'em none."

As Clara started graciously and sweetly to comply with Will's request, the theatre went suddenly dark and spotlights flashed down upon her; the audience proving it's enjoyment of Will's treat with ear-splitting acclamation.

The interesting part of it all was, as he divulged to me later, Will was really worried—about me, I mean.

Despite Will's richly deserved fame and popularity which grew to such outstanding proportions through the years, he never forgot or neglected old friends. Time and again where their lives had been dealt with harshly,—as in the case of Fred Stone,—he healed their situations with direct personal action, or financial balm. Lowly bootblacks knew his friendship. He swapped jokes and horses with royal Princes.

1932

Will's inborn, noble character was further revealed ten years or so after our Goldwyn days together. Again residing in California, he organized a "round-up", or, social get-together, to which he invited all who had, in any way, been associated with our picture unit at Goldwyn's those many years before. For instance, there was our esteemed and ingenious head cinematographer, Marcel Le Picard, who had filmed all our productions. There were other cameramen, too,—now aces, themselves—who had been Marcel's assistants those days; electricians, make-up men, studio cooks and waiters, the ageing darky bootblack. . . . Will also invited Fred Stone, who was visiting him at the time, and who, happily, was now enjoying good health.

The "round-up" was held in a gardened area of "Big Boy" Guinn Williams' San Fernando Valley ranch; "Big Boy" being a years-long friend of ours. There was hearty browsing by all upon the barbecued spread and much quaffing of loving cups; the gathering becoming one of never-forgotten camaraderie.

At one point during the festivities, Will ambled over to me and placing an arm around my shoulders, requested—in a loud voice—everyone's attention. Response immediate, he then said something like this:

"Now, if all you pioneer picture folk of this here round-up don't mind listenin' to Clarence an' me for a spell, then perk up you're ears for one out of Ripley's."

Silence reigning, he said, glancing my way, "Clarence, you any notion of how many pictures the two of us hashed up together?"

"Sure have, Will," I answered, wondering what he was up to now. "Fifteen."

"I'm takin' it, folks," he went on to the "perked-up" ears, "you all heard Clarence's total. Fifteen. Now, I'm requestin' you study the pair of us an' ponder over what you're witnessin'." Hearing him say this, coupled with the fact that his arm was still around my shoulders, prompted me to slide my arm nearest him around his waist. "My point bein', folks," Will was continuing, "is that mighty few directors an' stars—an' there ain't none I know of —teamed up cheek by jowl like Clarence an' I was, ever made so many pictures without coming out of it showin' signs of wear an' tear; such as bein' antagonistic-like, feudin' an' wranglin', havin' lawsuits in the offin', bein' at loggerheads, displayin' frigidity, or, actin' up like a couple of fightin' cocks when meetin' face on; but, instead, comin' out of it like you're witnessin', an' the way we've been stringin' along through the years since Goldwyn's—each gettin' from tother the kind of comradship an' harmony honest to God friends enjoy an' treasure an' cling to for dear life in this here uncertain old world. . . ."

1935

I braked to a screeching stop. Time and time again during the last year or so,—because of the convenient way it cut around these Santa Monica foothills—I had used this highway; and this was the first time, when passing it, I had ever noticed that big wooden gate back there standing open like that! Always before, it had been closed and padlocked.

I backed up. Stopped before it. What an alluring, come-hither picture it now presented! An "open" invitation, if ever there was one! Accept? Why not? Scorning further argument, I shot the car through the gate's welcoming arms; sped up an ever-rising dirt road that wound it's way through wild holly, sycamores, crossed sylvan dells and came out, finally, atop a high mesa. Here I stopped.

On my right arose a hacienda-type residence—superbly-designed. On my left, framed by a white, one-railed fence, lay spread a polo field. In the distance gleamed the Pacific Ocean; on the horizon paraded the Santa Barbara Islands.

A lone rider was galloping about the polo field, teaching his mount the game. My first glance identified him. Will Rogers. I knew that he had identified me, too, for as I backed from the car I heard, "Clarence!" then the sound of approaching hoof beats.

He leapt from his pony, vaulted the fence and grasped my hand.

"Howdy, Clarence," he panted, "gosh, long time."

'Yes,—three years, I'd say—anyway, since the 'round-up.' You've sure got a glorious place here, Will. Absolutely wonderful—first time I've seen it. And how's the family? O.K.?"

"Yep,—all doin' first rate. Will Junior an' Jimmy not those kids anymore you once romped with. Takin' to sproutin' whiskers. Been aborrowin' my razors for long time now. An' Mary's back East tryin' her hand at actin'. But why we doin' our gabbin' here? House'd be better. Come along—besides, got a couple of Charlie Russells I've been itchin' to show you,—you know, 'cause you knew the old buzzard. An' a new Navajo rug—one of them there sand ones,—sure classy weavin'. An' more important-like, there's the Missus,—Betty. Golly, will she be glad to see you! Come on, let's hand her a surprise."

We all gathered later out on their charming patio, with it's little sparkling fountain and gorgeous view. Here we spent an hour or so reminiscing. There was much to recall that was of interest to each of us. It was a treasured, never-forgotten hour.

When taking my leave, Will ambled along with me down to my car. As I climbed aboard, he said warmly:

"No foolin', Clarence, sure a treat seein' you again. Nobody more welcome. Jus' drop in any time you all so inclined."

"Thanks, Will." Then I laughed—could not help it. "But there's one thing that sure would stop me, inclined or not."

"Stop *you?* Why,—why—what?"

"Well,—not that I don't appreciate plenty your reasons for it, Will—that padlocked gate,—you know, down below at the highway."

"Jehoshaphat! Clean forgot! Look, Clarence, ring us when you get that there inclination, an' you'll find that blasted gate wide open." He gave me his private number. I noted it down. "Oh, tell you what," he went on suddenly, "I'm expectin' to take off from these here parts next couple of weeks or so—got planned a little air hop with Wiley Post—an' when I get back I'll straight-away get in touch with you an' we'll have a real nice evenin' together with dinner, a good pow wow an' all the fixin's."

"That would be wonderful!" I exclaimed. "Sure be looking forward to it. And this little hop with Post? Which way are you heading, Will? that is, if it's for publication?"

"Japan, we're aimin'—maybe take a squint at China. Post reckons we can make it by way of Alaska an' them there Aleutian Islands; steppin' stones, he reckons 'em."

"Sounds great. Gosh darn it, Will, how I envy you—the trip." We shook hands. "Anyway, I'll be waiting for you to get in touch with me. All the best—and good flying. . . ."

I often think of Will, and sometimes when his noble image visits my thoughts, I wonder why he made no mention that day of plans for that side flight which he and Wiley Post attempted after refueling at Fairbanks; Will venturing it with the intention—as was reported at the time—of dropping in on an old and close friend, who, in Government employ, was posted at Point Barrow, Alaska's desolate, northernmost tip of land, and who was grievously in need of inspiriting and cheering-up treatment. My guess is, that Will made no mention of it because it was *not* for publication, as he had a way of keeping all such benign, kindly intentions to himself.★

*Hitherto unpublished manuscript in the collections of the Department of Film, International Museum of Photography at George Eastman House, Rochester, New York, George C. Pratt, curator.

ALMOST A HUSBAND

Goldwyn Pictures Corp., Copyright August 30, 1919, LP 14139; renewed October 15, 1946, R 11829; b&w; silent; 5 reels. Release: October 12, 1919, Strand, NYC. Review in *New York Times*, October 13, 1919, 16:3. Extant: trims and clips only.

Production Staff: Director: Clarence G. Badger; cameraman: Norbert Brodin; based on the story "Old Ebenezer," by Opie Read; titles by Will Rogers.

Cast:

Will Rogers	Sam Lyman	Clara Horton	Jane Sheldon
Peggy Wood	Eva McElwyn	Ed Brady	Zeb Sawyer
Herbert Standing	Banker McElwyn	Sidney DeGrey	John Caruthers
Cullen Landis	Jerry Wilson	Gus Saville	Jasper Stagg

Synopsis: Sam Lyman takes a job as a schoolteacher in a small town in the South. During a forfeit game at a social gathering, the penalty for Sam and Eva, the banker's daughter, is to go through a mock marriage ceremony, performed by the first man to enter the house. This turns out to be a newly ordained minister, and the ceremony is perfectly legal. Zeb Sawyer, who has been pursuing Eva without encouragement, demands that Sam divorce Eva at once. But Eva, to avoid the unwanted suitor forced on her for financial reasons by her father, asks Sam not to release her. Zeb now sets night riders on Sam and decides to ruin Eva's father, Banker McElwyn, by starting a run on his bank. Having just sold a novel, and by a ruse of pretending to bring new money into the bank, McElwyn is saved, and Sam now musters enough courage to propose.

Reviews: ★ "The inimitable Will Rogers . . . has the gift of perfect composure, which, with his seeming indifference, give the impression of simplicity and spontaneity, the two highest attributes of an actor's art."

Motion Picture News, October 25, 1919

★ "[In *Almost a Husband*] Will Rogers is the finest comedian in the world."

London Daily Mail

Interview with Peggy Wood, September 10, 1970

S: *Almost a Husband*, which was Will Rogers' second film for Goldwyn—was it your first?
PW: Yes. He was so easy to work with. He was a pro.
S: I have always wondered what actors said to each other in those silent films, when they were supposed to have a conversation. Obviously there wasn't any written dialogue.
PW: We just talked about anything that had to do with the situation.

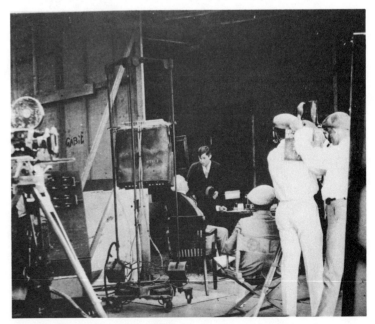

On set of *Almost a Husband;* Rogers faces Herbert Standing, 1919.

S: Were you ever concerned about anybody lip-reading?

PW: I wasn't about to use some nasty swear words or obscenities that they could lip-read. But do you remember in that famous war film *What Price Glory?*—that was a silent film—do you remember what a soldier said? It was very carefully photographed so that it could be lip-read. Do you remember what he said? The captain had given him an order and the soldier said, "That lousy son of a bitch!" And everybody in the audience roared. That was so clearly shot, the camera was aimed at this doughboy, who had just been taken down a peg or two. He didn't say it out loud, even if it had been a sound film; it was his fury of saying it under his breath.

S: In your work with Will Rogers, did you find him sometimes taking over the director's job, by wanting to do scenes his way?

PW: He had a great sense of taste, and if things weren't right, he would do them over. He, being a sensible man, didn't have to be told. He knew.

S: Do you know that there is no copy available of *Almost a Husband?* Almost all of Mr. Rogers' early silent films were allowed to hypo [decompose] in the cans and had to be thrown away.

PW: I'm not surprised. The motion-picture people at that time were just out after what was quick money, and they had no idea that they could save these films, that it was probably an art form.

S: Do you recall any idiosyncrasies Mr. Rogers might have had?

PW: No, because he was a typical Oklahoman, and to a person from New York, that was idiosyncrasy enough. The language was different, the choice of phrases was different, there are lovely locutions they use—sure, he was full of idiosyncrasies! He was a puncturer of self-made balloons. If it was the truth, he said it! The most devastating thing that can happen to pomposity is comedy! The comedian can destroy so much better than the invector, the one who rages. George Bernard Shaw was the same. By way of comedy he punctured things that were the shibboleths of the Victorian era. And so Will Rogers punctured the poses and pomposity, or even slyness, or even lies—all he had to do was say what it really was in simple words. As my father used to say, "I can only understand words of one syllable and one letter." Also the similes he used were things of the earth; they are eternal. What he meant was that people who lived by the earth, on the earth, have to do with living things. Therefore, his similes—I suppose the cliché is homilies—were so true. And further, he put a little twist on the end of them, and that is where the corkscrew was that pulled out the cork! The funny part was that he was his own straightman, or the newspapers were his straightman, but he never used a dirty word, and he never was sly. He didn't have to be.

WILL ROGERS' FOURTEEN POINTS

President Wilson and I each have fourteen points. He took his to Paris where they not only saw his fourteen, but raised him twelve more. I brought my fourteen to the coast.

The first five and principal points of mine are a wife and four children, which in itself constitutes a novelty in this business—that is provided you still live with them.

Point number six: I heard there was a movement on to revive moving pictures.

Point number seven: Producers decided to make fewer and worse pictures. They may make fewer, but they will never make worse.

Point number eight: I hold the distinction of being the ugliest man in pictures.

Point number nine: Caruso and I and Jesse Willard were the last to go in.

Point number ten: Goldwyn figured by getting a good cast and a great story, it would about offset the action of the star.

Point number eleven: I can't roll a cigarette with one hand and can't whip but one man at a time—and he must be littler than I am.

Point number twelve: I made a picture last year and some theaters bought it. So they figured if I made another one they could double the sale on this one. Get two to use it.

Point number thirteen: Moving pictures are the only way in the world that you can play and tour and not have to worry about hotels.

Point number fourteen: `It's the only business where you can sit out front and applaud yourself.

Press Release

From the Goldwyn office comes the news that *Almost a Husband* which is based on Opie Read's *Old Ebenezer*, will be Will Rogers' first photoplay under his present contract. Peggy Wood has the leading woman's role and Clarence

Badger is directing the production. *Mabel Normand will appear in the picture as an "extra." Rogers having agreed to make a similar appearance in one of her photoplays.* (italics added) From the *New York Times*, Sunday, July 20, 1919

Whether or not the announced reciprocal appearances took place is impossible to trace at this time. Camaraderie among actors on the individual studio lots makes the above arrangement quite likely. In those days stars would think little of making cameo visitations in one another's films, just as a lark. (See the pictures in this book of Charlie Chaplin visiting Will Rogers' An Unwilling Hero *set.)*

Since we have seen only clips and trims of Almost a Husband, *we do not know whether Miss Normand appeared in it. The Mabel Normand film in which Will Rogers could most easily have appeared as an extra is* Pinto, *the next film Miss Normand began after her possible visit in* Almost a Husband. *It would have been easy for Will Rogers to simply walk over to the set where* Pinto *was being shot. The plot seems to be an ideal vehicle for Rogers to mix with the cowboys, especially as there was considerable roping. Since we have not been able to find a copy of* Pinto, *we could not verify an appearance by Mr. Rogers. As a publicity stunt, the announcement in the* New York Times *is definitely to be considered as a fact, though we cannot claim that Will Rogers actually appeared in* Pinto; *chances are that he did.*

We will not count Pinto *as one of Mr. Rogers' films, but we will supply the facts about the film. Perhaps some copy in private hands will become available at some future time, and the mystery can be solved.*

PINTO

Goldwyn Pictures Corp., Copyright December 9, 1919, LP 14524; b&w; silent; 5 reels.

Production Staff: Director: Victor L. Schertzinger; cameraman: George Webber; written by Victor L. Schertzinger, scenario by Gerald C. Duffy.

Cast:

Mabel Normand	Pinto	Andrew Arbuckle	Guardian
Cullen Landis	Bob De Witt	Richard Cummings	Guardian
Edward Jobson	Looey	George Kunkle	Guardian
Edythe Chapman	Mrs. Audry	John Burton	Guardian
George Nichols	Pop Audry	Joseph M. Hazelton	Guardian
William Elmer	Lousy	Manuel R. Ojeda	Mexican
Hallam Cooley	Armand Cassel	Dwight Crittenden	De Witt, Sr.

Synopsis: Pinto is a girl of the West who has grown up under the guardianship of five ranchmen in whose care her father left her when he died. Her daring exploits on her pony Legs nearly drive the cowboys on the ranch to distraction. Consequently, they are overjoyed at the news that Pinto is to go to New York for a year to visit with Pop Audry.

Pinto's first shock in the East comes with the knowledge that New York is not a ranch, as she had thought. A young fellow of engaging personality named Bob De Witt helps her find Pop Audry's home, and they decide to become very good friends. Pinto's second shock comes when she finds herself snubbed by Mrs. Audry. Rather than stay under the same roof with the girl, the aristocratic lady goes to her summer home. Pinto thinks it about time that Pop should know of his wife's deceptions, and during the Wild West show that she stages for his society friends, she informs him of Mrs. Audry's affairs. He returns to Arizona with the girl, and Bob accompanies them, for he and Pinto have come to a complete understanding.

Review: ★ "*Pinto* comes near being the best of all the Mabel Normand releases and again proves that it isn't what you do; it's the clever way you do it."

The Moving Picture World, February 7, 1920

JUBILO

Goldwyn Pictures Corp., Copyright November 15, 1919, LP 14437; b&w; silent; 6 reels (as per copyright registration); running time 80 minutes. Release: December 7, 1919, Strand, NYC. Review in *Motion Picture News*, December 20, 1919. Extant. Location shots: New Orleans.

Production Staff: Director: Clarence G. Badger; cameraman: Marcel Le Picard; based on *Saturday Evening Post* story "Jubilo," by Ben Ames Williams; adapted by Robert F. Hill; art director: Gilbert White.

Cast:

Will Rogers	Jubilo
Josie Sedgwick	Rose Hardy
Charles French	James Hardy
Willard Louis	Sheriff Nate Punt
James Mason	Bert Rooker

Synopsis: Jubilo, so named by his fellow hoboes for his cheery habit of singing the old spiritual, witnesses a train robbery. Fearing embarrassing involvement with the sheriff if he came forward to testify, Jubilo decides to move on. On his wanderings he comes to a ranch and asks for food. He is taken in, fed, and treated kindly by Jim Hardy, the owner, and by his daughter Rose. Asked to help out, he breaks the habit of a lifetime and for the first time performs manual labor. While helping the rancher out of his difficulties, and repaying him for his kindness, Jubilo falls in love with Rose and asks her to marry him.

Reviews: ★ "Will Rogers firmly establishes himself as a screen star of the first magnitude."

Motion Picture News, December 20, 1919

★ "The screen adaptation measures up in no sense whatever to the original story and some of the most potential elements of the story were either lost or neglected for the screen version.
"The story seems somewhat inconsistent throughout and if Rogers has any ability as a screen actor, he is not able to show it here."

Variety, December 19, 1919

★ "If the part of 'Jubilo' had been written with the inimitable Will Rogers in mind, it could not suit this kindly and humorous player better. He seems to be Jubilo, instead of simply impersonating the character.

Houston Chronicle, January 6, 1920

An Advertisement

Now I was asked to write my own ad. Now that is a pretty tough job. At that I am glad they asked me to write it instead of paying for it. Jubilo means a song, an old-time Negro camp meeting song "In the Land of Jubilo." I sing this song, but fortunately the voice don't register on the film, so you needn't stay away on that account.

It was originally before we got ahold of it a very good story and appeared in the *Saturday Evening Post* (I get nothing extra for mentioning their name). This character Jubilo is a tramp. Mr. Goldwyn, after see-

On set of *Jubilo,* with director Clarence Badger, Charles French, and Josie Sedgwick, 1919.

Trouble afoot, in *Jubilo*, with Charles French and Josie Sedgwick, 1919.

Rogers sings "Jubilo," in a silent film. (*Jubilo*, 1919)

ing me several times in my street clothes, he said, there is the fellow to play the tramp.

You know, come to think of it, it ain't such a bad picture at that; it had father, girl, villain who makes play for girl, tramp hero, dirty but honest. Pickford, Fairbanks, and all of them have the same layout, only they get real dough for theirs; story, same as usual. Looks bad for the hero right up to the last close-up; first reel introduces hero dividing last crumb of bread with dog, which they all do in the movies but nobody ever did in real life. Second reel looks bad for hero; third reel looks even worse for hero; fourth reel evidence all points to hero being the robber, villain looks slick and satisfied. End reel five: the winners—the tramp wins 100 percent HERO.

Several times during the picture I am asleep, so the audience will have nothing on me. The photography was mostly shot in focus, the camera used was a Brownie No. 2.

The sets, Goldwyn really spread themselves in this picture. There is one scene with mountains in the background that if you had to build it, it would have cost a million dollars. To give you an idea, we trav-

eled over two miles from the studio to get it.

Interior sets, well there is a barn showing real hay, no fake stuff but real hay, and a kitchen scene that I'll bet didn't cost under twenty-five dollars but very realistic dirty dishes in the sink and everything.

Yes, Ben Ames Williams wrote *Jubilo*. I like to play tramps. There is something about an old tramp that kinder hits me, especially a kind of good-natured one that don't take things too seriously. Anyway, *Jubilo* was the only story ever made out here where there was no scenario made. We just shot the scenes from the various paragraphs in the story in the *Saturday Evening Post*. When we took a scene, we just marked it off, and went on to the next. I think that it was the only story ever made that was absolutely filmed as it was written. And here is the novelty to it, we didn't change the main title either. They will film the Lord's Supper, and when it's made, figure that that is not a good release title and not catchy enough.

Sometimes you just think there ain't enough crazy titles to go round, and that when they end, that will be the finish of pictures.

A Telegram

THOUGHT I WAS SUPPOSED TO BE A COMEDIAN BUT WHEN YOU SUGGEST CHANGING THE TITLE OF JUBILO YOU ARE FUNNIER THAN I EVER WAS. I DONT SEE HOW LORIMER OF THE SATURDAY EVENING POST EVER LET IT BE PUBLISHED UNDER THAT TITLE. THAT SONG IS BETTER KNOWN THROUGH THE SOUTH BY OLDER PEOPLE THAN GERALDINE FARRAR'S HUSBAND. WE HAVE USED IT ALL THROUGH BUSINESS IN THE PICTURE BUT OF COURSE WE CAN CHANGE THAT TO "EVERYBODY SHIMMY NOW." SUPPOSE IF YOU HAD PRODUCED "THE MIRACLE MAN" YOU WOULD HAVE CALLED IT "A QUEER OLD GUY." BUT IF YOU REALLY WANT A TITLE FOR THE SECOND PICTURE I WOULD SUGGEST "JUBILO." ALSO THE FOLLOWING:

A POOR BUT HONEST TRAMP

HE LIES BUT HE DONT MEAN IT

A FARMER'S VIRTUOUS DAUGHTER

THE GREAT TRAIN ROBBERY MYSTERY

A SPOTTED HORSE BUT HE IS ONLY PAINTED

A HUNGRY TRAMP'S REVENGE

THE VAGABOND WITH A HEART AS BIG AS HIS APPETITE

HE LOSES IN THE FIRST REEL BUT WINS IN THE LAST

THE OLD MAN LEFT BUT THE TRAMP PROTECTED HER.

WHAT WOULD YOU HAVE CALLED "THE BIRTH OF A NATION?"

WILL ROGERS

Lunch break on location, *Jubilo*, 1919. *From left, at back:* C. E. Thurston, Charles French, Willard Louis, Johnny Mescal, Marcel Le Picard (cameraman). *Seated in foreground:* Josie Sedgwick, James Mason, Buster Trow, Jimmy Flood, Clarence Badger, Will, Jack Leys. (*Academy of Motion Picture Arts and Sciences*)

WATER, WATER EVERYWHERE

Goldwyn Pictures Corp., Copyright December 31, 1919, LP 14676; renewed June 29, 1947, R 20345: b&w; silent; 5 reels. Release: February 8, 1920. Review in *Variety:* February 6, 1920, p. 54. Extant: clips only. Location shots: Mojave; Kern River near Bakersfield.

Production Staff: Director: Clarence G. Badger; cameraman: Marcel Le Picard; original *Saturday Evening Post* story "Billy Fortune," copyrighted by William R. and Louise D. Lighton; screenplay by Robert F. Hill.

Cast:

Will Rogers	Billy Fortune	Victor Potel	Steve Brainard
Irene Rich	Hope Beecher	William Courtwright	Daddy Sammett
Roland Lee	Lyman Jennings Jordon	Sydney De Grey	Red McGee
Wade Boteler	Ben Morgan	Lillian Langdon	Fay Bittinger
Margaret Livingston	Martha Beecher	Lydia Yeamans Titus	Mrs. Red McGee
Milton Brown	Sam Beecher		

Synopsis: In a western town, the local saloon has been the target of the ladies of the local temperance society. Finally they manage to convert it into a soda-water parlor; but the men have the last word when they import the prettiest girls as waitresses to cater to their thirst. Billy Fortune is a wholesome, self-sacrificing cowboy who forgoes his love for Hope Beecher when he suspects that she is interested in another. The other man is the town doctor, who has taken to drink and appears a failure, until a mine explosion gives him a chance to prove to himself that he can function without first taking a drink. When Billy sees that the doctor has lost his need for alcohol and is engaged to Hope, he leaves town.

Reviews:

★ "It must be a joy for his director to work with him [Will Rogers], and if he had as sound a story sense as he has a comedy sense, he would be an unbeatable combination . . . I suspect him of writing half his own titles—the better half, and of developing many of his own scenes."

Burns Mantle in *Photoplay Magazine*, March 1920

★ "Rogers does some corking stunts, several close shots disclosing him doing real wild west dare-devil antics, standing erect on a spirited bronc."

Variety, February 6, 1920

★ "Will Rogers measured from the feet up to the neck looks something like other men, but when the face is brought into play, the difference is seen and felt. It is difficult to watch a Rogers smile . . . he is irresistible when it comes to the smile . . . there is no other man like him on the screen today. . . ."

Dramatic Mirror, February 7, 1920

Music: *Water, Water Everywhere* (Goldwyn—Will Rogers) Specially selected and compiled by M. Winkler

The timing is based on a speed limit of 14 minutes per reel (1,000 ft.).

Theme: "Humorous Drinking Theme" (characteristic), Roberts

1 Theme (40 seconds), until—S: At screening.

2 "Stampede" (for western scenes), by Simon (35 seconds), until—S: Close-up of running cattle.

NOTE: To action pp. or ff.

3 "Babillage" (entr'acte), by Castillo (2 minutes and 15 seconds), until—T: Redstone.

4 "Legend of a Rose" (allegretto), by Reynard (2 minutes and 30 seconds), until—T: "Nobody had ever called."

5 Continue pp. (30 seconds), until—T: "You poor kid, wait."

6 "Impish Elves" (intermezzo), by Borch (4 minutes and 10 seconds), until—T: The next day.

7 "Why?" (song ballad), by Levy (1 minute and 5 seconds), until—S: Girl at piano.

NOTE: To be played as piano solo

8 Theme (45 seconds), until—T: "I ain't pullin' any."

9 "Gavotte Piquante" (allegro grazioso), by Pierson (1 minute and 15 seconds), until—T: "The Welfarers come to."

10 "Dainty Daffodils" (moderato), by Miles (2 minutes and 55 seconds), until—T: Lyman Jennings Jordon starts.

11 "Western Rodeo" (cowboy descriptive), by Minot (1 minute), until—T: "Eighty-six, there ain't."

12 "Birds and Butterflies" (intermezzo), by Vely (1 minute and 40 seconds), until—T: "Billy decides there are."

13 Theme (3 minutes and 45 seconds), until—T: So Billy pulls a Romeo.

14 "Comedy Allegro," by Berg (1 minute and 5 seconds), until—T: "Now, Billy, dear."

15 "Hunkatin" (half-tone jazz), by Levy (2 minutes and 20 seconds), until—T: A week later.

16 "Valse Danseuse" (moderato), by Miles (1 minute and 35 seconds), until—T: "Billy, dear, tell me what."

17 Theme (2 minutes and 30 seconds), until—T: A package of dry literature.

18 Continue pp. (50 seconds), until—T: "Your friend is certainly———"

19 "May Dreams" (and. con moto), by Borch (3 minutes and 10 seconds), until—T: Morgan leaves the decision———"

20 Theme (3 minutes and 30 seconds), until—T: finding consolation at———"

21 "Hurry" (for pursuit and races), by Minot (1 minute and 40 seconds), until—T: "Premature explosion at———"

22 Continue to action (1 minute and 25 seconds), until—T: The ordeal of his life———"

23 Continue pp. (30 seconds), until—T: "He's pulling through."

24 "Sparklets" (moderato), by Miles (1 minute and 50 seconds), until—T: "Billy and Hope bring him———"

25 Theme (1 minute and 25 seconds), until—T: "Redeye goes back on the———"

26 "Scherzetto" (from Symphonette Suite), by Berge (1 minute and 55 seconds), until—T: "That don't look good to———"

27 "Gallop No. 7," by Minot (1 minute and 50 seconds), until—S: Billy galloping down hill. The end.

Will Rogers Said

One time, in the old silent picture days, it was in 1919, we made a picture near Mojave at a big old mine, and Irene Rich was with us. It was her first picture with us and she was just breaking in as a leading lady. She is a big star now. In those days I was one of the love interests. (Nowadays I just have to fix it for some young ones. They won't let me have anything to do with it personally. I guess it's just as well, I never was so hot as a screen lover.) But in those days your age never mattered. Audiences figured that old people fell in love, too, but now that's out. Modern audiences think that old folks are just to be the fathers and mothers of the young ones.

And too, Margaret Livingston, who is now Paul Whiteman's wife, was with us. It was called *Water, Water Everywhere* and it was a western, and I had to swim out into a river and rescue her from drowning. Well, we had to go another two hundred miles to find a stream. We took it on the Kern River, out of Bakersfield. It's as hard to find a running river in southern California as it is a drowning man. You know, this water thing out there ain't just water, it's gold.

Well, anyhow, I was supposed to swim in on a horse and rescue her, and as I dragged her ashore, pull her up on my horse and run to the doctor with her. Well, say, you get on dry land and try to stay up on your horse and pull a fair-sized old girl up on there with you, when she is supposed to be plum dead—and here was a drowning woman that was all wet. I tell you, it was mighty hard to carry her on a running horse, and it was mighty hard on the lady, too. Say, she had to reduce before I could get her up there. There is nothing heavier than a person that is wet, even a little person. And I never see Margaret that I don't think of that ride.

I love westerns. They won't let me make one. They say they can only get just so much money with it, as they have a kind of set price for westerns, but I would like to get to make a good one.

Now about a wet person, you dip one of Singers' Midgets in the water and let him soak awhile, and I bet you Jack Dempsey wouldn't lift him up in front of him.

THE STRANGE BOARDER

Goldwyn Pictures Corp., Copyright March 11, 1920, LP 14869; renewed August 5, 1947, R 21702; b&w; silent; 5 reels. Release: May 1920.

Production Staff: Director: Clarence G. Badger; cameraman: Marcel Le Picard; based on a story by Will Payne.

Cast:

Will Rogers	Sam Gardner	Lionel Belmore	Jake Bloom
Irene Rich	Jane Ingraham	Jack Richardson	Westmark
Jimmy Rogers	Billy Gardner	Sydney Deane	Dawson
James Mason	"Kittie" Hinch	Louis J. Durham	Sergeant Worrill
Doris Pawn	Florry, his wife		

Synopsis: Sam Gardner, a simple-hearted Arizona rancher, promised his dying wife to take their son east, so he could be well educated. He mortgages the ranch, and with $10,000 in his pocket, he heads for Chicago. Here he is almost immediately relieved of his fortune. The plot was simple. Met by the crooks in the entrance to the bank, Sam is introduced to the "bank president," to whom Sam trustingly hands the entire amount. Sam refuses to pursue the crooks, for he believes that even should they be caught, the money would have been spent.

Sam befriends a gambler, "Kittie" Hinch; Kittie threatens to kill a Chicago ward heeler who has been making advances to Florry. When the politician is found dead, Sam is mistakenly arrested and accused of the murder.

A girl, Jane Ingraham, whom Sam had met in his boardinghouse, and who had fallen in love with him, perjures herself trying to clear him. It does not work. Only when Kittie confesses before crossing into Mexico, is Sam released and he rushes into Jane's embrace.

Reviews: ★ "As photoplay entertainment 'The Strange Boarder' is big league stuff."

Variety, April 23, 1920

★ ". . . it is Will Rogers' personality upon the screen and his droll, quiet way of picturing the character he plays in this feature that account for its success."

Motion Picture News, 1920, p. 3907

Music: *The Strange Boarder* (Goldwyn—Will Rogers) Specially selected and compiled by M. Winkler

The timing is based on a speed limit of 14 minutes per reel (1,000 ft.)

Theme: "Jubilo," by J. Kern

1 Sinister Theme (for scenes of impending danger), by Vely (1 minute and 5 seconds), until—S: At screening.

NOTE: Watch shot

Father and son Jimmy, in a dramatic scene, c. 1920.

2 Theme (2 minutes and 30 seconds), until—T: "Business Chances."

3 "Adoration" (moderato), by Barnard (4 minutes and 20 seconds), until—T: "And I promised your mother."

4 "Adieu" (12/8 moderato), by Favarger (2 minutes and 35 seconds), until—T: "Wait here while I phone."

5 "Adagietto" (from Symphonette Suite), by Berge (3 minutes and 15 seconds), until—T: "After an hour's wait for———"

NOTE: To action pp. or ff.

6 Theme (1 minute and 45 seconds), until—T: "Accepting things as they———"

7 "May Dreams" (and. con moto), by Borch (2 minutes and 35 seconds), until—T: "The hardest thing to find———"

8 "Gallop No. 7" (characteristic), by Minot (25 seconds), until—S: "Scene on ranch."

9 "Spring Blossoms" (novelette), by Castillo (2 minutes and 55 seconds), until—T: "I wish I had you out there."

10 Continue pp. (50 seconds), until—T: "What have you done about?"

11 "Rêve d' Amour" (allegretto), by Zamecnik (1 minute and 45 seconds), until—T: "He was not a gambler."

12 "This Is the Life" (popular song) (3 minutes and 20 seconds), until—T: "While sweetheart's away."

NOTE: To be produced on phonograph

13 "Allegro Agitato" (for general use), by Kiefert (2 minutes and 30 seconds), until—T: "If I ever see you with him."

NOTE: To action pp. or ff.

14 Theme (1 minute and 30 seconds), until—T: "There's sure a lot of people."

15 "Love Song" (moderato), by Puerner (2 minutes), until—T: "Thirty days and out."

16 Repeat Sinister Theme, by Vely (3 minutes and 45 seconds), until—S: "Kittie" with gun.

17 Half Reel Storm Furioso, by Levy (1 minute and 20 seconds), until—T: "Sam wonders has he———"

18 Continue to action (3 minutes and 55 seconds), until—T: "Jake Bloom always went to———"

19 Repeat Sinister Theme, by Vely (2 minutes and 15 seconds), until—T: "On wash day the boarding———"

20 "Dramatic Tension," by Andino (3 minutes and 30 seconds), until—T: 'Gardner was not hard to———"

21 Theme (2 minutes and 25 seconds), until—T: "You may go for the present."

22 "Pizzicato Mysterioso" (for burglary or stealth), by Minot (3 minutes and 45 seconds), until—T: "Inspector Ryan stages a———"

23 "Dramatic Reproach" (dramatic), by Berge (1 minute and 30 seconds), until—T: "That afternoon Jake Bloom's———"

24 "Dramatic Conflict" (hurry heroique), by Levy (1 minute and 20 seconds), until—T: "A week later Florry follows."

25 Theme (2 minutes and 10 seconds), until—T: "That afternoon." The end.

Interview with Miss Irene Rich, January 3, 1971

S: Your first picture with Will Rogers was *Water, Water Everywhere*.

IR: Yes, and I have some pictures from that film; that was August 1919. You know I was in fourteen films with Will Rogers. Some of them were made for Goldwyn; those were in the silent days. Then later, we were together in some of the Fox films. Let me show you some of the pictures I have.

S: That is Jimmy, Will Rogers' younger son.

IR: Yes, and do you see here, I'm holding little Jimmy in my arms? Well, when the scene was being taken, with me facing the camera and Jimmy in my arms, at right angle to it, his little hand behind my back was inside my dress, going up and down my spine. Now, don't think I didn't have a hard time doing that scene. I still remember little Jimmy. He was a sweet, cuddly little kid.

S: This is such an unusual photo album; these are all candid snapshots, taken long before the usual movie stills.

IR: Here is one of Will! Did anyone ever tell you how Will concentrated on his little column? How he would sit with his typewriter between his knees, and he'd sit there, and he'd chew his glasses till the wing would be all chewed down, and only a little stub would be left? And then he would start chewing on the other side.

S: Tell me, what kind of an atmosphere did you have when you went on location?

IR: You see, that was the thing. They would get a story, then they would talk it over what they would do, "We'll get old Irene, and then we'll go up in the mountains, and do the film." They would gather the whole cast, everybody; maybe it would take a couple of carloads on the train, but we would all go. We would live in a hotel, but it was just like one big happy family—everybody was happy, everybody liked each other. It's not like that today.

JES' CALL ME JIM

Goldwyn Pictures Corp., Copyright April 27, 1920, LP 15058; renewed April 14, 1948, R 30117; b&w; silent; 6 reels (as per copyright registration); running time 75 minutes. Release: May 30, 1920, Strand Theatre, NYC. Extant.

Production Staff: Director: Clarence G. Badger; cameraman: Marcel Le Picard; based on the novel *Seven Oaks*, by James G. Holland; adapted by Thompson Buchanan; screenplay by Edward T. Lowe.

Cast:

Will Rogers	Jim Fenton	Bert Sprotte	Buffum
Irene Rich	Miss Butterworth (the milliner)	Nick Cogley	Mike Conlin
Lionel Belmore	Belcher (the thief)	Sidney De Grey	Sam Yates
Raymond Hatton	Paul Benedict	Seldon, the "hound dog"	
Jimmy Rogers	Harry Benedict		

Synopsis: Jim Fenton is a simple, happy-go-lucky man of the woods, a hunter and trapper. Paul Benedict, his friend, has been taken to the county asylum. Jim learns from Miss Butterworth—with whom he is in love—that Paul has been the victim of a plot to keep him confined, so that others (Belcher) may profit from his invention. While Paul is held in the asylum, Miss Butterworth is taking care of Paul's son, Harry. Jim Fenton sets to work. He is able to effect Paul's release, hides him in his cabin, misdirects the pursuers, and helps Paul to regain his health and win the court case, proving that he is the rightful owner of patents that have made a fortune for Belcher. Miss Butterworth consents to marry Jim, who almost manages to disrupt the ceremony.

When the minister starts to say: "Do you, Jim Fenton . . ." Fenton interrupts with: "Jes' call me Jim."

From Columns:

★ "The filming of scenes for 'Jes' call me Jim' was delayed this week because of the illness of little Jimmy Rogers, who is absent from the studio because of measles."

Motion Picture News, February 28, 1920

★ "Irene Rich rescued Nick Cogley from certain death when a canoe was turned over in a stream recently, during the filming of Will Rogers' latest picture 'Jes Call Me Jim.' A swift current, many rocks and a water-fall a short distance down stream made the rescue one that would never have been staged for publicity purposes."

Variety, February 12, 1920

Reviews:

★ "It is one of the real films of the month."

Burns Mantle

★ "In this picture Rogers gives the lie to all those who have been insisting that he is only a rough comedian blessed with a likeable personality. Show me an actor who can play with more genuine feeling than Rogers does the basicly theatrical scene in which Jim sends Benedict's little boy into the woods to pray for the recovery of his father, and I'll introduce you to one of the leaders of his profession."

Photoplay, August 1920

Music: *Jes' Call Me Jim*   Specially selected and compiled by M. Winkler

The timing is based on a speed limit of 14 minutes per reel (1,000 ft.)

Theme: "Jubilo," by J. Kern

1   "Woodland Whispers" (characteristic), by Blon (1 minute and 55 seconds), until—S: At screening.

2   "Poeme Symphonique" (4 minutes), until—T: "The Seven Oaks asylum and————"

3   "Flirty Flirts" (mel. rubato), by Levy (5 minutes and 20 seconds), until—T: "Seven Oaks."

4   "Adieu" (moderato), by Karganoff (1 minute and 20 seconds), until—T: "When I think of the man."

5   Continue to action (3 minutes and 45 seconds),

Irene Rich with Jimmy Rogers in scene mentioned in interview.

until—T: "The comfortable Mr. Belcher."

6 "Dramatic Recitative" (for heavy and intensive dramatic situations), by Levy (3 minutes and 30 seconds), until—T: "True to her threat."

7 Theme (1 minute), until—T: "Now don't worry too."

8 "Mysterioso" (for general use), by Andino (1 minute and 50 seconds), until—T: "Something does happen to————"

9 "Dramatic Suspense," by Winkler (2 minutes and 35 seconds), until—T: "Missing Paul Benedict."

10 "Turbulence," by Borch (2 minutes and 10 seconds), until—T: "Sleepy Seven Oaks."

11 "Perpetual Motion," by Borch (2 minutes and 40 seconds), until—T: "He's a dying man, Jim."

12 "Rêve d'Amour" (allegretto), by Zamecnik (3 minutes and 20 seconds), until—T: "Little feller, we're in————"

13 "Chanson Melancolique" (3/4 andante), by Collinge (3 minutes and 50 seconds), until—T: "The Valley of the Shadow."

14 "Ave Maria" (dramatic melody), by J. Ascher (4 minutes), until—T: "Don't you suppose you————"

15 Theme (1 minute and 5 seconds), until—S: "Jim feeding Paul."

16 Continue to action (2 minutes and 15 seconds), until—T: "The next morning."

17 "Spring Blossoms" (characteristic intermezzo), by Castillo (2 minutes and 30 seconds), until—T: "As the passing days————"

18 "Gavotte & Musette" (allegro), by Raff (1 minute and 10 seconds), until—T: "Jim gets his ideas."

19 "Grotesque Mysterioso," by Lake (1 minute and 30 seconds), until—T: "A spooky errand."

20 "Furioso" (depicting conflict and riot), by Shepherd (1 minute and 40 seconds), until—T: "Wait, I want you to————"

NOTE: pp. during interior scenes

21 "Heavy Mysterioso" (for general use), by Levy (2 minutes and 30 seconds), until—T: "Midnight."

22 "Reverie," by Drumm (3 minutes and 45 seconds), until—S: Close-up of newspaper clipping.

23 "Mysterioso Dramatico" (depicting mystery and agitation), by Borch (1 minute), until—T: "Tell the court what————"

24 "Dramatic Reproach," by Berge (4 minutes and 50 seconds), until—T: "Your honor, I move to strike————"

25 Theme (3 minutes and 15 seconds), until—T: "I'll issue a bench————." The end.

Interview with Miss Irene Rich, January 3, 1971

IR: "There was one thing Will did in one picture we did together that was positively awful. I don't remember the name of the film, but I know it was silent. Will played the part of a woodsman, or something like that, and we had shot part of the film. [*Jes' Call Me Jim*, ed.]

He came in one morning after having his long hair cut the night before. Here he had gone through a door with long hair and was about to come out the other side with short hair. They had to paste on part of a wig on the back of his head. Everybody was just so upset.

Then there was one other thing. He wouldn't let anybody put makeup on him. Well, it got so that he needed some, and he had a little bag with a powder puff in it, and he'd go way out behind a bush to put it on. He wouldn't let anybody see him do it. He had to put on just a little dab of powder, but no other makeup.

CUPID, THE COWPUNCHER

Goldwyn Pictures Corp., Copyright July 17, 1920, LP 15369; renewed May 22, 1948, R 34318; b&w; silent; 5 reels. Release: July 25, 1920, Capitol Theatre, NYC. Review in *New York Times*, July 26, 1920, 9:5.

Production Staff: Director: Clarence G. Badger; cameraman: Marcel Le Picard; based on novel *Alec Lloyd, Cowpuncher,* by Eleanor Gates; screenplay by Edfrid A. Bingham.

Cast:

Will Rogers	Alec Lloyd ("Cupid")	Tex Parker	Monkey Mike
Helene Chadwick	Macie Sewell	Roy Laidlaw	Dr. Billy Trowbridge
Andrew Robson	Zack Sewell	Katherine Wallace	Rose
Lloyd Whitlock	Dr. Leroy Simpson	Nelson McDowell	Sheriff Bergin
"Big Boy" Guinn Williams	Hairoil Johnson	Cordelia Callahan	Mrs. Bergin

Synopsis: Alec Lloyd is nicknamed "Cupid" by his friends because of his insatiable urges to get all of his fellow cowpunchers married off—even though quite a number of the matches he has engineered have not exactly provided the bliss promised. Every time Alec feels the desire for matchmaking coming on, he breaks into song—the old-fashioned "In the Shade of the Old Apple Tree."

When the first raising of Alec's voice in the familiar song is heard, eligible townspeople take off, for "Cupid" is out to snare another unsuspecting victim.

At last, Alec, himself, falls in love; it is his boss's daughter Macie. He manages to have her elected winner of a beauty contest conducted by a traveling medicine show, while he wins the "Homeliest Man" title. Even though he has a rival for Macie's love, an eastern doctor, Alec gets the girl of his own choice.

From Column: ★ "Everyone who saw Will Rogers in 'Jubilo' will recall that in the character of the happy-go-lucky tramp of this great picture the famous comedian sang a little song called 'Jubilo' on every possible occasion and the number became very popular, and is used now in cabarets as a fox trot."

Unidentified newspaper column

Review: ★ "This picture belongs to Will Rogers, lock, stock and barrel. He appears in 99 44/100 per cent of the scenes, does his famous rope stunts, rides a bucking broncho and has quite evidently contributed most of the titles along with his share of the entertainment."

Motion Picture News, August 7, 1920

Music: *Cupid, the Cowpuncher* (Goldwyn)

The timing is based on a speed limit of 14 minutes per reel (1,000 ft.)

Theme: "Under the Shade of the Old Apple Tree"

1 "Western Rodeo" (cowboy descriptive), by Minot (2 minutes and 15 seconds), until—S: At screening.

2 Theme (40 seconds), until—T: "With a heart."

3 Continue to action (1 minute and 20 seconds), until—T: "We don't go nowhere."

4 "Laughing Beauties" (2/4 moderato), by Berge (1 minute and 3 seconds), until—T: "Zack Sewell, owner."

5 Theme (1 minute and 35 seconds), until—T: "The next morning."

6 "Continue to action" (2 minutes and 10 seconds), until—T: "Teeth like hell."

7 "Stampede," by Simons (2 minutes and 30 seconds), until—T: "Back home after———"

8 Theme (50 seconds), until—T: "Say, you're some cowboy."

9 "Wigwam" (Indian fox-trot), by Samuels & Sanford (3 minutes and 15 seconds), until—T: "The renowned Blackfoot."

On location for *Cupid, the Cowpuncher;* Will gets directions, 1920.

Riding "School Girl," a horse Will used here in *Cupid, the Cowpuncher*, 1920, and again in *Two Wagons, Both Covered*, 1923.

10 Continue to action (50 seconds), until—T: "Here's eight dollars."

11 "Frivolettes" (allegretto), by Baron (3 minutes), until—T: "Cupid canvasses the town."

12 "Comedy Allegro," by Berg (2 minutes and 55 seconds), until—T: "The battle has raged."

13 Continue pp. (1 minute), until—T: "It was mean of them."

14 Theme (1 minute and 20 seconds), until—T: "The last few weeks."

15 Toreador Song from "Carmen," by Bizet (35 seconds), until—T: "Please don't do to———"

16 "Rêve d'Amour" (Romance), by Zamecnik (4 minutes and 50 seconds), until—T: "I see myself."

17 "Mamselle Caprice" (allegretto grazioso), by Baron (2 minutes and 35 seconds), until—T: "Humble pie."

18 "Hurry" (for pursuit and races), by Minot (2 minutes and 30 seconds), until—T: "At the busiest hour."

19 "Gavotte and Musette" (allegro), by Raff (4 minutes), until—T: "I'll do the best I can."

20 "Half Reel Hurry," by Levy (2 minutes and 15 seconds), until—T: "On the road to———"

21 "Impish Elves," by Borch (1 minute and 35 seconds), until—T: "You come with me."

22 Theme (1 minute and 50 seconds), until—T: "I wanted to see———" The end.

HONEST HUTCH

Goldwyn Pictures Corp.,   Copyright September 14, 1920, LP 15551; renewed August 13, 1948, R 37110; b&w; silent; 6 reels (as per copyright registration); 5,349 ft. Release: September 19, 1920. Working title: *Old Hutch.*

Production Staff: Director: Clarence G. Badger; cameraman: Marcel Le Picard; based on the *Saturday Evening Post* story (February 28, 1920) "Old Hutch Lives Up to It," by Garret Smith; screenplay by Arthur F. Statter.

Cast:

Will Rogers	Ort ("Honest Hutch") Hutchins	Eddie Trebaol	
Mary Alden	Sarah ("Sary") Hutchins	Jeanette Trebaol	The Hutchins children
Priscilla Bonner	Ellen	Yves Trebaol	
Tully Marshall	Thomas Gunnison	Byron Munson	Thomas Gunnison, Jr.
Nick Cogley	Hiram Joy	and 9 dogs from the pound	

Synopsis: Ort Hutchins, "Honest Hutch," is a shiftless, lazy, happy-go-lucky loafer in a small town on the banks of the Mississippi who will exert himself just enough to hunt up excuses to keep out of work. Day after day finds him sitting on the riverbank, fishing, while his jewel of a wife, "Sary," supports their dirty, ragged brood of children.

One day while digging for bait, Honest Hutch discovers a buried box, containing what seems like the loot from a bank robbery. It is $50,000—all in thousand-dollar bills. Hutch realizes that the money is useless to him, as nobody would ever believe him to be the possessor of such a fortune. To account for his sudden prosperity, he must first acquire the reputation of a successful farmer and businessman. Carefully he selects a new hiding place for the money and reburies it.

Reluctantly Hutch goes to work. The farm, long in a sorry state, now becomes productive; the house is cleaned, the family becomes neat and orderly. Through his own efforts, Hutch makes a success of farming and other investments—he becomes prosperous.

Eventually, when old Hutch goes to dig up the treasure, he finds that the bank robbers have reclaimed their loot. But by now Hutch is well established in his new, well-ordered life, which he has created.

Reviews: ★ "The new Will Rogers' picture [is] called 'Honest Hutch.' It is the best Will Rogers' picture we have ever seen, which is perhaps the best thing that could be said of any comedy now on the film market. Indeed, if we were not somewhat coy about superlatives, we would say that it is the most delightful picture of this type ever screened."

Theatre, December 1920

★ "An odd and homely little tale, shining out of an exceedingly dull photoplay month is 'Honest Hutch,' an unpretentious Will Rogers effort which, to our way of thinking, is the best thing ever done by Goldwyn. Interesting it is to see this simple story of a village loafer easily displace all the expenditure and elaborateness of a long line of Goldwyn productions."

Motion Picture Classic, December 1920

Music: *Honest Hutch*   Specially selected and compiled by M. Winkler

The timing is based on a speed limit of 14 minutes per reel (1,000 ft.)

Theme: "Scherzetto" (from Symphonette Suite), Berge

1 Theme (4 minutes and 5 seconds), until—S: At screening.

2 "Adolescence," by Collinge (3 minutes and 55 seconds), until—T: "Ellen Hutchins with ribbons."

3 "Twilight Reverie," by Berge (4 minutes), until—T: "Mrs. Hiram Joy, wife of the ———"

4 "Norma" (valse lente), by Luz (1 minute and 45 seconds), until—T: "If he didn't have to watch."

5 "Laughing Beauties," by Berge (2 minutes and 25 seconds), until—T: "Tom Gunnison, son of the ———"

6 "Dramatic Suspense," by Winkler (4 minutes and 10 seconds), until—T: "I've told you to quit."

7 Theme (2 minutes and 45 seconds), until—T: "How can he realize?"

8 "Babillage" (entr'acte), by Castillo (3 minutes and 55 seconds), until—T: "Gunnison's store the clearing———"

9 "Pizzicato Mysterioso" (for burglary or stealth), by Minot (50 seconds), until—T: "Yes, sir, $50,000."

10 "Serenade Romantique" (and. con moto), by Borch (1 minute and 40 seconds), until—T: "The next step in the ———"

11 "Frivolette" (entr'acte), by Baron (4 minutes and 40 seconds), until—T: "If the Hutchins' table ever———"

12 Theme (4 minutes and 20 seconds), until—T: "If Sarah had seen Hutch the———"

13 "Spring Blossom" (novelette), by Castillo (1 minute and 25 seconds), until—T: "Durn wimin, anyhow."

14 Organ accompaniment to action (church services) (4 minutes), until—T: "The Hutchins family creates———"

15 "Lovelette" (allegretto grazioso), by Levy (3 minutes and 20 seconds), until—S: People leaving church.

16 "Chiribiribim" (Italian waltz), by Pestalozza (50 seconds), until—T: "Afore leaving I'll be———"

17 "Skeleton Dance," by Stevenson (3 minutes and 5 seconds), until—T: "Someone had told Hutch."

NOTE: Watch shots

18 Theme (1 minute and 25 seconds), until—T: "What have you got thar?"

19 "At Twilight," by Golden (2 minutes and 25 seconds), until—T: "Supernatural means having———"

20 "Kiss a Miss" (valse chantee), by Baron (4 minutes and 5 seconds), until—T: "With the harvest season."

21 "Recuerdos" (Spanish caprice), by Santos (25 seconds), until—T: "Hutch makes a slight————"

22 "Rêve d'Amour," by Zamecnik (3 minutes and 45 seconds), until—T: "Well I hope some poor man————"

23 "Flirty Flirts," by Levy (3 minutes and 45 seconds), until—T: "Now listen to what————"

24 Theme (50 seconds), until S: Close-up of woman with wash basket." Until—the end.

Will Rogers Said

I will never forget one time, I made a picture where I was fishing and found some money. It had been stolen and hidden, and it was all in one-thousand-dollar bills, and here I was and couldn't pass 'em.

Well, just even in a picture, it was annoying.

Syndicated column, January 28, 1934

GUILE OF WOMEN

Goldwyn Pictures Corp., Copyright December 26, 1920, LP 15975; renewed November 17, 1948, R 40458; b&w; silent; 5 reels, 4,496 ft. Release: December 26, 1920, California Theatre, L.A.; March 1921, Capitol Theatre, NYC. Location shots: San Francisco.

Production Staff: Director: Clarence G. Badger; assistant director: James Flood; cameraman: Marcel Le Picard; based on the *Saturday Evening Post* story (April 10, 1920) by Peter Clark MacFarlane; screenplay by Edfrid A. Bingham.

Cast:

Will Rogers	Hjalmar ("Yal") Maartens	Nick Cogley	Captain Stahl
Mary Warren	Hulda Swanson	Doris Pawn	Annie
Bert Sprotte	Skole Knudson	John Ince	Butler
Lionel Belmore	Armstrong	Jane Starr	Maid
Charles A. Smiley	Captain Larsen		

Synopsis: "Yal" is a fisherman who left his sweetheart Hulda back in Sweden and sailed for America to make his fortune. When he had saved some money, he sent Hulda $1,000 to come to him. But five years have passed and Yal never again heard from her. Despite this unhappy experience, Yal has a new girl, Annie. With $3,000 he has saved, Yal opens a delicatessen and puts Annie in charge. When he tries to sell the store to use the money to purchase a partnership in a ship, Annie lies and insists that he never gave any money, and that the store is hers. As Yal has no papers, he cannot prove that the store had been bought with his money. He becomes even more distrustful of women.

Then, one day, he sees Hulda on the waterfront. Yal is torn between the love he still feels for his Swedish sweetheart and his fear of women's guile. The former wins and he learns from Hulda that she never received the money he sent, and that she came to America on her own, to look for him. She found a position with Captain Larsen and his wife. What Hulda does not tell him is that the Larsens—being childless—adopted her. While Yal thinks Hulda just a maid, she is really their daughter.

When Yal has saved enough money to furnish a house, he asks Hulda to marry him. But on the evening before his wedding, Yal is being shanghaied by Armstrong, who wants to marry the prospective heiress himself. But Yal dives off the ship into San Francisco Bay, gets aboard a fishing boat, and arrives back—wet and barefoot—in time to be married.

Captain Larsen dies and Hulda confesses that she is now the new owner of the captain's fishing fleet, and Yal is made president of the company.

Music: *Guile of Women*   Specially selected and compiled by M. Winkler

The timing is based on a speed limit of 14 minutes per reel (1,000 ft.)

Theme: "Capricietta" (allegro moderato), by Varley

1   "Swedish Peasant" (¾ allegretto), by Translateur (2 minutes and 20 seconds), until—S: At screening.

2   "Saeterjentens Sandag" (Swedish song), by Ole Bull (1 minute and 20 seconds), until—T: "Just before the great war."

3   "Caprice Joyeaux" (melodious allegretto), by Seeligson (1 minute and 35 seconds), until—T: "So she came to you."

4   Continue to action (1 minute and 15 seconds), until—T: "The Howe delicatessen shop."

5   "Serenade Lointaine" (6/8 moderato), by Berge (2 minutes and 45 seconds), until—T: "The office of the White Bean."

6   "Dramatic Agitato," by Simon (1 minute and 35 seconds), until—T: "Eager to tell Annie."

NOTE: Begin pp. then to action

7   Theme (3 minutes), until—T: "If you are going to have———"

8   "Adagietto" (from Symphonette Suite), by Berge (3 minutes and 50 seconds), until—T: "You haven't got any proof."

9   Theme (2 minutes and 35 seconds), until—T: "Never again, Skole."

10   Repeat: "Swedish Peasant," by Translateur (1 minute and 30 seconds), until—T: "Crow's Nest —Captain."

11   "Courtesy" (Langey moderato), by Langey (5 minutes and 5 seconds), until—T: "Why are you dressed like———"

12   "Serenade Romantique" (and. con moto), by Borch (2 minutes and 55 seconds), until—T: "Skole was right."

NOTE: Effect of steam whistle

13   Theme (1 minute), until—T: "Remembering with shame."

14   "Sparkles" (6/8 moderato), by Miles (3 minutes and 30 seconds), until—T: "Two months after."

15   "Love Song" (moderato), by Puerner (2 minutes), until—T: "The evening before the———"

16   "Sinister Theme" (for scenes of impending danger), by Vely (50 seconds), until—T: "Yet that's most of bad———"

17   "Lento Allegro" (from Symphonette Suite), by Berge (3 minutes and 5 seconds), until—T: "The wedding morn finds———"

18   "Dramatic Suspense," by Winkler (1 minute and 50 seconds), until—S: Close-up of bride.

19   Theme (1 minute and 30 seconds), until—T: "Two minutes to twelve."

20   "Comedy Allegro," by Berg (3 minutes and 25 seconds), until—T: "Two hundred dollars he———"

21   "Gavotte & Musette" (allegro melody), by Raff (2 minutes and 25 seconds), until—T: "Where is Hulda?"

22   "Dramatic Narrative" (for scenes of reminiscence), by Pement (2 minutes), until—T: "You'd better go."

23   Theme ff. (1 minute and 25 seconds), until—T: "I can't be just." The end.

Rehearsal on location for *Guile of Women*, 1920.

BOYS WILL BE BOYS

Goldwyn Pictures Corp., Copyright January 27, 1921, LP 16077; renewed December 10, 1948, R 40933; b&w; silent; 5 reels, 4,300 ft. Release: February 27, 1921, California Theatre, L.A.; May 15, 1921, Capitol Theatre, NYC. Review in *New York Times*, May 16, 1921, 20:2.

Production Staff: Director: Clarence G. Badger; cameraman: Marcel Le Picard; based on *Saturday Evening Post* story (October 20, 1917) by Irvin S. Cobb, and a three-act play (NYC, 1925) by Charles O'Brien Kennedy, screenplay by Edfrid A. Bingham.

Cast:

Will Rogers	Peep O'Day	C. E. Thurston	Sheriff Breck
Irene Rich	Lucy	May Hopkins	Kitty
C. E. Mason	Tom Minor	Cordelia Callahan	Mrs. Hunter
Sydney Ainsworth	Sublette	Nick Cogley	Aunt Mandy
Edward Kimball	Judge Priest	Burton Halbert	Farmer Bell
H. Milton Ross	Bagby		

Synopsis: Peep O'Day lives in the livery stable of a small Kentucky town. Born on the Poor Farm, raised in the orphanage, an illiterate, he has never had more than eighty cents in his pocket at any one time. He is the town character, good-natured and dreamy, befriended only by Lucy, the local schoolteacher.

He suddenly becomes the town's richest and most important citizen when he inherits $40,000 from an uncle in Ireland. For the first time in his life, Peep can fulfill his dreams, yet all he wants is to make up for the lost pleasures of his childhood—candy, picnics, children's games, stealing watermelons (after first paying for them). To enjoy these pleasures even more, he shares them with the children of the orphanage where he once lived. But Sublette, the crooked lawyer, plots to have Peep declared insane and produces a "niece"—scheming manicurist—to claim the inheritance.

Judge Priest, who hears the case, finds that Peep is perfectly rational and entitled to the joys he seeks; he even gets the larcenous "niece" to confess.

Reviews: ★ "As a featured photoplay . . . this comedy would be disappointing. Save for the homely grace of Rogers and a number of deft strokes of characterization he is able to get in, it is pretty flat."
New York Times, May 16, 1921, 20:2

★ "The result of combining Will Rogers with Irvin S. Cobb is a simple excellently titled, quaintly humorous, but rather weak feature."
Motion Picture News, May 28, 1921

On location for *Boys Will Be Boys,* 1921; director Clarence Badger serves cake to cast. (*Academy of Motion Picture Arts and Sciences*)

WHAT? ME AN ACTOR?

I'm not an actor, I'm a rope thrower. I can't act. I can't be nothing but myself. And I don't aim for an argument with a picture taker, but I can't see any sense in an awkward maverick like me tryin' to look sweet and pretty before a camera.

And I don't want to be a hero. Let Bill Hart and Tom Mix do that. Heroes are right good to look at and we all like to see thrillers, but I don't aim to play in those parts. I was never much on killin' people and I'd rather not gallop through my pictures armed like a battleship and linin' a dozen bad men against the Arizona skyline, dyin' of fright.

I'm friendly by nature, I guess, and in my pictures I'd like to smile a lot and make everyone feel sociable at home-like. Then, maybe, we could tack a wedding on the end, with some love scenes and all—you know.

But movie people are funny! They send me a book to read and ask if I'd like to do it in pictures. I read the book and write back that I would. Then they don't buy it. And if I say I don't like a story, they buy it. I don't know much about pictures, though.

Yet I like pictures, but then I like whatever I'm working at. I think we all like to be where things are going kinda good and coming our way. And I'm going to see that my kids have everything. I just bought a new place in Beverly Hills and I have everything I could think of for them: circus, swimming pool, animals, toys, everything to make kids happy. But I'm not fooling myself like a lot of these people 'round here, counting on good things to come. No siree! Just now I'm doing fine—but it ain't going to last—all luck!

But I ain't counting on no luck. If anything ever happens, I've got a whole bunch of new rope tricks up my sleeve and just let 'em give me time to read the evening papers and I'll have a vaudeville act ready. I ain't getting rusty and don't you think it—I don't trust this lady luck.

I always was that way. In vaudeville I'd always think each week would be my last and I'd plan what I'd do when I had to shove off. I was always ready for the worst that could happen. Same way when I was in New York in the *Follies*—each season I'd think would be my last. Every first night would go bad. Nobody would laugh at my gags. You see, a first-night audience at the *Follies* is made up of Broadway people. Very few of them ever read the current events in the newspapers. They didn't know what I was talking about. But when the second night came with a few honest-to-God people in the audience, the act went fine. Always was that way. I never had a good first night in the *Follies*.

So when I decided to go into the pictures I just packed my rope and chewing gum, and westward, ho! with my wife and kiddies and their ponies and cats and dogs and toys. Anyhow, I had made up my mind that I would not wait a minute after my first two pictures were made if they were a failure.

The thing that struck me most when I saw myself on the screen was I never knew before how homely I was. I never did think I was an Apollo, but I didn't think I was as ugly as that face that grinned at me. But there ain't no bitter that hasn't got something sweet about it, and if you look long enough you can find it. I was the homeliest man on the screen. It was unique, distinguishing! Whatever you are, be that thing just a little better than anyone else, and you are all right.

So my grin came back.

AN UNWILLING HERO

Goldwyn Pictures Corp., Copyright April 28, 1921, LP 16433; b&w; silent; 5 reels, 4,759 ft. Release: May 8, 1921, L.A. Location shots: New Orleans.

Production Staff: Director: Clarence G. Badger; cameraman: Marcel Le Picard; art director: Cedric Gibbons; screenplay by Arthur F. Statter, based upon the short story "Whistling Dick's Christmas Stocking" (c. 1909), by O'Henry (William Sydney Porter).

Cast:

Will Rogers	Whistling Dick	George Kunkel	
Molly Malone	Nadine	Dick Johnson	Hoboes
John Bowers	Hunter	Larry Fisher	
Darrel Foss	Richmond	Leo Willis	
Jack Curtis	Boston Harry	Nick Cogley	Negro servant
		Edward Kimball	Lovejoy

Synopsis: Whistling Dick is a good-natured, ragged, work-shunning hobo who likes to whistle classical tunes. He arrives at the winter meeting of his tribe in New Orleans, only to learn that some of the tramps are scheming to rob a plantation on Christmas Eve. They have inside information from Richmond, who is not only a guest at the plantation but seeks to marry Nadine, the daughter of the house. Nadine, however, is in love with Hunter, the plantation overseer.

Dick will have no part of the plan and moves on, but by chance he meets Nadine and Hunter, who are driving along the same road. They offer him a ride and even give him a Christmas present. Dick warns them of the planned robbery, and in gratitude he is welcomed as a guest at the plantation, is given new clothes, and is offered employment, but Dick manages to escape the threatening respectability.

Review: ★ "It is difficult to choose between Will Rogers and his titles. Certainly the New York audience appreciated to the fullest Rogers' powers as a humorous writer. From the time the shivering tramp looks heavenward at the flock of wild geese flying southward over New England and says: 'Just to show that I have as much intelligence as those geese, I'm going south too,' up to the time when he exclaims 'I'm one of the few men that prohibition hasn't driven to drink,' the titles are exhilarating in their originality. Not one is trite or forced."

Motion Picture News, July 23, 1921

Censorship

A Will Rogers film had always seemed censor-proof. Not so with *An Unwilling Hero*. In Pennsylvania, censors ordered the following deletions:

1. View of hobo holding gun up close to Rogers' back, following subtitle: "You stick right here!"
2. Subtitle: "We'll set fire to the sheds. That'll get the men out of the house and leave only the women inside."
3. Subtitle: "Then we'll rush the house, grab the money, and scoot."
4. Views of hoboes seen gathering and placing brush around shed.
5. All views of hoboes kneeling down, lighting and setting fire to brush.
6. View of hobo opening safe and taking out bag of money and placing it inside his coat.

Charlie Chaplin visits set of *An Unwilling Hero*, 1921, and inspects "wine." *From left:* John Bowers, Molly Malone, Will, Chaplin, and Ed Kimball. (*Academy of Motion Picture Arts and Sciences*)

An Unwilling Hero, 1921.

On set of *An Unwilling Hero*, 1921. Will tries to teach visiting Charlie Chaplin the secret of twirling a lariat. (*Academy of Motion Picture Arts and Sciences*)

DOUBLING FOR ROMEO

Goldwyn Pictures Corp., Copyright November 2, 1921, LP 17141; renewed October 17, 1948, R 53125; b&w; silent; 6 reels (as per copyright registration), 5304 ft.; running time 70 minutes. Release: October 23, 1921, Capitol Theatre, NYC. Review in *New York Times*, October 24, 1921, 13:1. Extant. In March 1921, exterior shots were made at Jackson, California, where Will Rogers gave a benefit performance for charity.

Production Staff: Director: Clarence G. Badger: cameraman: Marcel Le Picard; based on the outline by Elmer L. Rice and Will Rogers, "assisted" by William Shakespeare; screenplay by Bernard McConville; titles by "Will Rogers and a few borrowings from Wm. Shakespeare."

Cast:

Will Rogers	Sam "Slim" Cody (Romeo)	C. E. Thurston	Duffy Saunders (Benvolio)
Sylvia Breamer	Lulu Foster (Juliet)	Cordelia Callahan	Maggie (maid)
Raymond Hatton	Steve Woods (Paris)	Roland Rushton	Minister (Friar Lawrence)
Sidney Ainsworth	"Buck" Pendleton (Mercutio)	Jimmy Rogers	Jimmie Jones
Al Hart	Big Alec (Tybalt)	William Orlamond	Movie director
John Cossar	Robert Foster (Capulet)	with Kate Lester	

Synopsis: Sam Cody, called "Slim," is an Arizona cowboy in love with Lulu, who can't decide between the tongue-tied ranch hand and the smooth-talking, handsome soda jerk from the village drugstore. Lulu wants to be courted in the romantic ways she has seen in the movies. So Slim quits his job and goes to Hollywood to learn lovemaking from the movie heroes. He gets a job as a "double," but not for any hero's love scenes. Slim is to stand in for the villain's losing fight scenes, and he gets slammed and battered. He quits when, after a bruising fight, the director insists on a retake.

When given a copy of *Romeo and Juliet*, he falls asleep and dreams of being Romeo, and of his friends taking other character parts of the play; there are sword fights and romantic love scenes. When Slim wakes up, he combines the eloquence of Romeo with the brute strength tactics of the cavemen, and wins Lulu.

Reviews: ★ " 'Doubling for Romeo' is about the most hilarious thing Mr. Rogers has done."
New York Times, October 24, 1921

★ "The personality of Will Rogers, titles contributed by the star, which are the acme of wit and appropriateness, a wealth of truly humorous incidents and one of the most ingenious picture ideas ever to be used, all contribute in making 'Doubling for Romeo' fine entertainment. . . . The picture is pretty much Will Rogers' from beginning to end, which is as it should be. It also looks as if he had something to do with the direction. There is so much typical Rogers stuff used, to be otherwise."
Motion Picture News, November 8, 1921

Recognitions: ★ On list of Best Pictures of 1922, *Photoplay Magazine*

★ #8 of Year's Best Films, *The Reel Journal*

Will Rogers' Comment

I made *Doubling for Romeo* for Sam Goldwyn. It was the story of a cowhand who went to sleep and dreamed he played Romeo in Shakespeare's immortal drama. I like my work in this one a lot, but they had a sales convention at the studio and showed the film to the gang. Although I thought the picture was very funny, the boys seemed to think different and refused to laugh. At the time I was nearly heartbroken. I felt that I was a flop and was about to quit pictures. Gosh it was awful!

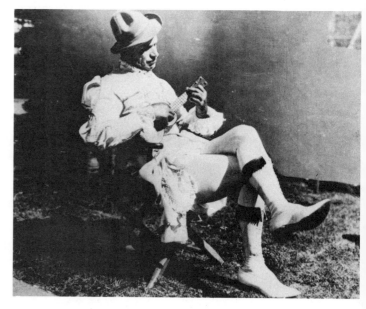

Between scenes on the set of *Doubling for Romeo*, 1921.

A POOR RELATION

Goldwyn Pictures Corp., Copyright November 29, 1921, LP 17243; renewed September 30, 1949, R 52585; b&w; silent; 5 reels, 4,609 ft. Release: December 1921.

Production Staff: Director: Clarence G. Badger; cameraman: Marcel Le Picard; based on three-act comedy/drama of same name by Edward E. Kidder; screenplay by Bernard McConville.

Cast:

Will Rogers	Noah Vale	Molly Malone	Scallops
Sylvia Breamer	Miss Fay	Robert De Vilbiss	Rip
Wallace MacDonald	Johnny Smith	Jeanette Trebaol	Patch
Sydney Ainsworth	Sterrett	Walter Perry	O'Halley
George B. Williams	Mr. Fay		

Synopsis: Noah Vale lives in poverty, spending every minute on perfecting an invention. He is barely able to keep his head above water and raise the two orphans he adopted, Rip and Patch. He is helped considerably by a girl, Scallops, who occasionally brings them food.

Trying to enlist the help of well-to-do relatives, Noah asks Mr. Fay for funds to complete and market his invention. Fay is not impressed, but his daughter becomes interested. Sterrett, Fay's partner, steals Noah's model and tries to market it in his own name, only to discover that it has no commercial value. He returns it.

Johnny Smith, Fay's secretary, is in love with his employer's daughter, and when it is learned that he has proposed to her he is dismissed. Hoping to find a kindred soul, he visits Noah, who reads him his philosophical witticisms. Impressed by what he hears, Smith takes Noah's work to a publisher, who decides to publish them in book form, promising fame and fortune to both men. Vale decides to give up inventing and concentrate on his writing, while Johnny decides to marry the girl he loves, even without her parents' consent.

Review: ★ " 'A Poor Relation,' enforces what many people have long contended, that Rogers is one of the most versatile character actors the screen boasts today, and that he is not by any means limited to the shy cowboy or self-sacrificing, bashful tramp role. Unless the writer's memory is at great fault, the comedian has not played a role like it before. He gives one of his superlative performances."

Moving Picture World, April 15, 1922

Earliest surviving film poster for *Laughing Bill Hyde*, 1918. (*Courtesy Charles Banks Wilson*)

WILL ROGERS SUGGESTS

- Use your audience for a press agent instead of hiring one.
- Don't tell your audience what your picture cost; they know what they were stung by the price of admission.
- You hear it asked: Are movie audiences getting smarter? The answer is No! Ain't more people going to movies than there ever was?
- There is only one thing that can kill the movies, and that is education.
- What movies need is another name for an All-Star Cast.
- What the picture business needs is a picture.
- What the movie audience needs is endurance.
- What the movie actor needs is better doubles, so they can do better stunts.
- What the weeping movie heroine needs is glycerin that won't stay in one place but will run down the face.
- What the entire industry needs is a sense of humor.
- If the movies want to advance, all they have to do is not get new stories but do the old ones over as they were written.
- Producers say pictures have improved, but they haven't. It's only that audiences have got used to them.
- The finish of the movies will be when they run out of suggestive titles.
- Some cynics ask, Is movies really an art yet? Yes, selling 'em is.
- The average life of the movie is till it reaches the critic.
- The average life of the movie hero is till he is found out.

Will Rogers, Pioneer

I was in pictures before they were referred to by the press agents as an art. I was in Hollywood away back, when some of these big stars now were just learning to get married.

In other words, I am what you call a pioneer. I am all right in anything while it's in its crude state, but the minute it gets to having any class, why, I am sunk. After anything begins to take itself serious, I have to gradually drop out—sometimes suddenly.

You see, pictures have to undergo a poor, or what Will Hays would call "mediocre," stage before they can get to be big. Well, there is the stage that I assisted the great film industry through. The minute they commenced to getting better, why, my mission had been fulfilled.

Syndicated column, August 22, 1926

2
THE ILLITERATE DIGEST

The Humorist

The Gaumont people are to add a monologue feature to their News and Graphic releases. Will Rogers is to do the talking for them on matters topical."

Variety, May 23, 1919

Will Rogers and his principals felt that his humorous views of events should not remain confined to Ziegfeld's stage, but could be disseminated via film strips to any motion picture theater. His one- and two-liners would be flashed on the screen, together with his image. Even though Rogers' words—now in written form—lacked the warmth and impact of his unique delivery, people laughed at his observations. His fame spread into the remotest towns, provided they had one of those newfangled film theaters.

The idea of such short film strips was not new. One Aaron Hoffman had originated a humorous series called Topplitsky Says: *And then there were comments on the daily news by* The Literary Digest Topics of the Day. *These strips were prepared by the prestigious periodical,* The Literary Digest. *Founded in 1890 by Isaac K. Funk and Adam W. Wagnalls, it enjoyed nationwide circulation and influence. And the powers-that-be at* The Literary Digest *looked asquint at this upstart competition, calling itself* The Illiterate Digest.

One William Beverly Winslow, a lawyer with offices deep in New York City's financial center, represented The Literary Digest.

In his book The Illiterate Digest, *Will Rogers dedicates the volume to lawyer Winslow, and explains the entire incident:*

Two Letters and a Dedication

Most books have to have an excuse by some one for the author, but this is the only book ever written that has to have an alibi for the title, too. About four years ago, out in California, I was writing sayings for the screen and I called it The Illiterate Digest. Well one day up bobs the following letter from this N.Y. lawyer. It, and the answer are absolutely just as they were exchanged at that time.

William Beverly Winslow
Lawyer
55 Liberty Street,
New York, N.Y.

Nov. 5th, 1920.

Will Rogers, Esq.,
c/o Goldwyn Studios,
Culver City, Calif.

Dear Sir:-

My client, the Funk & Wagnalls Company, publishers of the "Literary Digest" have requested me to write to you in regard to your use of the phrase, "The Illiterate Digest," as a title to a moving picture subject gotten up by you, the consequence of which may have escaped your consideration.

For more than two years past it (my client) has placed upon the moving picture screen a short reel subject carrying the title "Topics of the Day," selected from the Press of the World by "The Literary Digest." This subject has achieved a wide popularity both because of the character and renown of "The Literary Digest" and through the expenditure of much time, effort and money by its owners in presenting the subject to the public. "The Literary Digest" is a publication nearly thirty years old, and from a small beginning has become probably the most influential weekly publication in the world. Its name and the phrase "Topics of the Day" are fully covered by usage as trademarks as well as by registration as such in the United States Patent Office.

Overleaf: cartoon by famous Oklahoma artist, Charles Banks Wilson.

During several months past your 'title,' "The Illiterate Digest" has been repeatedly called to our attention and we are told that the prestige of "The Literary Digest" is being lowered by the subject matter of your films as well as by the title of your film because the public naturally confuse the two subjects. We are also told that exhibitors are being misled by the similarity of titles and that some of them install your subject in the expectation that they are securing "The Literary Digest Topics of the Day."

It seems to me self-evident that your title would scarcely have been thought of or adopted had it not been for our magazine and for our film. If this were not the case the title which you use would be without significance to the general public.

I have advised the publishers that they may proceed against you through the Federal Trade Commission in Washington calling upon you to there defend yourself against the charge of "unfair competition," because of your simulation of their title, or that they can proceed against you, the producers of your film, its distributors and exhibitors in court for an injunction restraining you from use of the title, "The Illiterate Digest."

Before, however, instituting any proceedings in either direction, they have suggested that I write directly to you to see if your sense of fairness will not cause you to voluntarily withdraw the use of the objectionable title.

Unless I hear favorably from you on or before the first of December, I shall conclude that you are not willing to accede to this suggestion and will take such steps as I may deem advisable.

Yours truly,
WBW/als   (signed) William Beverly Winslow.

Los Angeles, Cal.
Nov. 15, 1920

Mr Wm Beverly Winslow,

Dear Sir,
Your letter in regard to my competition with the Literary Digest received and I never felt so swelled up in my life. And am glad you wrote directly to me instead of communicating with my lawyers, as I have not yet reached that stage of prominence where I was committing unlawful acts and

requiring a lawyer. Now if the Literary Digest feels that the competition is too keen for them—to show you my good sportsmanship I will withdraw. In fact I had already quit as the gentlemen who put it out were behind in their payments and my humor kinder waned, in fact after a few weeks of no payments I couldn't think of a single joke. And now I want to inform you truly that this is the first that I knew my title of the Illiterate Digest was an infringement on yours as they mean the direct opposite. If a magazine was published called Yes, and another bird put one out called No, I suppose he would be infringeing. But you are a lawyer and its your business to change the meaning of words, so I lose before I start.

Now I have not written for these people in months and they haven't put any gags out unless it is some of the old ones still playing. If they are using gags that I wrote on topical things 6 months ago then I must admit that they would be in competition with the ones the Literary Digest Screen uses now. I will gladly furnish you with their address, in case you want to enter suit. And as I have no lawyer you can take my case too, and whatever we get out of them, we will split at the usual lawyer rates of 80:20, the client of course getting the 20.

Now you inform your editors at once that their most dangerous rival has withdrawn, and that they can go ahead and resume publication. But you inform your clients that if they ever take up rope throwing, or chewing gum, I will consider it a direct infringement of my rights and will protect it with one of the best lawyers in Oklahoma.

Your letter to me telling me I was in competition with the Digest would be just like [President] Harding writing to [losing Democratic candidate] Cox and telling him he took some of his votes.

So long Beverly, if you ever come to California, come out to Beverly where I live and see me.

Illiterately yours
Will Rogers.

When I sent him my answer I read it to some of the movie company I was working with at the time and they kept asking me afterwards if I had received an answer. I did not, and I just thought, oh well, there I go and waste a letter on some high brow lawyer with no sense of humor. I was sore at myself for writing it. About 6 months later I came back to join the *Follies* and who should come to call on me but the nicest old gentleman I had ever met, especially in the law profession. He was the one I had written the letter to, and he had had photographic copies made of my letter and had given them around to all his lawyer friends.

So it is to him and his sense of humor, that I dedicate this volume of deep thought. I might also state that the Literary Digest was broadminded enough to realize that there was room for both, and I want to thank them for allowing me to announce my illiteracy publicly.

★

Samples from *The Illiterate Digest*

• If they convict General Billy Mitchell for talking too much, when will they start trying the Senate?

• A man must say something worth remembering, or there should be no use to hush him up.

• I see America is selling Russia meat now. If they charge them as much for it as they do us, no wonder they are Bolsheviks.

• My idea of an honest man is a fellow who declares income tax on money he sold his vote for.

• If you don't care to sell your vote outright, the Democrats will pay you just for an option on it.

• Ohio claims they are due for a president as they haven't had one since Taft; but look at the United States, it hasn't had one since Lincoln.

• The California delegation to the convention took a carload of Poppies, California's national flower, and they were met by thousands of drug addicts who wanted a bouquet.

• If the Tennessee delegation had brought her national commodity, which is moonshine liquor, they could have broken up the convention.

• We have had six months of Prohibition and the casualty list from drinking wood alcohol reads like the war.

• It has carried away some of our best Prohibitionists.

• They are using airplanes to bring booze from Mexico. One guy is an ace, he has brought down 500 quarts.

• Headline in the papers says: Thieves Get 2,000 Dollars Worth Liquor—must have taken two bottles.

• The worst crime a child can commit nowadays is to eat the raisins his father brings home for fermenting purposes.

• Do your Christmas brewing early!

• Prohibition has done one thing—it has drove whiskey prices up.

• Well, this looks like it will be a wonderful year, if we can only afford to live through it.

• A committee who were investigating the high cost of living turned in a report: We find the cost of living very high and recommend more funds to carry on the investigation.

• That's one advantage of the cafeteria. You get to see the food even if you can't afford to buy it.

• Most places are using girl waitresses. Well, they can do it. Even a child could carry all you can afford to order nowadays.

• A rich New York divorcee sues for more alimony. She claims she can't support their child on 50 thousand a year. Somebody's been feeding that kid meat.

• Headline in the paper says: Bandits from other cities are coming to Los Angeles. The landlords here are going to have competition.

• I see where the courts here are going to be more strict with burglars. They are going to take their guns away from them.

• One burglar was caught twice on the same block and I understand they took his license away from him.

- One fellow robbed five banks and still needed money, another guy robbed one bootlegger, and was able to retire.
- Headline in the papers says: Five Autos Held Up. Didn't say whether it was a bandit or a garage.
- New traffic laws go into effect this week. They change 'em here every ten years whether they need it or not.
- Why do they call it the traffic problem, when things cease to move it's not traffic.
- Here's a way to solve the problem. Eliminate all turns to the right and the left. Everybody traveling West go on Mondays, East—Tuesdays, and so on.
- Sundays are reserved for just the weekend drivers, Sunday night for caring for the injured.
- I see they are tearing down a church here to build a movie theater. Going to keep on building till they find something people will go to.
- You know, if the prices of automobiles keep on going up, that will solve the traffic problem itself.
- Raise the speed limit to 55 miles per hour and make them go that fast or be pinched, that would eliminate the slow, or undesirable element, and kill off the fast.
- Be a good joke on Ireland, if England said we give you freedom just like America, including Prohibition.
- The Republicans built their political platform not only to stand on, but it's in such shape they can crawl under it and hide behind.
- San Francisco children are taught two things, one is to love the Lord, and the other is to hate Los Angeles.
- Over six-hundred delegates instructed by the voters went to Chicago to nominate either Lowden or Johnson, then they nominate someone they never heard of—yet you meet men who will tell you our presidents are chosen by the people.
- People had never heard of Harding but after nomination you would have thought he was dead, the nice things the papers said about him.
- Only two detrimental things have come out in Harding's whole record; one is his middle name, Gamaliel, and the other was he used to play a B-Flat cornet in a band.
- This fellow Watson says he will put up one-hundred thousand dollars to back a third party. At the present price that would buy about eight votes.
- It took six months and about 50 million dollars to nominate a Republican for president, and they nominated a vice-president while they were putting on their hats.
- I used to write gags for Mr. Rothafel at the Rivoli, in New York. He was the first manager to discover that motion pictures were bad. So he had a large orchestra to offset the picture.
- Now he is looking for something to offset the orchestra.
- See where the coal strike was settled in the usual way—by the public paying more for their coal.
- President Wilson lays all the world's troubles on the Peace Treaty not being signed—suppose when it is signed you can even find a place to park your car.
- He says the income tax should be lowered. It will have to be, people are not making enough to pay it.
- Income tax has made liars out of more men than golf has.
- And to make this tax business even more difficult, it's harder to make out than it is to pay.
- In his message the president spoke of the high cost of living; that's all they ever do—just speak of it.

3
MR. WILL ROGERS, PRODUCER

Will Rogers has completed his term with the Goldwyn Company, it is reported, and will head his own organization for the production of two-reel comedies, thus reversing the order of stars whose ambition it is to spread themselves, quantitatively speaking, rather than concentrate on quality. Clarence G. Badger, who has directed the former Rogers pictures, will be associated with him, it is said.

From the *New York Times*, Sunday, July 10, 1921

Will Rogers' venture into independent motion-picture production proved disastrous. He had been in films long enough to know about the possible pitfalls, but he never considered that he could fail. After all, he had been involved in every phase of production, and his ideas had always been sound. Now all he had to do was to put his own ideas on film.

Despite the artistic success and the critical acclaim, Will Rogers' losses were monstrous. His personal savings, bonds put aside for the children, the family assets, all had to be liquidated—and were gone in a moment. And still the creditors came.

For the next seven years Will Rogers worked harder than he had ever done before. Every last bill would be paid in full, and equities would be rebuilt.

With Mary, Will, Jr., and Jimmy, who may need a little help to stay in the saddle.

Aboard liner *Ile de France*, September 1934.

Jimmy, Mary, Betty, Will, and Will, Jr.

While Will, Jr., spins the lariat and Jimmy listens, Will talks to Snowy Baker, Australian sportsman.

Having roped the goat, Jimmy Rogers ponders next step while Dad looks on. (*Academy of Motion Picture Arts and Sciences*)

THE ROPIN' FOOL

Pathé Exchange, Inc., Copyright November 11, 1922, LU 18398; b&w; silent; 2 reels, 2,000 ft. Release: October 29, 1922, Roxy Theatre, NYC. Extant.

Production Staff: Producer: Will Rogers; director: Clarence G. Badger; cameraman: Marcel Le Picard; screenplay and titles by Will Rogers.

Cast:
Will Rogers	"Ropes" Reilly, "The Ropin' Fool"
Irene Rich	The girl
John Ince	The stranger
Guinn ("Big Boy") Williams	The foreman
Russ Powell	The medicine doctor
Bert Sprotte	The sheriff

Synopsis: Little pretense is made here to claim that this film has an important plot; it is basically a vehicle to display Will Rogers' extraordinary skill with the lariat. In short, Rogers, as "Ropes" Reilly, eats, drinks, and even dreams roping. Too shy to propose marriage, he mimes the question by throwing a miniature rope around his girl's ring finger. "Ropes" Reilly will rope anything that moves, be it dog, goose, cat, goat, the medicine doctor's hat, or a prowling rat.

But suddenly, accused of a fictitious crime, "Ropes" almost ends up with a lynch mob's rope around his neck. He is saved—at the proverbial last minute—when it is revealed that his tribulations, including the lynch mob, were engineered by a film company that secretly filmed the exploits of "Ropes" Reilly, and were simply looking for a spectacular ending to their motion picture.

Review: ★ "Now Will of the homely but likable physiognomy comes forth with a two-reel film that is reminiscent of his earlier entertainments, for numerous subtitles written in conversational tone, provocative of hearty laughter, and views of a bewildering variety of roping stunts afford a permanent record of Will Rogers' famous stage stunts and the uniqueness of his monologue.

A Will Rogers Advertisement for the Roxy Theatre, New York City

I got a little two-reel picture here I would like to have you folks stay and look at if you are not in too big a hurry to have your today's prescription filled. I didn't think Mr. Rothafel would run it in a swell joint like this, but he said: "Sure, I will run it, I have put over worse pictures than it in here."

You see, I made this picture myself. It's my own dough in it, so you critics and bootleggers, treat it kindly. Being a cowboy, they always put me in some acting part, and 90 percent of the moving pictures

Showing off with the "Texas Skip," for Irene Rich. (*The Ropin' Fool*, 1922)

Buck McKee on the pony Dopey, caught in a figure eight. (*The Ropin' Fool*, 1922)

have no story, but this is the only one ever admitted it. Theater owners tell me it's generally about the middle of the third reel when audiences go to sleep. I am going to beat them to it with this short picture. I tried to get D. W. Griffith to direct it, but he would be too old by the time he finishes *Two Orphans*. Griffith, they say, advances four years with one of his pictures. Well, here's one that will set 'em right back where they started. If it flops, I will put on a beard and swear it was made in Germany, then it will be a riot. I don't know what you might consider art, but there is thirty years of hard practice in it.

★

An Advertisement

A great many so-called wise guys have said, "Isn't it kinder goin' back to go from five reels to two?"

I say, no, not when you can tell the same story in two reels. I have made fourteen two-reel pictures, which were released in five reels. I'd rather have the credit of making a split reel, if it was any good, than to make the longest picture ever made."

In a little picture called *Ropin' Fool*, where I did all my little fancy catches in slow motion, Dopey was the pony that run for them. He was coal black, and I had my ropes whitened with shoe polish, and the catches showed up fine.

★

Rogers Answers a Critic

Someday I'm going to get me an education and be a critic. I'll learn all about algebra, the fourth dimension, Einstein, psychoanalysis, and flapdoodle—then I'll go out and criticize somethin' I didn't take up.

That sounds like I'm sore, maybe. I ain't sore and I don't think I've got to that point where I'm one of the sacred cows of the movies, or anything like that. This is what I'm crabbing about: I spent thirty years to get so's I could do my ropin' tricks good enough for a picture like *A Ropin' Fool* and then somebody said there wasn't much to it. It didn't have enough plot in it, this critic said, and somebody else said I wasn't as funny as Charlie Chaplin or Harold Lloyd. I found out the first was a lady—a New York lady a-criticizing a ropin' stunt—for that's all the picture was.

I sweat blood and then some making that ropin' picture, especially the part where I snare the rat. It took me two days to get that rat so it wasn't camera shy and another day to get the hang of twirling a line small enough to noose the rat. After I learned the trick it came as easy as throwing a man-size lariat. Like everything else, it's easy when you know how.

★

In making a movie, I can throw a rope without hav-ing a crowd out in front waiting to see me miss. You have to hand it to the movies for that. If you don't do a thing right the first time, the director will make you do it again, and nobody will be wise to the fact that you gummed the job several times before you got it right.

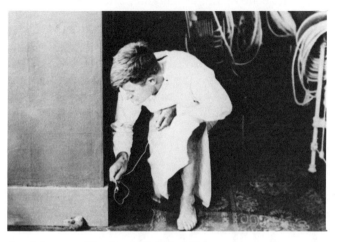

Ropin' a rat. *The Ropin' Fool*, 1922.

A proposal of marriage with a rope engagement ring, with Irene Rich in *The Ropin' Fool*, 1922.

FRUITS OF FAITH

Pathé Exchange, Inc., Copyright December 1, 1922, LU 18438; b&w; silent; 3 reels (as per copyright registration); number of prints: 56. Release: December 24, 1922, Rialto Theatre, NYC. Review in *New York Times*, January 15, 1923. Extant: trims and clips only.

Production Staff: Producer: Will Rogers; director: Clarence G. Badger; cameraman: Marcel Le Picard; original story and screenplay by Mildred and William Pigott; titles by Will Rogers.

Cast:
Will Rogers	Larry, an amiable and likable tramp
Irene Rich	The girl who becomes his wife
Jimmy Rogers	The child found in the desert

Synopsis: In his wanderings, Larry, a likable tramp, happens to meet an itinerant preacher who tells of all the wonders of faith. Larry has only one belief: to shun all work. Persuaded to give faith a chance, he prays for food. His hunger is almost immediately gratified when a passerby's paper bag of groceries bursts open spilling food at his feet.

Larry moves on and in the desert, "beyond the cactus line," he comes upon a small boy and a mule; through the power of prayer, the three manage to survive. When the boy cries for a mother, Larry cannot deny him his desire. He marries and settles down to the life of a useful citizen.

Larry's newfound faith is tested when the boy's real father appears, prepared to take him away; but seeing his child's happiness and his wholesome homelife, he legally turns the boy and his property over to the new parents and moves on.

Reviews: ★ "If there is any fault to find with this . . . it is that the picture is so strong that unless the feature to follow is 'sure fire,' the short subject is bound to be the best part of the program. . . . Three more reels of the same entertainment would not have been amiss."

Motion Picture News, December 23, 1922

★ "[At the Rialto, with *Drums of Fate,* starring Mary Miles Minter.] Let the Drums of Fate sound as loud as they will, they cannot arouse the echo of smiles, laughter and applause called forth by the quiet little film "Fruits of Faith" in which Will Rogers, his baby and a mule take possession of the program at the Rialto this week. After you have sat through the featured photoplay, you come to this real feature of the bill. It's only some two or three reels long and it makes no pretensions as to plot or magnificence of setting. It probably cost less than one reel of the intercontinental concoction which precedes it. But there is more genuine entertainment in any hundred feet of it than in all the celluloid mile of agony and adventure that prolongs the heavy hour of the photoplay. . . . story made human and humorous by the humanness and humor of Will Rogers."

New York Times, January 15, 1923

ONE DAY IN 365

Working titles: *Home Folks; No Story at All.*
Production Staff: Producer: Will Rogers; director: Clarence G. Badger; screenplay and titles by Will Rogers.

Cast: The Will Rogers family

Synopsis: A day in the life of the Rogers family, with the rigor of living in Beverly Hills—just down the hill from famous movie stars.

NOTE: This film was never released, and today only clips and trims remain. It was b&w and silent. The shooting script is at the Will Rogers Memorial, Claremore, Okla.

As for a copyright, none could be located under any of the above titles. However, Pathé Exchange, Inc., filed an application for copyright through Hal Roach on December 1, 1922 (# 18442), with the notation that forty prints would be issued. The name of that film is *365 Days.* It is interesting to note and compare the copyright dates and numbers for *Fruits of Faith* and *365 Days.* The dates are identical, and the numbers are within four digits. It is quite possible that *One Day in 365* and *365 Days* are indeed one and the same film. Pathé would have applied for the copyright had the above film been completed. It would seem strange to have one studio register two such similar titles at precisely the same time. Extant: clips, only.

From *One Day in 365* with Will, Jr., Mary, and Jimmy Rogers, 1922.

Spending hours every day pointing out Mary Pickford's house to visiting Iowans.

4
HAL E. ROACH, AUTHOR

Having lost his savings and reserves, and faced with staggering debts, Will Rogers began the climb back to financial solvency. First of all, he went back into the Follies. Friend Ziegfeld welcomed him with open arms, and so did the theater crowds. In addition to nightly performances, Rogers became the most celebrated after-dinner speaker in New York City and would "address every known organized form of graft" from the National Association of Bankers to the corset manufacturers, from traffic chiefs to building superintendents. In addition, he began to write a syndicated weekly column, about fifteen hundred words, which he would continue until his death.

On March 10, 1923, Will Rogers signed a contract with Hal Roach. Wrote the New York Times, *Sunday, February 11, 1923 (one month before the contract was signed:*

As soon as he finishes his present engagement with "The Follies" Will Rogers will go to the Coast to make his announced series of thirteen two-reel comedies under the management of Hal Roach, producer of the Harold Lloyd works, for distribution by Pathé Exchanges. Mr. Rogers says that he will make five-reel features in two reels.

Visit to the Goldwyn lot, *from left:* Will, Jr., Mary, Betty, Jimmy, and Will.

On the porch of the Beverly Hills home, Jimmy, Betty, Will, Jr., and Mary, c. 1927.

Wrote Will Rogers

So me for Los Angeles and the movies for at least a year, and perhaps two. You see, when I left there a year and a half ago, they were cleaning up the morals of Hollywood and I had to get out. But now that we both have reformed, I am returning.

Syndicated column, June 24, 1923

★

From Goldwyn's I went to work for Hal Roach and made a series of two-reel comedies there. It's a serious business—this making people laugh. One time I was supposed to get on a bucking horse in a corral and he was supposed to buck out of the gate and down to the creek, where he was to throw me off and into the water. Then the leading lady was supposed to come up and see me as I was crawling out of the water, and I was to register embarrassment and try to conceal my wetness at the same time. It was in the wintertime when we took it. The fellow that wrote this little by-play in the scenario did so in a nice, warm, dry room.

Well, I got on the horse and got almost to the gate, when he bucked me off. We caught him and did it over again. And the next time I stayed with him until he got out of the gate, and that was all.

The director said, "That's no good. You'll have to

try it again. You are supposed to stay on until you get to the creek and then get bucked off."

I says, "Say, listen, if you want me to do this scene, you get a corral that's nearer the creek; or better still, find some creek that's nearer a corral."

But wisecracks and picture work pays better than the old rope-throwin' act, and that salves my bruised feelings considerably.

★

Been doing a little prowling around here lately, kind of broke out socially. Mr. Hal Roach, an old employer (don't that mean the guy that hires you? I never could get those two words straight, employer and employee), well, whichever one it is that does the work, why I was him. Roach dug up the money, and I expect sometimes when I hadn't earned it. (Maybe all the time.) It was the twentieth anniversary of his entry into pictures. I think he entered pictures as a cowboy. In those days, if you played in pictures at all, you played a cowboy, for that's all there was to 'em, a cowboy running down a hill and having a fight at the bottom. Hal at that time couldn't ride a horse, especially downhill. He has since learned, and plays an excellent game of polo. But, in those days he must have played the rancher, whose daughter was stolen, and he stayed at home and pointed out which way they went. You remember, there was always one fellow left, just to point.

It was a grand party, the biggest thing I ever saw. It would take me three columns to tell you who all was there. The list read like one of those "Who's delinquent in their income tax?"

I run into Groucho Marx, out by one of the orchestras. I say "one of those orchestras," for there was orchestras for you to get out of your car by, another for you to check your hat by and dance. Why, every couple had their own orchestra. Well, this one I was talking about was Hawaiian and was playing "The Last Round-Up." Groucho suggested that a cowboy tenor voice would be just about what was lacking in this whole musical setup. Now I have a voice—it's what you call a fresh voice. You know, I got resonance without any reason, and I've got tone without any tune, and volume with practically no control whatever. You can just go wherever you want with it. I'm kinder like a crooner. I've got an ideal voice for everything—outside of a satisfied listener.

I told Groucho I would sing it, if he would join me with his alto. Now here is a funny thing about those Marxes: Groucho can play as good on the guitar as Harpo can on the Harp, or Chico on the piano. But he never does. So he is really what I call an ideal musician; he can play, but don't. In New York, when I was playing with Miss Dorothy Stone, he even tried to learn me to play the guitar. He would come over to my dressing room before our two shows started, and he would play, and we would sing these old songs. And so this thing was really nothing new we was pulling, but it was new to the gang. And for a half hour we totally ruined (musically) Mr. Roach's party —course lots of folks joined us to try to drown us out. But not us.

The next night, Mrs. Rogers and I had dinner over at Groucho's and we took up right where we had left off. Only he played the piano that night. I love to sing old songs, and anytime anybody will start, I am the loudest. And if they won't start 'em, I will myself.

But we did have a good time at Hal's party, and I believe everybody did. And when he is in pictures for forty years, I am going to go to another one for him.

Roach says he will hire Groucho and me the next time.

Syndicated column, December 24, 1933

Interview with Hal Roach, January 2, 1971

HR: We made a deal with Will to come to work for us—I think the salary was twenty-five hundred dollars a week, which at that time was a lot of money for anybody. My Irish dad, who I don't think ever earned more than ten dollars a week before we got into the picture business, was treasurer of the company. One of his jobs was to give out the checks, and when anybody got over five dollars a day, the old man thought it was absolutely ridiculous. So as he handed out the checks, he would hand them out with a great deal of profanity, saying things like, "Here, you so-and-so, here is your lousy check that you're not entitled to!"

Well, when Will came to work for us, his was the biggest check up to that time. Harold Lloyd, who was on a percentage, did not draw a very big check. But Dad thought, of course, that Harold was entitled to it, because Harold was our bell ringer. Well, anyway, all of a sudden, Dad saw this check for twenty-five hundred dollars. I could just imagine what he built up in his mind as to what he was going to say to Rogers the first time he picked up his check.

A week went by, and Rogers didn't come to get his check. Now Dad had two checks, each for twenty-five hundred dollars, and he couldn't stand it. And a third week went by, and Will still didn't come in to pick up his check. Now the old man was about to have a nervous breakdown. I happened to be on the porch, near my dad's office, as Will was walking by, and Dad walked over to him and said very humbly, "Please, Mr. Rogers, would you mind picking up these checks?"

Instead of the profanity he had already set up —well, it never happened.

From left: Mrs. Will Rogers, Mrs. Will Rogers, Jr., Mrs. James Rogers, Will, Jr., and James.

Will with Hal Roach, on the old Roach ranch on La Cienega Boulevard, Culver City, c. 1922.

HUSTLING HANK

Pathé Exchange, Inc., Copyright November 23, 1923, LU 19649; b&w; silent; 2 reels; 36 prints. Release: November 11, 1923. Extant.

Production Staff: Producer: Hal E. Roach; Director: Perc. Pembroke; Author: Hal E. Roach; Titles by H. M. Walker; Cameramen: Robert Doran and Otto Himm; Editor: T. J. Crizer.

Cast: Will Rogers
Marie Mosquini
Billy Engle
Eddie Baker
Vera White
Gus Leonard

Synopsis: Rogers becomes a cameraman to a militant feminist, determined to get some photographs of wildlife.

As a rule, shorts (one- and two-reelers) were not reviewed, but it is a sign of Rogers' importance that quite a few of his short films were mentioned.

Review: ★ "Will Rogers scores again. . . . the scenes where he pursues a bear in an effort to get his picture, are hilarious, as are some of Rogers' esthetic poses and his manners at the first tea party. It is all very good entertainment, well marked with the star's distinctive personality and talent."
Moving Picture World, November 10, 1923

From *Hustling Hank*, 1923.

TWO WAGONS, BOTH COVERED

Pathé Exchange, Inc.,   Copyright December 14, 1923, LU 19713; b&w; silent; 2 reels; 40 prints. Release: January 6, 1924. Extant. Location shots: Lake Elsinore.

Production Staff: Producer: Hal E. Roach; director: Rob Wagner; screenplay by Will Rogers.

Cast: Will Rogers   { William Banion   Earl Mohan   Sam Woodhull
                               { Bill Jackson   Charles Lloyd   Jesse Wingate
              Marie Mosquini   Molly Wingate

Background: In March 1923, Paramount released a ten-reel western epic, *The Covered Wagon*, presented by Jesse L. Lasky. It was based upon the *Saturday Evening Post* story by Emerson Hough and was one of the outstanding pictures of the year. The scenario was by Jack Cunningham, and the producer/director was James Cruze. (c. March 14, 1923, LP 18770)

Will Rogers' Comment:

I was on location, making a covered-wagon picture (I found two covered wagons that had not worked in the original, so I decided to put them on the screen, as I think that every wagon that has a clean sheet should be seen by the multitudes).

Synopsis: This film tells the "saga" of a wagon train, consisting of only two wagons, taking weeks and months to traverse hundreds of miles—yet every location looks ludicrously like the one before. Rogers imitates actor Ernest Torrence as the scout and, in his dual role, also imitates J. Warren Kerrigan, the hero of *The Covered Wagon*. As the scout, Rogers appears with a full, though disreputable-looking, beard; as the hero, he insists on careful shaves every morning, and in an area overrun by hostile Indians, he insists that the wagon top be properly washed.

Approaching California, the two wagons separate, one heads northward, while we follow the one heading south. As that wagon nears the area of the future Los Angeles, its occupants are attacked by the feared "Escrow Indians," fully armed with lengthy real estate contracts, and dedicated not to depart without a sale. By the time the "Escrow Indians" leave, having successfully waged their sales campaign, the new immigrants are left without even their one covered wagon.

Review: ★ ". . . a splendid burlesque on 'The Covered Wagon' . . . Will Rogers is the stellar quantity in this laughable parody. . . . It is as funny as anything we have ever seen . . ."
New York Times, January 27, 1924, sect. 7, 4:2

The Director's Story

Our first meeting with Will was at Irene Rich's house; we immediately got on Will's wire, and he on ours. A few months later we had a call from the Roach Studio. "Will isn't satisfied with the stuff he's doing here, and he has asked us to let you direct him in a picture," said Warren Doane, the studio manager. "Have you any ideas?" he asked.

"Only this," we replied. "Metro-Goldwyn-Mayer played Will as the character actor, which he isn't, and you have been playing him as a red-nosed comic, which is profane. How would it do to get on the screen what the *Follies* are paying him three thousand dollars a week for? If we could get Will Rogers up there, we'd have something."

"Sounds okay," replied Warren, "let's go."

"Why are you unhappy here?" we asked Will, as we horned into his little, crowded dressing room while he was making up as a small-town loafer.

"Well, I'll tell you, Rob. All I ever do on the Roach lot is run around barns and lose my pants."

We then told him that we had been signed to work with him. Pretending surprise, he asked us to come to his house that night and talk it over. Will had an idea that he would have a lot of fun with *The Covered Wagon*, then a tremendous box-office success. Not merely a burlesque of it, but simply by using the characters and incidents to put over his own satirical humor.

"We'll just have two wagons, an oxteam from Hoboken and a swell horse-drawn coach from Palm Beach. The two parties join and go west to found an 'empire,' which in itself would be unpatriotic in a republic. We could load up on Mayflower furniture, and then for stock to start our empire, take just one bull and a crate of roosters."

After a week or two of collaboration, of discussing various gags, we got completely set on our story—the first complete working script the Roach lot had had, and for which we were "kissed" by the entire technical staff from carpenters to prop boys.

We ran into one difficulty in collaborating on this. Will's mind works in quick, brilliant flashes, but it lacks continuity. It was our job to prepare a stout cord upon which to hang his pearls. Will, however, would become excited over a certain sequence, and the first thing we knew, he'd cut the cord and be off, up another alley. The stuff would be gorgeous, but it led nowhere. Finally we managed to get a straightforward story that carried the two wagons to a point in California where they parted, one going orth to Sacramento, the other south to Los Angeles. As we couldn't go both places, Will, as Torrence, in charge of the oxteam, said good-bye to Will, as Kerrigan, in charge of the horse-team—he played both parts—and we stuck to the oxteam headed for Los Angeles (Will could never quite get over the fun he missed by not going to Sacramento).

When everything was set, Will said: "Rob, let's go a couple of hundred miles away to shoot the picture, for if we stick around here, they'll be building barns for me to lose my pants behind." So we went to Lake Elsinore, where we had locations for water, desert, and mountain stuff.

Will sits beside Hal Roach in this 1923 version of a ranch wagon. Author/director Rob Wagner is farthest left.

One of Will's phobias was his objection to close-ups of his "homely mug," as he called it. We then explained that close-ups were used merely for emphasis, to exclude everything else from the field of vision while the character was registering. "Will," I went on, "these arguments hurt my feelings."

Will must have thought that like all directors, we were more or less crazy, but when our feelings were hurt—well, he threw his arms around our shoulders, and that was the last time he ever argued against our direction.

Will's best wit was inspirational. The immediate business was likely to bring forth the best gag in the picture. We let him talk and kid all he wished to (you could always cut it out), but took no chances on losing one of his priceless pearls.

Our budget was thirty-one thousand dollars; we finished for twenty-eight thousand. Our schedule at Elsinore was for two weeks; we smilingly returned in eleven days. But our smiles vanished as we realized that we had returned to the world's largest mortuary—everybody as glum as a bunch of undertakers.

"Will, it looks as though they didn't like the picture," we said.

"No, I've found that out," he replied. "But I'll tell you what I'm going to do. I'm going to offer to buy the darned thing."

But the studio couldn't sell. A release date had been announced in the East, and as rotten as they considered the picture, the date must be met. We were fired gracefully: "Rob, we love you to death; you're a good executive and you shot the picture underschedule and underbudget, but there isn't a laugh in it."

Some six weeks later we received a phone call from the office girl at the studio, who told us the picture was to be previewed at Santa Monica. We dreaded going, for by this time we had begun to have qualms. "Will, maybe they're right," we said. "They've been in the business of making comedies for fifteen years, and they ought to know. Maybe we're just a pair of half-baked highbrows who think we're funny."

Will shook his head. "No, Rob, I still think the picture is funny."

That preview in Santa Monica was one of the most extraordinary adventures of our very full and snappy life. Sneaking in early on rubber shoes so as to escape the glares of the studio bunch who were bound to be there, the Wagner family took back seats and waited the blow. A George Ade feature comedy came on first and got a grand hand. A tough one to follow. Finally a scratch-title was flashed on the screen—"Hal Roach presents Will Rogers in *Two Wagons, Both Covered*." We almost slid under the seats in shame.

Bam! With the first narrative title the crowd began to laugh. Then as the story progressed, the laughter grew and grew until we thought the audience would pull up the seats. At the end a tremendous cheer. Flushed with excitement, the Wagners proudly made

Will is on white horse, director Rob Wagner with megaphone, filming *Two Wagons, Both Covered*, 1923.

Will as the Yale graduate pioneer, in *Two Wagons, Both Covered*, 1923.

their way through the burbling auditors, and sure enough, they ran smack into the inevitable sidewalk conference.

"Well, you never can tell," said Warren Doane, smiling at last. "Bob, I hear you are under negotiations with Paramount again. Well, come on over and see us tomorrow." So we returned to the Roach lot under much more agreeable terms than we left it. Nor was the preview a flash in the pan. *Two Wagons* went on at the old California, and so sensational was its two weeks run that it went over to Miller's and ran seven weeks as the feature!

With *Two Wagons* as a credential, the Rogers-Wagner combination got under way, but the studio fellows had been thinking, thinking, and thinking and had just about decided *Two Wagons* was a freak that couldn't be repeated. We were back at the studio now, so they began to muscle in so as to be "sure" of the next one.

"I'll walk through this stuff until my contract's ended," said Will. "Then back to the *Follies!*"

Thus the happy combination that promised so much dissolved.

★

Postscript: "Incidentally, it's really too bad that the public won't see this picture at its full length. When I saw it (at the preview) it was 2,600 feet, but the demands of exhibitors, I was told, would necessitate shortening it to 2,000 feet. Which is a pity, for it was a gem as it stood." *Los Angeles Times*, December 12, 1923

JUS' PASSIN' THROUGH

Pathé Exchange, Inc., Copyright December 14, 1923, LU 19714; b&w; silent; 2 reels; 40 prints. Release: October 14, 1923. Extant.

Production Staff: Producer: Hal E. Roach; director: Charles Parrott (also known as Charley Chase); author: Hal E. Roach.

Cast: Will Rogers

Synopsis: A hobo in a small town, dodging work, trying to get a square meal, hopes to stay in prison so as to be fed.

This film is rare; the only copy we know of is in the vaults of the Museum of Modern Art in New York City. This copy was found in Czechoslovakia and still has Czech titles. There are plans to have those titles translated, photographed, and inserted into a copy of the original film. There will be no way to make certain that the English copy will be identical to the one issued in 1923.

WILL ROGERS WANTS TO PUT MOVIE EXPERIENCE TO WORK

President of these United States
Viceroy of the District of Columbia,
Chevy Chase Golf Club, Washington, D.C.

My Dear Mr. President:

I see where Ambassador Harvey is coming back here again from England. Now I don't know if it's a slumming trip or just what it is, as he was here a few days ago. Maybe he forgot something in one of his speeches and is coming back for an encore. But in a later paper I see where he is talking of resigning and not going back. Mr. President, if that is the case, I hereby make this an open letter as an application to take said Mr. Harvey's place.

I can tell by observation that it does not come under the Civil Service or competitive examination. Neither, on the other hand, is it a purely political appointment, as Mr. Harvey adapted his politics to fit the occasion. Now that would not even be necessary in my case, as I have no politics. I am for the party that is out of power, no matter which one it is. But I will give you my word, that in case of my appointment, I will not be a Republican. I will do my best to pull with you, and not embarrass you. In fact, my views on European affairs are so in accord with you, Mr. President, that I might almost be suspected of being a Democrat.

Now I want to enumerate a few of my qualifications for the position of Ambassador to the Court of St. James. My principal qualification that must not by any means be underestimated is my moving-picture experience. You see, for an official position nowadays, we must pay more attention to how our public men screen if we are to have to look at them every day in the news films. We must not only get men with screen personality, but we must get men who know camera angles and know when you are getting the worst of it in a picture and not be caught in the background during the taking of some big event.

Europeans are far ahead of us in this line of diplomacy, and if you don't watch them you are liable to be found photographed with the mob, instead of the principals. The thing to do is to do some little thing during the taking of the picture that will draw the audience's attention to you. For instance, during some court ceremony, I could just playfully kick the king. Now you don't know how a little thing like that would get over with the public. Or at one of the big weddings in the Abbey, I could just sorter nonchalantly step on the bride's train, as they passed by, perhaps ripping it off, or any little diplomatic move like that. You don't realize how just little bits like that would make our Ambassador stand out over all the other countries.

We have had an example of screen training right here at home. Take Josephus Daniels, our former secretary of the navy, when he was working. We spent four years sitting in picture houses watching him launch ships, and at every launching he could place himself at such an angle that you not only could not see the Democratic governor's daughter who was breaking the ginger ale, but you couldn't even see the ship! Now that was not accident; that was art.

And did you ever notice in the weekly news pictures how some senators can take a chew of tobacco right in the scene and you watch yourself watching them and no one else? Now those are just a few of the little things we have to look after if we want to hold our own as the greatest credit nation north of Mexico.

Now as to salary, I will do just the same as the rest of the politicians—accept a small salary as pin money, and take a chance on what I can get.

Awaiting an early reply, I remain,

Yours faithfully,
Will Rogers

Syndicated column, April 22, 1923

UNCENSORED MOVIES

Pathé Exchange, Inc.,   Copyright December 14, 1923, LU 19717; b&w; silent; 2 reels; 38 prints. Release: December 9, 1923. Extant.

Production Staff: Producer: Hal E. Roach; director: Roy Clements; cameramen: Robert Doran and Otto Himm; author: Hal E. Roach; titles by H. M. Walker; editor: T. J. Crizer.

Cast: Will Rogers   Earl Mohan
Guinn ("Big Boy") Williams   Noah Young
Marie Mosquini   Ena Gregory

Synopsis: Rogers appears as an investigator, sent by a village reform society to Hollywood, and also impersonates Tom Mix, Willam S. Hart, Rudolph Valentino, and others.

Reviews: ★ "Will Rogers tries very unsuccessfully to be killingly funny. . . .The title writer throws in a word now and then and makes things worse. Why did Will leave his rope out of the script anyway? And why is this called a comedy?"

Photoplay, February 1924

★ "This is one of the very best of the new series of Will Rogers two-reelers, distributed by Pathé. . . . The titles and action are in Rogers' best style. . . ."

Moving Picture World, December 1, 1923

My old pal William S. Hart killed more people in one reel of *Wild Bill Hickok* than ever lived in Dodge City. But he afterward explained it to me, he said: "Will, my public likes to see me shoot actors; in fact, I think most audiences like to see not only me but anybody shoot actors."

He was just reloading his gun—a thing he seldom does—so I thought, as he was looking straight at me, I better be leaving.

★

Tom Mix and I arrived in New York back in 1905. We showed in Madison Square Garden. We got twenty dollars a week and was both overpaid. Well, we wasn't exactly overpaid, because we didn't get the twenty. The show closed and Tom went back to Oklahoma and I didn't have enough to get back on.

Tom always had plenty of money, even in those days. You know Oklahoma was always "dry" when it was the Indian Territory—you know, no liquor—and Tom was the first of an industry which has since become world renowned. He was the first bootlegger I ever met.

When Prohibition come in and everybody took to drinking, and what they couldn't drink themselves, they tried to sell to somebody else. Why, that put Tom out of business. The competition was too keen.

The biggest graft in the world, next to bootlegging, was the movies, and he drifted into them.

Imitating Rudolph Valentino, in *Uncensored Movies*, 1923.

Imitating Tom Mix, in *Uncensored Movies*, 1923.

In a typical Tom Mix pose, just for the camera. (*Uncensored Movies*, 1923)

With a tough *hombre* look, Will imitates William S. Hart, in *Uncensored Movies*. With Snub Pollard and Stan Laurel.

Will, on one of his favorite horses, Chapple, performs one of Tom Mix's impressive stunts. (*Uncensored Movies*, 1923)

THE CAKE EATER

Pathé Exchange, Inc.,   Copyright January 26, 1924, LU 19859; b&w; silent; 2 reels; 40 prints. Release: March 2, 1924. Extant.

Production Staff: Producer: Hal E. Roach; director: Jay A. Howe; author: Hal E. Roach.

Cast: Will Rogers   Grace Woods
         Marie Mosquini   Patsy O'Byrne
         Billy Engle   Al Forbes

Synopsis: Rogers appears as a cowboy, pursued by two spinsters—the owners of the ranch—trying to catch him as a husband. They smother him with attention, persisting in baking cakes for him, and looking after him when he feigns sickness.

Review: ★ "There are quite a few laughs and some of Rogers' characteristically witty subtitles. It is up to his usual standard in entertainment value."

Moving Picture World, March 1, 1924

Temptation, from *The Cake Eater*, 1924.

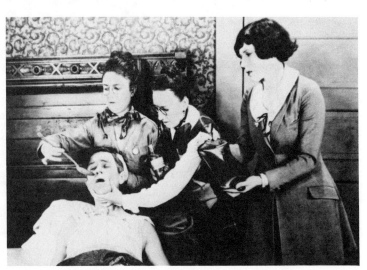

Suffering the agonies of overeating. (*The Cake Eater*, 1924)

THE COWBOY SHEIK

Pathé Exchange, Inc.,   Copyright January 26, 1924, LU 19860; b&w; silent; 2 reels; 40 prints. Release: February 3, 1924. Extant. Working title: *Two-Straw Bill*.

Production Staff: Producer: Hal E. Roach; director: Jay A. Howe; author: Hal E. Roach; titles by Will Rogers.

Cast: Will Rogers   "Two Straw" Bill
Marie Mosquini   Schoolteacher
Earl Mohan   Slicky
Helen Gilmore   The cook

Synopsis: Rogers plays a bashful cowboy who solves his problems by drawing straws to find out which of two alternatives to choose. This makes for interesting situations, right in the midst of complications.

Reviews: ★ "This picture follows along more familiar lines than the average Rogers offering and there is not so much of his distinctive humor present. A good fight adds to the interest."
Moving Picture World, February 2, 1924

★ "This is just an average two-reel comedy, the kind made in from six to eight days. It lacks originality of plot, and is made acceptable only by the work of Rogers."
Los Angeles Times, December 12, 1923

BIG MOMENTS FROM LITTLE PICTURES

Pathé Exchange, Inc.,   Copyright April 18, 1924, LU 20102; b&w; silent; 2 reels; 40 prints. Release: March 30, 1924. Extant.

Production Staff: Producer: Hal E. Roach; director: Jay A. Howe; author: Hal E. Roach.

Cast: Will Rogers

Synopsis: This, as the title tells, shows Rogers impersonating famous stars in famous films; there are Rudolph Valentino in the bullfight scene from *Blood and Sand*, Douglas Fairbanks in *Robin Hood*, Ford Sterling and his Keystone Kops. Also shown is how some stunts are accomplished in films.

Review: ★ "Will Rogers shows that he is a real travesty artist when he burlesques several big scenes from successful feature pictures. . . .This one should register pleasantly anywhere."
Motion Picture News, March 29, 1924

Will's imitation of Ford Sterling of Keystone Kop fame, in *Big Moments from Little Pictures*, 1924.

Will's impersonation of Rudolph Valentino in *Blood and Sand*, in *Big Moments from Little Pictures*, 1924.

Will (*far right*) impersonating Ford Sterling and his Keystone Kops, during filming of *Big Moments from Little Pictures*, 1924.

HIGH BROW STUFF

Pathé Exchange, Inc.,   Copyright April 18, 1924, LU 20090; b&w; silent; 2 reels; 40 prints. Release: April 27, 1924.

Production Staff: Producer: Hal E. Roach; director: Rob Wagner; author: Hal E. Roach.

Cast: Will Rogers

Synopsis: Satire of the Little Theatre groups. Rogers is signed to a movie contract on the insistence of the wife of a motion-picture magnate. Looking behind the screen, the director does not approve of the actor and hopes to have him break his contract by pasting him with pies, punching him, and so forth.

Reviews: ★ "Satire of the so-called Little Theatre movement for the uplift of dramatic art. Rogers' carica-
ture is of the imported actor, who is willing to suffer everything for his art, provided there is

enough money in it . . . a somber Russian drama, where everybody is killed but the orchestra and stage hands and a few other members of the union."

Motion Picture News, April 26, 1924

★ "Clever burlesque."

Moving Picture World, April 26, 1924

As Director Graves, Will listens to advice, in *High Brow Stuff*, 1924.

Will directs a royal scene, with regal demeanor. (*High Brow Stuff*, 1924)

GOING TO CONGRESS

Pathé Exchange, Inc.,   Copyright May 12, 1924, LU 20187; b&w; silent; 2 reels; 40 prints. Release: May 25, 1924. Extant.

Production Staff: Producer: Hal E. Roach; director: Rob Wagner; cameraman: Robert Doran; titles by Will Rogers; editor: T. J. Crizer.

Cast: Will Rogers   Alfalfa Doolittle   Marie Mosquini   His daughter
Mollie Thompson   His wife   Jack Ackroyd   Adviser

Synopsis: This film, the first in a series, deals with politics as seen through the eyes of Rogers. Here we see the first step—the behind-the-scene selection, nomination, and election of an obviously unqualified party faithful. This film shows the campaign and the activities of the new congressman until he reaches Washington.

Review: ★ "It should prove especially timely in view of the political activities at the present time."
Moving Picture World, July 19, 1924

NOTE: *This film was shown in Cleveland during the Republican National Convention and in New York City during the Democratic National Convention.*

Arriving in Washington, D.C., in *Going to Congress*, 1924.

The humble start of a political career. (*Going to Congress*, 1924)

DON'T PARK THERE

Pathé Exchange, Inc., Copyright May 28, 1924, LU 20252; b&w; silent; 2 reels; 36 prints. Release: June 22, 1924. Extant.

Production Staff: Producer: Hal E. Roach; director: Fred L. Guiol; author: Hal E. Roach.

Cast: Will Rogers
Marie Mosquini

Synopsis: Rogers, as the owner of the White Horse Ranch, is on his way to town to purchase some Doan's horse liniment. He spends his time trying to find a parking space, only to lose out to faster or more experienced drivers, or by violating every conceivable traffic regulation, and in the process amassing all kinds of subpoenas.

Failing to find a parking spot in Los Angeles and San Francisco, he finally succeeds in Seattle, only to learn that the liniment has not been manufactured for years.

Review: ★ "Typical Rogers humor pervades this subject. While there is much to laugh at in this comedy, there is a lot of duplication of idea and the action is not always swift. The general idea, however, is quite satisfactorily funny and most of the incidents will succeed in arousing laughter."
Moving Picture World, June 21, 1924

A traffic problem in *Don't Park There*, 1924.

Discussing next scene with director Fred L. Guiol, in *Don't Park There*, 1924.

JUBILO, JR.

Pathé Exchange, Inc., Copyright June 5, 1924, LU 20278; b&w; silent; 2 reels; 40 prints. Release: June 29, 1924. Extant. (In series of *Our Gang* comedies)

Production Staff: Producer: Hal E. Roach; director: Robert F. McGowan; cameraman: Frank Young; author: Hal E. Roach; titles by H. M. Walker.

Cast:

Will Rogers	Jubilo	Allen ("Farina") Hoskins
Mickey Daniels	Jubilo, Jr.	Leo Willis
Noah Young	Jubilo's father	Andy Samuels
Lyle Tayo	Jubilo's mother	Allen Caven
Charley Chase		Richard Daniels
Mary Kornman		Joy Winthrop
"Fatty" Joe Cobb		Otto Himm
Jackie Condon		

Synopsis: Set into the background of a movie company on location, Will Rogers is a track walker. When one of the boys, "Freckles," wants to buy his mother a birthday present, a hat, Rogers remembers the hat he once bought for his mother.

Once again, playing a tramp, in *Jubilo, Jr.*, 1924.

OUR CONGRESSMAN

Pathé Exchange, Inc.,   Copyright August 2, 1924, LU 20465; b&w; silent; 2 reels; 40 prints. Release: July 20, 1924. Extant.

Production Staff: Producer: Hal E. Roach; director: Rob Wagner; author: Hal E. Roach; titles by Will Rogers.

Cast: Will Rogers   Congressman Alfalfa Doolittle   Sammy Brooks
Mollie Thompson   His wife   Chet Brandberg

Synopsis: In this, the second in a short series of political satires, Rogers, as the handpicked congressman, arrives in Washington, D.C., to take his seat. His family now starts to get social recognition. The family commits social errors due to ignorance of etiquette and the intentional misdirection of newspaper reporters who try to make the congressman believe he is a great man.

Review: ★ "Some of the satire is rather subtle and it is a picture that will have its greatest appeal with more intelligent patrons, who should find it a delight. It is fully up to the standard of 'Going to Congress.' It is filled with typical Will Rogers stuff, including his inimitable subtitles."
Moving Picture World, July 19, 1924

A TRUTHFUL LIAR

Pathé Exchange, Inc.,   Copyright July 31, 1924, LU 20443; b&w; silent; 2 reels; 40 prints. Release: August 17, 1924. Extant. Original title: *The Truthful Liar*.

Production Staff: Producer: Hal E. Roach; director: Hampton Del Ruth; cameraman: Robert Doran; author: Hal E. Roach; titles by H. M. Walker; editor: T. J. Crizer.

Cast: Will Rogers   Ambassador Alfalfa Doolittle
Mollie Thompson   His wife   Beth Darlington
Jack Achroyd   Flunkie   Madge Hunt
Richard Pennell   Jack Cooper

Synopsis: This is the third, and last, in the political satire series, which included *Going to Congress* and *Our Congressman*. Doolittle is back home, surrounded by his former neighbors, and he recounts his almost-incredible exploits as ambassador. We see him rehearse how to first meet the king, not in the traditional silk pantaloons, but in a cowboy outfit, complete with chaps; he slaps the king on the back, in a friendly gesture, saves him from an assassination attempt, and introduces him to a card game—winning money and even the miniature crown this king wears under his bowler hat.
These are the tales Doolittle tells to an incredulous crowd. Sensing their disbelief, Doolittle offers as proof

of his honesty that the chimney of the house where he stands should topple on him if he has been fibbing. Naturally, the chimney crashes down.

Review: ★ "Because of its extreme burlesque qualities, this Will Rogers number should be classed as one of his greatest mirth provokers."

Moving Picture World, August 16, 1924

"Our Ambassador" receives a warning by arrow-mail, from *A Truthful Liar*, 1924.

"Ambassador" Will is presented to the king, in *A Truthful Liar*, 1924.

Having dared the chimney to fall if he has told a lie, Will ducks. *A Truthful Liar*, 1924.

"Ambassador" Will teaches his majesty an ancient American pastime—poker, in *A Truthful Liar*, 1924.

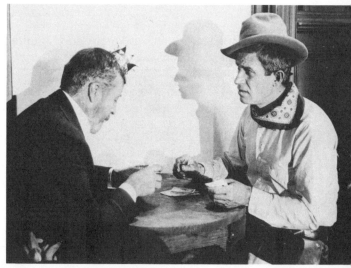

GEE WHIZ, GENEVIEVE

Pathé Exchange, Inc., Copyright August 2, 1924, LU 20587; b&w; silent; 2 reels; 40 prints. Release: September 28, 1924. Original title: *Sweet Genevieve.*

Production Staff: Producer: Hal E. Roach; director: Jay A. Howe; author: Hal E. Roach.

Cast:
Will Rogers
Marie Mosquini
Ena Gregory
Laura Roessing
May Foster
Don Maines
Earl Mohan

Synopsis: Rogers again plays his favorite character, a tramp, who while being held by health authorities for being in contact with a smallpox sufferer, is told about the easy life, plenty of food, and workless days. The catch is that he will have to go to the restaurant run by the sick man's sister and marry her. She is described as a former circus performer, and the tramp visualizes an airy, beautiful young woman, such as are seen on posters of the circus.

At the restaurant he meets Genevieve, who is long past the prime of her life, but the tramp must go through with the planned marriage. After the wedding, the tramp's faithful dog cannot stand the surroundings and leaves him, and it is revealed that the tramp only contemplated marriage and settling down in order to provide a home for his dog.

Review: ★ "The second series of two-reel comedies in which Will Rogers is starred by Hal Roach, reaches its conclusion in 'Gee Whiz, Genevieve.' It is the thirteenth Rogers picture to be released by Pathé in this series. If the films had been released in the order in which they were produced, we would be advising Mr. Rogers to place thirteen on his list of pet superstitions. The result of all the work by scenarist, director and star has not been crowned by any conspicuous luck, and the spectator must be content with Will Rogers, alone, unaided, if not hampered by the poverty of the plot and the lack of spirit, or life, or whatever you will, in the staging of this piece."

Motion Picture News, October 11, 1924

The "happy" couple, from *Gee Whiz, Genevieve,* 1924.

Will in typical Hal Roach sight gag.

Interview with Hal E. Roach, Sr., January 2, 1971

HR: Will loved brown Mexican beans. One day he told Betty, "Betty, I want those Mexican beans every night." So the first night Betty had a rather modest little dish of beans prepared, and Will said, "Betty, that's not what I want. I love them, I want a lot of these beans." Well, the next day, there was a bowl containing at least four quarts of beans sitting in front of Will. And for the next month, a bowl with four quarts of beans was in front of Will every night until he got so damn sick and tired of Mexican beans that he had to call it quits.

5
INDEPENDENT WORK FOR HIRE

Even though Hal Roach and Will Rogers were good friends, Will did not enjoy the type of films he made on the Roach lot. Since motion pictures still had no voice, most of the humor had to be visual. That was not what Rogers wanted. His humor was mostly in the titles, the so-called voice of the young film industry.

When the second year of Will's contract with Roach was completed, Rogers made two independent films— One Glorious Day and The Headless Horseman. He also returned once more to the Ziegfeld Follies.

In October 1925, Will Rogers set out on one of the most grueling endeavors of his life—the lecture tours. For several months at a time he would perform every night, always in another city, without rest, and with no time off in between. Each day was like the one before: a strenuous performance, a trip through the night or most of the day, and on to the next engagement. At first there was an all-male quartet, the DeReszke Singers, that opened the performance, then it was Will Rogers, alone. Performances would last two hours, some more, with just one man holding an audience. And still, there was the weekly column, the reading of newspapers to keep up with the news and find new material for the lecture, and, after 1926, another chore, the "Daily Telegrams"; only a squib, true—but what a squib. Forty million Americans read it at breakfast. First there were seven columns a week, later "only" six. These, too, would continue until Rogers' death.

In 1926, during the five off-months of summer, Rogers went to England, the Continent, and as far as the Soviet Union. He wrote ten major articles for the Saturday Evening Post, called "Letters of a Self-Made Diplomat to His President." Naturally, the daily and weekly columns continued, winter or summer, even from Europe. While abroad on his "vacation," Rogers made the film Tip Toes, appeared for six weeks in London in a Charles Cochran Revue (he was considered the British Florenz Ziegfeld, Jr.), and gave benefits for several worthy causes, including one for the survivors of an Irish fire disaster. And just in case there was too much free time left over, Rogers had with him producer and director C. S. Clancy and a cameraman, who filmed enough footage for thirteen one-reel films, a type of travelogue with the distinctive Rogers touch.

One week after Rogers' return from abroad, he was off once again on the lecture tour—an effort he kept up until 1928. But in some manner, he found time to make independent motion pictures, write his columns, write captions for the travel films, change routines, and go on benefit tours (at his own expense) for the victims of the disastrous 1927 Mississippi flood.

At the very end of the 1927 lecture tour, Rogers suffered a severe gallstone attack. He arrived home in great agony, developed jaundice, and was rushed to the California Hospital, where surgery was performed. For days the outcome was in doubt; regular bulletins had to be issued to the nation. When Rogers was at last out of danger, congratulatory telegrams poured in from people in all walks of life, from the president of the United States to dirt farmers.

Rogers was now told to take it easy for months and keep off horses for a year. Within weeks, however, he was on location, shooting A Texas Steer. "Taking it easy" were words that probably did not exist in Will Rogers' vocabulary—besides, he never used a vocabulary.

Will showing his expertise, c. 1918.

Publicity photograph, c. 1920. (*Academy of Motion Picture Arts and Sciences*)

72

Interview with Patricia Ziegfeld Stephenson, January 4, 1971

S: Will Rogers thought of you almost as one of his own children.

PZS: He was such fun. The first year we came to California, he just did everything he could to make us like the place—and we certainly did. We used to go up to the ranch.

S: What year was that?

PZS: Late 1929, or early 1930, shortly after the stock market crash. Daddy came out to do *Whoopee* for Sam Goldwyn. When we came out here, we rented Marion Davies' guesthouse at the beach, which was very near the ranch. I was up there almost every day to ride with a girl friend, and Will Rogers gave us each a horse we could ride anytime we wanted to. And, of course, he was there, except when he traveled.

S: Did Will Rogers ever come to your house?

PZS: Oh, yes. The Rogerses came—Will loved to swim. I don't think anyone ever thinks of him as a swimmer. We had a pool at the house and Will would dive. You see, there was no pool at the ranch. They did have a pool when they lived in Beverly Hills. Will loved to clown in the water, race out on the diving board, plunge into the water—always that marvelous twinkle in his eyes. There was something special in those china-blue eyes.

S: Tell about your visits to the ranch.

PZS: He was such a warm person. I always felt at ease with him. He was always kidding you; he was always such fun. He would always say, "C'mon, let's do some roping!" or, "Let's go and catch a steer!" And he was such a dear after Daddy died. He took mother and me up to the ranch, and we spent about a week up there. Then the Olympics were that year in Los Angeles, and he gave us tickets. We went every day to the games. Mother adored Will. Next to my father, he was her favorite.

S: Is it true that there never was a contract between your father and Will Rogers?

PZS: As far as I know, there never was; they never had any written agreement, just a handshake. They were great friends, and I do not ever remember them having any problems. If they did, they ironed them out very quickly, because they had a mutual admiration society going.

S: Is this the trowel used at the dedication of the Ziegfeld Theatre?

PZS: Yes, it needs resilvering.

S: What year was that?

PZS: It says on the trowel, "December 9, 1926." Mother and I used it. Will Rogers was there, and he saw that I was not very charmed with the whole procedure. It was cold, and there wasn't much going on, so he said: "Here, Patricia, have a piece of gum." So I

Even a master roper has to get the kinks out sometimes. (*The Penguin Collection*)

Laying cornerstone of Ziegfeld Theatre (1926). *From left:* Will, Billie Burke (Mrs. Ziegfeld), daughter Patricia, and Florenz Ziegfeld, Jr.

was chewing the gum merrily, and my mother caught me, "What are you doing with that gum in your mouth?" I thought it would be perfectly all right if I said that Mr. Rogers had given it to me. But it wasn't. She said, "Spit it out!" But I tucked it up on the roof of my mouth, because it was sort of a sacred piece of gum, because Will Rogers had given it to me.

ONE GLORIOUS DAY

Famous Players-Lasky Corp., Copyright February 1, 1922, LP 17509; renewed February 4, 1949, R 44350; b&w; silent; 5 reels, 5,100 ft. Release: Paramount, January 29, 1922, Rivoli Theatre, NYC., Review in *New York Times*, January 30, 1922, 16:2. Working title: *EK*. Scenario and continuities in Paramount Collection, AMPAS, Beverly Hills, Ca.

Production Staff: Producer: Jesse L. Lasky; director: James Cruze; cameraman: Karl Brown; based on a story by Walter Woods and A. B. Barringer; screenplay by Walter Woods.

Cast:

Will Rogers	Ezra Botts, psychology professor
Lila Lee	Molly McIntyre
Alan Hale	Ben Wadley
John Fox	"Ek"
George Nichols	Pat Curran
Emily Rait	Mrs. McIntyre
Clarence Burton	Bert Snead

Synopsis: Professor Ezra Botts lectures on spiritualism. He is a meek, shy milquetoast who secretly loves Molly McIntyre, but could never summon enough courage to admit it. He will not even stand up to the bully Wadley, who pursues Molly.

In the dimension where as-yet-unborn spirits dwell, waits an impatient Ek, straining to get out. Somehow he misses the birth of the baby assigned to him and he wanders the earth in search of a body.

Professor Botts, at home one evening, tries to separate body from spirit. Successful at last, his gentle spirit temporarily leaves him, and Ek is ready to take his place, totally transforming Professor Botts. The new Botts, with Ek in control, surprises his friends and foes—indeed, the whole town. He smashes the Owl Club, headquarters for the corrupt political machine that has been ruining the town. And when Wadley annoys Molly, the incensed Botts thrashes him soundly.

Meanwhile Botts' gentle spirit longs to return to his accustomed body. When Ek finally gives up the borrowed body, Botts becomes his old self again—but not quite. He now knows that Molly loves him, and because of his action against the corrupt political machine, the town nominates him for mayor.

Reviews: ★ "Can anything imaginative come out of Hollywood? It can. It has. It is 'One Glorious Day,' and it is at the Rivoli this week.

"And the best of it is that the picture is imaginatively done. Such a story would be dreary without suitable settings, acting and cinematography. Everything depends on its treatment. So its high success is due, first of all, to the director, James Cruze, and his staff, including especially his cameraman. The production of the picture involved almost continuous double exposure, and some exceedingly difficult feats with it. It is a skillful and ingenious piece of work.

"But this is not all. There is also the acting. Will Rogers, as Professor Botts, is a revelation. See him first, when the professor's spirit is at home, and then when Ek occupies his body, and you'll say again that Will Rogers can be a good deal more on the screen than just himself."
New York Times, January 30, 1922, 16:2

★ "Not only is the picture a novelty in itself, but it furnishes Will Rogers with a role that is decidedly different from anything he has ever attempted. With it he is eminently successful."
Moving Picture World, February 11, 1922

Honors: #1 Film on list of 40 Best Pictures of 1922, chosen by National Board of Review of Motion Pictures

The following publications listed *One Glorious Day* among their top-ten films for 1922. The names of the reviewers are in parentheses.

#1, *Omaha Daily News* (E. M. Landale)

#3, *Picture Play Magazine* (Alison Smith)

#3, *Boston Post* (Prunella Hall)

#3, *Kansas City Star* (Catherine S. Prosser)

#4, *The North American*, Philadelphia

#5, *New York Times* (James O. Spearing)

#6, *Detroit News* (Harold Heffernan)

#8, *St. Louis Post Dispatch* (W. H. James)

#8, *The Film Daily* (L. W. Brennan)

#10, *Photoplay Magazine* (James R. Quirk)

NOTE: This film was in production in late 1921, then titled: *The Melancholy Spirit*, starring Roscoe ("Fatty") Arbuckle. When the scandal involving Arbuckle broke, Paramount dropped Arbuckle, scrapped the film, and started from scratch, this time with Will Rogers.

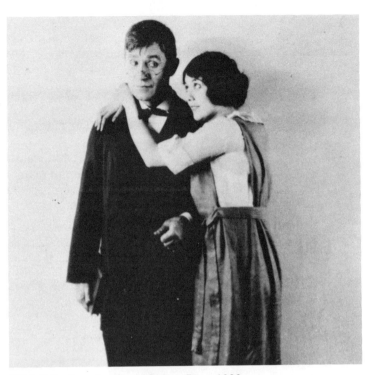

With Lila Lee, in *One Glorious Day*, 1922.

THE HEADLESS HORSEMAN

Sleepy Hollow Corp., Copyright 1922; b&w—tinted (early use of panchromatic film); silent; 7 reels, 6,145 ft. Release: W. W. Hodkinson Co., November 5, 1922, Capitol Theatre, NYC. Original title: *The Legend of Sleepy Hollow*. Location shots: Sleepy Hollow, N.Y.; Hackensack, N.J.

Production Staff: Producer: Carl Stearns Clancy; director: Edward Venturini; assistant director: Warren V. Fromme; from the original story by Washington Irving; screenplay and adaptation by Carl Stearns Clancy; spoken titles: Will Rogers; narrative: Roxanne White; titles: H. M. Walker; art titles: Warren A. Newcombe; photography and lighting: Ned Van Buren; film cutter: Helen Burgess; sets by Tec-Art Studios.

Cast:
Will Rogers	Ichabod Crane	Mary Foy	Dame Martling
Lois Meredith	Katrina van Tassel	Charles Graham	Hans van Ripper
Ben Hendricks, Jr.	"Brom" Bones		

Synopsis: The familiar story tells of the Yankee schoolmaster, Ichabod Crane, who comes to the small Dutch community of Sleepy Hollow on the banks of the Hudson River. To add him to her string of admirers, the local belle, Katrina van Tassel, encourages Crane. Considering it a great opportunity to marry into the wealthy Van Tassel family, Crane wants to wed Katrina. "Brom" Bones, one of Katrina's admirers, tries to eliminate this new rival by getting Crane tarred and feathered on a trumped-up charge of treating his students cruelly—but the truth is learned. Next, Bones uses Crane's interest in the legend of the headless horseman. Disguising himself as that phantom, he encounters Crane late one night at a lonely bridge and so frightens Crane that he leaves the area, never to return.

As Ichabod Crane, the schoolteacher, in *The Headless Horseman*, 1922.

In *The Headless Horseman*, 1922.

HOLLYWOOD

Famous Players-Lasky Corp.,   Copyright July 11, 1923, LP 19202; renewed July 24, 1950, R 64681; b&w; silent; 8 reels, 8,100 ft. Release: Paramount Pictures, August 19, 1923.

Production Staff: Producer: Jesse L. Lasky; director: James Cruze; cameraman: Karl Brown; from original story by Frank Condon; adapted by Tom Geraghty.

Cast (in story):

Hope Drown	Angela Whitaker
Luke Cosgrove	Joel Whitaker
George K. Arthur	Lem Lefferts
Ruby Lafayette	Grandmother Whitaker
Harris Gordon	Dr. Luke Morrison
Bess Flowers	Hortense Towers
Eleanor Lawson	Margaret Whitaker
King Zany	Horace Pringle
Roscoe ("Fatty") Arbuckle	Fat man in casting director's office

Cast (stars in Hollywood):

Gertrude Astor	Alan Hale	Jack Pickford
Mary Astor	Hope Hampton	Will Rogers
Baby Peggy	William S. Hart	Ford Sterling
Noah Beery	Jack Holt	Gloria Swanson
William Boyd	J. Warren Kerrigan	Estelle Taylor
Viola Dana	Lila Lee	Ben Turpin
Cecil B. De Mille	Bull Montana	and many more
Sid Grauman	Pola Negri	

Synopsis: Angela and her grandfather, Joel Whitaker, are visiting Hollywood, but for different reasons. The grandfather is there to recuperate in the sunny climate, while Angela wants to become a movie star. But it is Grandfather Joel who is discovered. When Angela's boyfriend, Lem, and the rest of her family hear of grandfather's new career, they all descend on Hollywood to protect the patriarch from all the rumored evils of moviedom. Every one of the newcomers is picked for movies, except Angela, the one who came there expressly for that reason. With everyone in front of cameras, they meet many celebrities. Angela's ambitions fade when she marries Lem. When she gives birth to twins, they, too, appear on the screen.

NEWS FROM HOLLYWOOD (1925)

I have often said if the public judges the movie people by some of the interviews that appear in print, they must wonder how they have ever kept out of the asylum.

If a president of the United States had as silly things written about him as appear in movie magazines and write-ups about movie people, he would be impeached in three months.

TIP TOES

British National Pictures, Ltd.
Paramount-Famous Players-Lasky Corp., Copyright May 16, 1927, LP 23960; b&w; silent; 7 reels, 7,514 ft. Release: Paramount, June 19, 1927. Shooting script extant.

Production Staff: Producer J. D. Williams; director: Herbert Wilcox; cameraman: Roy Overbaugh; screenplay by Herbert Wilcox; based on musical play (opened on Broadway, December 28, 1925, at Liberty Theatre for 192 performances; cast included Queenie Smith in title role, Andrew Tombes, Harry Watson, Jr., Allen Kearns, and Jeanette MacDonald; book by Guy Bolton and Fred Thompson; music: George Gershwin; lyrics: Ira Gershwin;) made at Elstree Studios, London; summer of 1926.

Cast: Dorothy Gish   Tiptoes Kaye
Will Rogers   "Uncle" Hen Kaye
Nelson ("Bunch") Keyes   "Uncle" Al Kaye
John Manners   Lord William Montgomery
Miles Mander   Rollo Stevens (Metcalf)
Annie Esmond   Lord William's aunt
Ivy Ellison   Lord William's sister
Dennis Hoey   Hotelier

Synopsis: Three American vaudevillians are stranded broke in London. To get out of the predicament, they pose as rich socialites to meet British nobility. When their mounting hotel debt forces Tiptoes to find work as a dancer in a nightclub, she meets Lord William Montgomery and marries him.

With Dorothy Gish and Nelson ("Bunch") Keyes in *Tip Toes*, 1927. (*Photo by James Abbe*)

British pictures needed a start, so I thought I just as well go and help them out. I being the one that started American pictures. So that is why they sent for me to get the British pictures through this early stage.

I wired London to get their camera ready and have an extra-strong lens, as they were about to shoot one of the most homely but practical faces that ever registered sex appeal.

But I won't last long here because they are a little too far advanced for me now. I was put in to try and handicap Dorothy Gish, who is the star in the picture. You all know Dorothy. She is one of the three Gish sisters, the mother and two daughters.

So I am here in London, uplifting the newest and greatest art. It's lots of fun over here making pictures. Every time you finish a scene, they bring you a cup of tea, and what makes me sore at myself is I am beginning to like the stuff. The picture is the story of three vaudeville actors that are playing in England and they are not so good. Well, if anyone was well cast, it's me. I have been in vaudeville and can fill the "Not So Good" part and, also, I remember when I was playing over here one time, using a horse and Buck McKee. Well, it looked like we were going to have to swim the horse back home and hang on to his tail as he did it. So I certainly know how to play a vaudeville actor that's not so good. If I can just stay natural, I will be a hit.

A TEXAS STEER

First National Pictures, Inc., Copyright November 29, 1927, LP 24702; b&w; silent; 8 reels, 7,418 ft. Release: December 4, 1927, Strand Theatre, NYC. Location shots: Washington, D.C.

Production Staff: Producer: Sam E. Rork; director: Richard Wallace; assistant director: James F. O'Shea; cameraman: Jack MacKenzie; comedy construction: Jack Wagner; production manager: Ben Singer; based on the stage comedy *A Texas Steer,* by Charles Hale Hoyt (c. 1899); screenplay by Bernard McConville; titles by Will Rogers and Garrett Graham; editor: Frank Lawrence.

Cast:

Will Rogers	Maverick Brander	Bud Jamieson	Othello
Louise Fazenda	Mrs. ("Ma") Brander	Arthur Hoyt	Knott Innitt
Sam Hardy	Brassy Gall	Mack Swain	Bragg
Ann Rork	Bossy Brander	William Orlamond	Blow
Douglas Fairbanks, Jr.	Fairleigh Bright	Lucien Littlefield	Yell
Lilyan Tashman	Dixie Style	Fred Lacey	Riding double
George Marion, Sr.	Fishbach		for Mr. Rogers

Synopsis: At the hub of this farce is the Eagle Rock Dam Bill (near Red Dog, deep in the heart of Texas) and the graft that shall flow from it.

The bad guys, Bragg, Blow, and Yell, want the bill passed, while the good guys, Brassy Gall and his loyal supporter, Dixie Style, want it blocked, or at least buried in committee.

The bad guys secure the unwitting aid of socially ambitious "Ma" Brander and her romance-seeking daughter, Bossy. Together they get gentle, plain, fabulously wealthy (this is Texas, sir) rancher Maverick Brander elected to Congress.

The good guys go to Washington, too, to try and stop Brander from supporting the bill, by threatening to publish certain photographs. When this fails, they leave him without clothes, tied up in his room, to keep him from casting his vote.

Somehow Brander frees himself, finds a nightgown for his modesty, locates a formal dress coat to be properly attired for the hallowed halls of Congress, jumps on his trusted charger, and—having seen the truth along the way—reaches Congress in time to foil the bad guys.

Oh, yes; Bossy gets Fairleigh Bright.

Review: ★ "Rogers now enjoys a national and international fame as a humorist and a figure in public life, and it is unquestionably a great coup to present him in a film feature, closely associated with his activities as a commenter on events political and social. This, as it happens, is just what 'A Texas Steer' in its modernized adaptation from the old Hoyt stage farce aims to be. It is what may be termed a 'natural,' a striking example of good showmanship.

"The picture kids politics. Upon Rogers' arrival at Washington, a newsboy, remarking on Rogers' extraordinary appearance in an old frock coat and ten-gallon hat, asks him: 'Where is the circus?'

" 'Right over there,' replies Rogers, pointing to the Capitol, 'the biggest circus in the world, and I've just joined it.'

"Another line refers to the hotel where Rogers stops as the one 'where honest citizens like to be mistaken for statesmen, and where statesmen like to be mistaken for honest citizens.'

"The picture is continually punctuated with laughs of the type for which Rogers' name is synonymous."

Motion Picture News, November 18, 1927

Will Rogers Tells About Film

Now take this here *A Texas Steer*. Even if I say it and it sounds like boasting, it's a good picture. It is the movie of the old stage play, Hoyt's *A Texas Steer*.

It was the story of a Texas cowman elected to Congress on bought votes. We brought it up to date by not changing it at all. In the stage version he didn't know what to do when he got in Congress. That part is allowed to remain as it was.

The cattleman-congressman used to play poker more than legislate, and that's left in the movie. There was a little drinking among the members at the time. For correct detail, in our modern version that has been allowed to remain in.

Of course, I'm the cowman who's elected to play dumb in Washington. I never did claim to be a Barrymore or Warfield, and you folks ought to be warned about that, but Sam Rork, the producer, rushed me with a contract and a pen and said: "Will, all you've got to do is act natural."

Well, that's easy enough to say, but it was mighty hard in a couple of scenes trying to act natural with a lot of people around, cameras and director and whatnot, and me in my underwear in what they call a "kidnapping episode."

You see, Sam Rork says he picked me out of all the Hollywood actors because all the rest of them have morality clauses in their contracts and are afraid to act like a congressman.

Sam Rork sure got some real actors, and our picture has got sex appeal, production value, clothes, melodrama, and everything else. We've been so faithful in detail of making the story that we haven't changed the price of votes in the Red Dog election, and anybody knows these days a dollar don't buy what it used to.

Yes, sir, Sam Rork got real actors in *A Texas Steer*. Take Louise Fazenda, for example. She has the part of "Ma" Brander, who sort of got tired of hanging around the ranch house and wanted to get her daughter married to a title, or some other clotheshorse.

With producer Sam Roark and director Richard Wallace, discussing their film, *A Texas Steer*, 1927.

There's one scene the ladies will sure enjoy. It's where "Ma" Brander gives a big highfalutin reception in Washington. Talk about clothes. Some of the ladies have on evening gowns that would shock Ziegfeld.

George Marion, Sr., who created the part of Fishbach, the Negro in the political woodpile of Red Dog, Texas, in the original stage play, has the same part in the film. He's the best all-around performer on the American stage. He's the only man equally at home acting or producing drama or dances in musical comedies.

Sex appeal? Every film has that, so we got Lilyan Tashman. She starred in the *Follies*. She holds a record, five years out of the *Follies* and married to one man all that time and still living with him. I guess that's an American record, including Hollywood and Beverly Hills, which I've always thought were Free States in Matrimony.

Douglas Fairbanks, Jr., has the juvenile lead with Ann Rork, who is climbing fast these days to be a star in pictures. When I say Douglas looks like his dad, acts like him, and is just as regular a fellow as his dad, that ought to be recommendation enough to make you want to see the movie twice. You are going to like Ann, I'm sure.

Sam Hardy is the "heavy." He was in the *Follies* with me, too.

Mack Swain, Lucien Littlefield, and William Orlamond are the Texas politicians, Bragg, Blow, and Yell, and they are right convincing in proving politics ain't on the level. Arthur Hoyt has a funny part. He is the social secretary to "Ma" Brander, and he's a book of etiquette animated. Bud Jamieson has a good part, too. He's the valet who knows where I keep the congressional liquor supply.

Sam Rork took us all to Washington to get what they call the correct background for the Washington exteriors.

Only one unfortunate thing happened, and I guess you have already read about that. Some of the boys of the National Press Club didn't have much to do with Coolidge and Congress out of town, so they appointed me congressman-at-large. They had six thousand people there to see me publicly appointed a congressman. My folks always raised me right and warned me about being a congressman. I guess I am one of the few persons for whom they ever got a gang together, to humiliate publicly.

I hope you like the movie *A Texas Steer*. I did my darnest to act natural like a congressman. And any congressman acting natural can give me a laugh every day in the year.

News Report

Will Rogers, ex-mayor of Beverly Hills, objected strenuously when it became known that a chauffeur was the actual rider taking a dashing ride down Pennsylvania Avenue instead of the famous cowboy star. The matter of the double raised eyebrows. Was it that he was not permitted to take the ride because his life as a movie star was too valuable, or was his riding ability unequal to the task?

New York Times, September 2, 1927

Will Rogers Answers

Huh, I may be a bum rider, but I figure that I'm still man enough to lope down the avenue in my ripe old age. I've just been out of the hospital five weeks. You know the big thing about an operation is keeping it quiet when it's over. The doctors told me I couldn't work on this picture at all. As for riding a horse—I hate not being able to get on a horse back at home.

It's a big joke there. I've got a polo field that cost me all the money I made in a year, and a dozen polo ponies. Other people come over and ride 'em while I stand around and watch. The doctors told me I couldn't ride for a year. I broke my fifteen-year-old son in at polo the other day. He can ride pretty well. Wish I had him here. Maybe I could have used him for my double.

New monument at Barrow, Alaska, near crash site, dedicated 1982. (*Elberton Granite Association, Inc.*)

Monument to Hollywood stars; Will is on left, as he appeared in *Lightnin'*; also seen are Mary Pickford (*center*) and Douglas Fairbanks.

6
SIGHTSEEING, BY PATHÉ

Now I haven't bothered you in a long time. I layed off you and let you all get rich and prosperous. Now this little mess I got here now, that these fellows are trying to sell you, won't hurt you much; they will just about give you time to go out and get asmoke while they are on. I don't know what they are—they ain't exactly travelogues; they ain't comedies 'cause comedies are gags that the people are used to laughing at. The plots are a little too clean for dramas.

Well, to be honest, they are just about nine hundred feet of celluloid and take up about the same amount of time that a couple of close-ups in a love picture would take up. They ain't good and they ain't bad, they just take up fifteen minutes of a class of people that time don't mean a thing in the world to. The *Saturday Evening Post* has already payed for the trip, talking about all over the country has made me more than I ever could have made in pictures, even if I had been a real star; the book of the trip has brought enough to pay for another trip. The Vitaphone staggered me to tell about it before their double-barrel contraption, and this is just another by-product; I wanted the reels to keep myself to show at home in my old days, and I just had them make another print.

In fact, there's the radio, that's another by-product I just thought of, that has already paid me for them too. I was raised on a ranch, but I never knew there was so many ways to skin a calf. I like to forget Bull Durham paying me to tell also about the same trip.

And, oh yes, my old friend Sam Goldwyn wants the dramatic rights to the book; I sold Keystone the still pictures; the syndicated strip cartoon rights are being negotiated for now.

Well, so long, the mayor has got to get busy. There is a lot of new divorced people standing here, waiting to get remarried again. That's a better sideline than all of them.

Your old friend,
Mayor Rogers

Rogers to Show Trip

"Will Rogers, 'Unofficial Ambassador' of the United States to Europe last summer, is going to prove to all America that his famous and humorous trip abroad really happened, and that the foreign experiences which he detailed in pungent and uproarious magazine articles, were not fiction.

"Not since Mark Twain chronicled his immortal tours abroad, has any private citizen of Yankeeland described so remarkable a trip as did Rogers in his recent series of articles on the adventures of a 'Self-Made Diplomat,' and the cowboy had the advantage of Clemens, in that he had a motion picture camera and a crack Hollywood cameraman along.

"Although Rogers has had years of experience as an actor in motion pictures, he has broken away from all film traditions in photographing his own tour, and has produced 12 reels of highly original and personally planned pictures, doing, for once, all his own directing, acting, and writing of subtitles.

"Rogers' star in those travelogues is, frankly, himself, and Mrs. Rogers is his leading woman. No other characters go through the entire series. Many of the sequences were made for the sole purpose of amusing himself and his family, and were not intended for the public eye, but the insistence of friends who have roared over them, has coaxed Rogers into including them."

Tulsa Daily World, December 19, 1926

Advertising poster for travelogues Will filmed during his 1926 European trip.

Pathé Ind., Inc., copyrighted the following twelve films originally. On April 29, 1946, all rights were assigned to C. S. Clancy, the producer. On that very same day, C. S. Clancy assigned all rights to Vitaphone Corp. In 1955, all but one copyright were renewed. In 1956, Vitaphone Corp. merged with Warner Brothers, Inc.

Warner Brothers' records indicate that all Will Rogers travelogues were shipped to the Eastman House, Roches- *ter, New York, in October 1958. The inventory list accompanying a substantial shipment of films from Warner Brothers, Inc., to the Eastman House in October 1958 is still available and shows not a single reel of a Will Rogers film.*

Warner Brothers, Inc., did at one time have in its possession a complete set of all twelve travelogues, but the entire set has disappeared.

WITH WILL ROGERS IN DUBLIN

Pathé Ind., Inc.,   Copyright February 4, 1927, MU 3774; renewed January 13, 1955, R 143005; b&w; silent; 1 reel, 20 prints. Extant. Distributed by Pathé Exchange, Inc.

Production Staff: Producer and director: Carl Stearns Clancy; cameraman: John LaMond; author and titles: Will Rogers.

Synopsis: The Capitol buildings; William T. Cosgrove welcomes Rogers; Vice-President O'Higgins; statues of two previous presidents, Arthur Griffith and Michael Collins; Trinity College; streets renamed in Gaelic, with English translations; Four Courts Building; American tourist shopping center; home of Guiness stout; various scenes of city life in the streets; military review in Phoenix Park.

Ireland welcomes you even if you don't buy something every minute.

★

It's so peaceful and quiet here in Dublin, it is almost disappointing. Even the Irish themselves are beginning to get used to it and like it. Imagine, they even have a representative at the peace conference!

★

I like Ireland perhaps better than any other foreign country. They got humor, and while they think they take life serious, they don't. They will joke with you, sing with you, drink with you, and, if you want, fight with you—or against you, whichever you want—and I think if they like you well enough, they would die with you.

★

I have been in twenty countries and the only one where American tourists are welcome wholeheartedly by everyone is in Ireland. They don't owe us, and they don't hate us.

The lakes of Kilarney is where Switzerland got their idea of lakes. Americans, go where you are welcome! Ireland is a friend to everybody—even England.

★

If a town had any culture, and tourists commenced hitting it, your culture is gone. Tourists rub it out of any town. Now you take tourists, there is one of the hardest working businesses that you could possibly adopt. They will leave a nice, comfortable home with all the conveniences and they will get them a ticket to Ireland, or any other country, and from then on they stop being human; they just turn sheep and the guide is the sheepherder.

Will in Ireland.

WITH WILL ROGERS IN PARIS

Pathé Ind., Inc.,   Copyright February 14, 1927, MU 3789, renewed January 13, 1955, R 143006; b&w, silent; 1 reel, 20 prints. Extant. Distributed by Pathé Exchange, Inc.

Production Staff: Producer and director: Carl Stearns Clancy; author and titles: Will Rogers.

Synopsis: American Express Company office; place de l'Opéra; Café de la Paix; Maxim's sidewalk café; les grands boulevards; Trocadero (auditorium); Eiffel Tower; book stalls; the Latin Quarter; the Tuileries (gardens); Le Louvre (interior, showing various paintings).

The taxicabs in Paris have the lowest start in the way of money of any taxicabs in the world; they start in at one franc. Now, a franc on the Tuesday afternoon at four-forty, when we were in this cab, was worth less than three cents, and there is, Lord knows, how many centimes in a franc. Well, at each turn of the front wheel of the car, the meter jumped ten centimes. Well, you have just settled back figuring here is something in Paris that I will get for nothing, for this thing is only one franc, and that is just about half a nickel. You have gone about a couple of blocks and you have just missed some dozen-odd people by less than a quarter of an inch, driven on every side of the street there is, over the edges of the sidewalk, down a couple of what we would call alleys, where you would say we are safe here; it's a one-way street because there is no one who could pass us in here. All at once here comes a truck loaded with French wine, labeled 1888. You say we can't pass that in this narrow place, and you can't—but you do. Then when your blood pressure is approaching normal again, you just casually glance at the taximeter. It registers in francs, fourteen, and in centimes, why, they are rolling by your eyes so fast you would have to stop to see what they did say. No human mind can read 'em as fast as they click by. The number of francs is caught up with the centimes. Now they are both chasing each other around the clock.

Traffic halts you, but it don't halt that thing. You arrive at your destination, some ten American blocks away, and you hand them a handful of francs, and then he comes back with: "Fer Me. You no pay Fer Me!"

You give him another baleful, and of course you tipped him, but this "Fer Me" comes anyway. That's an extra tip for giving him the first tip.

You think on account of these francs changing so fast in the rate of exchange that you should be getting the best of everything. Yes, that's another pet illusion. Say, they are up in the morning setting those prices, and no jump that that franc will make during that day will ever catch up with them. It could drop to one cent apiece in American money, and they would still be ahead of you.

Here is another great gag they have here in Paris. You know people in all these countries speak different languages, but they are supposed to write figures in the same language. For instance, when you get your bill in the café, all you should have to do is read the figures on it. But say, you can't read the figures on it. A handwriting expert can't read the figures. You start to add up the bill, because every American always warns every other one: "Oh, do add up your bill! You really are supposed to! It's not considered cheap like it is in America when you do it! So always add up!"

Well, here is what you are going to find. The threes are all made to add up and look like eights; sevens look like nines. So you take a figuring system where there is no such thing as threes and sevens and jump them up a few notches to eights and nines—why, you have a pretty good percentage system working for you. The men running Monte Carlo are just apprentices in the percentage-figuring game compared to these.

You see, there is another thing over here that we are slow getting accustomed to. Over home, if you go into a place and order ham, eggs, and coffee, why, when the bill comes, it would have those two objects on it: ham and eggs so much, and coffee so much. There would be two items, that's all. But here there would be a long slip. So many francs for waiter taking the order, so many for rent, so much for bread, so much for butter, and if by any chance you had a glass of water with it, that would be harder to get and cost more than the ham and eggs. Now these ham and eggs would be split in the addition. They don't pair any two things in the billing over there. Then there is the luxury tax. Then a cover charge; pepper and salt are only served on demand. So really what started out to be only a light breakfast will add up to be a dinner. Just try to find out what these twelve items are on the bill. They all speak English when selling you something, but if asked to explain a bill, their English gets back to native again.

So from what I have been able to learn about these people in a kind of offhand way is that they don't take bad care of themselves at all in any financial arrangements. Europe is supposed to be artistic, but if I had to judge, I should place their financial ahead of their artistic ability. So in offering prayers for downtrodden races, I would advise you not to overlook the "downtrodden tourist."

★

They call it the Latin Quarter because nobody speaks Latin, and nobody has a quarter.

★

See where they captured an American spy in France. He must have been working on his own, for we already know all we want to know about 'em.

★

I was passing through Paris and looking for a good show, and somebody suggested the House of Deputies. It's a satire on our Congress. It was the best thing I ever saw in Europe in the way of entertainment. They would get up and run at each other and shake their fists. You would think there would be murder, but they don't really fight any oftener than our heavyweight champion.

★

A bunch of American tourists were hissed and stoned yesterday in France—but not until they had finished buying.

★

Most of our secretaries of state I ever heard of gained fame by sending diplomatic notes to some nations. So why can't the present secretary send one too?

Why don't he send a note demanding protection of American tourists in France? They have been skinned alive there for years.

★

American tourists are still coming by the thousands and bragging about where they come from. Sometimes you think France really has been too lenient with them. Yours, for quieter visitors.

HIKING THROUGH HOLLAND WITH WILL ROGERS

Pathé Ind., Inc.,   Copyright February 14, 1927, MU 3792; renewed January 13, 1955, R 143007; b&w; silent; 1 reel, 20 prints. Extant. Distributed by Pathé Exchange, Inc.

Production Staff: Producer and director: Carl Stearns Clancy; author and titles: Will Rogers.

Synopsis: A boat trip on the canals of Amsterdam; a visit to Volendam, where the people wear wooden shoes and traditional costumes. The women and children pose for the camera; Rogers tries to walk in wooden shoes; Rogers describes Dutch customs and manners in wisecracking titles, speaking directly to camera. He walks out onstage at the outset, as though on a lecture tour.

In 1913 they christened the Peace Palace at The Hague, just prior to the world war.

★

Flying over Holland in an airship is the only real way to see it, 'cause if you are down on the level—and if you are in Holland you will be standing on the level—Holland's highest point is eight feet six and a third inches above sea level. That is called the mountainous region of Holland; that's where they do their skiing and winter sports.

★

She sure is a pretty dairying country. Those old big black cows with a white bandage around their stomachs don't seem to mind at all. You don't have to brand your cattle, and your herd will never get mixed up with your neighbor's, unless they develop webfeet or grow a rudder in place of a tail.

★

They got hundreds of canals and boats going along all of them. Your farm is not fenced off from your neighbor's; there is just a canal between you and him. You either visit by boat or holler over. If your next-farm neighbor starts to walk over to you some night, he may get there, but he will arrive wet.

★

I had always thought those windmills were located by a little white house. Say, there is not a little white house in Holland. There's not even a big white house there. It's the only country in the world where there is absolutely only one color, and a paintman would starve to death trying to sell any other. It's a kind of red, or a dark bay. So don't you believe pictures anymore. What makes everything look white is because it is so clean and neat and nice.

★

There is no road-contracting graft in Holland—no road commission. All roads come under the heading of Harbor and Dock Commission. If there is a flivver in Holland, it has oars on it, instead of wheels.

★

Look at Holland—great country, big as England, and they have colonies, but do you ever hear of them when they talk of what the big powers want? No! You would think they were Rhode Island. Why? No navy! We don't rate their culture, we don't rate their achievements, their art, their literature, their integrity, their population—in fact, nothing except: How big is their navy!

ROAMING THE EMERALD ISLE WITH WILL ROGERS

Pathé Ind., Inc., Copyright May 6, 1927, MU 4001; renewed April 1, 1955, R 147177; b&w; silent; 1 reel, 20 prints. Release: August 21, 1927. Extant. Distributed by Pathé Exchange, Inc.

Production Staff: Producer and director: Carl Stearns Clancy; author and titles: Will Rogers.

Synopsis: Village life in the Vale of Glendalough; home of Richard Croker, boss of Tammany Hall; Croker's tomb; burial place of Orby, Croker's famous racehorse; Mrs. Richard Croker; lakes of Killarney; Ross Castle; the earl of Killarney.

Ireland, that is where some of my folks come from. There is a fine breed for you, Irish-Indian. Ziegfeld says I have a touch of Hebraic in me, too. Which would make me an Irish-Jewish Indian.

★

Ireland treats you more like a friend than a tourist.

★

This is the home of Sir Thomas Lipton, the man who made more tea and drank less of it than any man living. He truly represents the British Isles, as he was born in Ireland, weaned on Scotch whiskey, and made English sportsmanship famous.

★

Of all the nationalities that have helped to root the Indians out over home, the Irish are the only ones that have made enough impression on everybody till we celebrate their Saint Patrick's Day. When you are laying out your European trip, don't overlook the old

88

Emerald Isle. It's got all of 'em beat for beauty, romance, humor, and hospitality, and the best horses in the world.

★

In the last Democratic political platform, at San Francisco, they officially expressed sympathy for Ireland. But from the looks of the casualty lists lately, England needs it more.

★

Well, if you get your schooling from an Irish history book, you shoot anybody. The theory is (and they are just about right) that everybody that ain't shot, should be shot.

★

Deer season opened; that's for all those who can't hit grouse.

★

If I was England, I would give Ireland home rule but

reserve the motion-picture rights for what follows.

★

The Irish Free State has an army of fifteen thousand men—that gives 'em a fighting force of sixty thousand.

★

These big wars over commerce are pretty bad. They kill more people, but one over religion is really the most bitter.

Syndicated column, September 8, 1929

THROUGH SWITZERLAND AND BAVARIA WITH WILL ROGERS

Pathé Ind., Inc., Copyright May 10, 1927, MU 4015; renewed April 1, 1955, R 147180; b&w; silent; 1 reel, 20 prints. Release: June 26, 1927. Extant. Distributed by Pathé Exchange, Inc.

Production Staff: Producer and director: Carl Stearns Clancy; author and titles: Will Rogers.

Synopsis: Mountain views in Switzerland; Grindelwald (town); lake at Zurich; Will at Lake Lucerne, with Swiss mountaineer, with German policeman; Munich (old section of town and the municipal brewery).

We were going along the other day—wasn't bothering a soul—and the first thing, we were stopped by a band of soldiers and they said that we were in their country. I said, "Whose country?" And they said: "Why, you are in the middle of Switzerland!"

I told him, "Why, we haven't been away from the hotel but a little while, how could we be in the middle of Switzerland?" But I couldn't argue with him. He evidently knew Switzerland better than I did. I would have sworn it wasn't Switzerland. I couldn't hear anybody yodeling, or falling off a mountain, or see feathers in anybody's hat. But the soldier told me to walk over here to the line and he would show me that I was in Switzerland, and sure enough, we walked over there and it said Switzerland on one side of the rock, and France on the other, and then a hundred yards to the north of us lay Germany, and one mountain south lay Italy.

Well, I had always heard a lot about Switzerland. Every time we read a headline in the papers about universal peace, or "War is expected to break out in the Balkans tomorrow afternoon," why, the dateline is always in Switzerland. It's the rumor factory of the world. When nations get ready to make peace or war (and they generally don't know which they are making), why, they always go to Switzerland. Geneva and Locarno are the principal conference towns. It's kinder like Atlantic City is for bathing contests (without water). Switzerland has a corner on all conferences. It has had fewer wars and has been the starting place of more of them than any nation that ever lived. They just sit around and remain neutral during these wars and then collect from all ends. It's the only country where both sides can go and meet and have a drink together during that particular war. Switzerland is a kind of speakeasy for any and all sides. There is little private rooms all over and anybody can come and meet anybody else and Switzerland just winks knowingly and says nothing.

They knew something when they settled there, too. They said to themselves: The best thing about a war is to keep out of it! But they also figured there is a lot of jack in them at that, if you are placed right. So they commenced to figuring: Where can a fellow go to be near enough to see a war but still not be in it? So they picked out the spot they have now, and they picked better than they knew, for it has never been necessary to even go out and get a better location.

Then, of course, you would think that it would be dull in between wars, but there is where you are wrong. They have what is really an all-the-year-round business. The minute a war was over, if there was none booked to start within the next few weeks, why, they would hold what they called a "Peace conference" to prevent other wars.

Yes, sir, the Swiss constitution is one of the shortest. It says: This nation must give aid and board lodging to any and all conferences to either prevent or start wars. No preference is to be shown. All conferences are to be held inside the home grounds of Switzerland, but all fighting is to be confined to the outside.

So in that way they have lived six hundred years in peace and have seen every war, and it hasn't cost them a nickel to do it. Confer or fight; it don't make any difference to Switzerland. They are going to get theirs either way.

★

I never could see much percentage in that mountain-climbing thing. Anytime I want to do any cliff hopping, I'm going to let a goat do it for me. Anytime I go up a mountainside, I'm not going to follow some guide; I'm going to go up after the surveyors have built a two-way road.

★

I've been away up in the mountains of Switzerland and couldn't get any news at all; if you didn't yodel it, they wouldn't read it.

★

Say, if the Mississippi ever flowed through Switzerland, why, there wouldn't be enough dry ground left to yodel in.

★

The League of Nations to perpetuate peace is in session in Geneva, Switzerland. On account of Spain not being in the last war, they won't let her in. If you want to help make peace, you have to fight for it.

★

Germany had an election to see if they approved leaving the League of Nations. There was one fellow voted against it, but they are on the track of him.

★

Before the war Germany led the world in lots of things. She lost all of them. Now, here she is, back where she was. It's a great argument against war. It just shows you can lick a nation, but when you let 'em up, they can still beat you at the same things they could before, which takes away the only reason left for having war.

★

Germany has a new airplane, with its tail where its head ought to be. They ought to call it the "congressional plane."

★

It looks to me like the last war ought to be the greatest example against any future wars. What I mean by that is the winners are the losers. I have been in every nation that was humorously supposed to have won the war, and then I visited Germany, which is humorously referred to as the loser, and I want to tell you that if the next war is to be anything like the last one, I wouldn't give you a five-cent piece to win it.

Wars strike me as being the only game in the world where there is absolutely no winner—everybody loses.

WITH WILL ROGERS IN LONDON

Pathé Ind., Inc.,   Copyright May 10, 1927, MU 4018; renewed April 1, 1955, R 147181; b&w; silent; 1 reel, 19 prints; tinted. Release: July 24, 1927. Extant. Distributed by Pathé Exchange, Inc.

Production Staff: Producer and director: Carl Stearns Clancy; author and titles: Will Rogers.

Synopsis: Parliament; interior of House of Lords; interior of House of Commons; London Bridge; Tower of London; Piccadilly Circus; the Strand; Regent Street (fashion center); American embassy; Westminster Abbey; entrance to Scotland Yard; Old Curiosity Shop; dog cemetery in Hyde Park; statue of Peter Pan; Buckingham Palace; Horse Guards; Grenadier Guards; changing of the guards.

England elected a Labour government, but nobody has ever accused ours of doing a tap of work. When a man goes in for politics over home, he has no time to labor, and any man that labors, has no time to fool with politics.

In England politics is an obligation; at home it's a business.

★

There is one thing about Englishmen: They won't fix anything till it's just about totally ruined. You couldn't get the English to fix anything at the start. No! They like to sit and watch it grow worse. If nothing was growing worse, they wouldn't have anything to debate and argue about. Then, when it looks just like the whole thing has gone up Salt Creek, why, the English jump in and rescue it. They seem to figure the whole expense of it makes it worth digging out of the fire in the finish.

★

Now there is one thing about England's government where they are more democratic than ours. When a guy don't suit 'em, there is no waiting to oust him. The minute the majority are at outs with the reigning premier, why, they can call for a new election and he is out, maybe before he even has time to learn where the icebox is at 10 Downing Street.

★

I see where England is having a royal wedding. Americans are flocking over to try and see it. That is one thing I will say for England—she is not mercenary. If she wanted to, she could charge Americans to get in to see the wedding and make enough to pay off the national debt. That is the unfortunate thing about our country: We have rich people who would pay to get into purgatory if they knew they were not wanted in there.

★

The English have a great royal family—they know just what they are to do, and they do it, and no more.

I imagine that is the best of systems, for it's worked for many years. There is not a well-trained servant in England that knows his place any more than royalty does in England. They would no more monkey with affairs of state than an English butler would monkey with slang.

★

I ain't going to tell you any jokes about the Prince of Wales falling off his horse. I fall just as much. Of course, my falls don't attract as much attention, but they hurt as much.

★

I guess you all have seen pictures of the English prince falling off his horse. Now people say, "He can't ride!" Well, I been riding since birth, and I learned that anytime your horse falls, you have a tendency to join him. It takes an expert rider to pause up there when your horse falls, until he comes back up under you.

★

I went over to Parliament—the House of Commons, rather. I have seen it now and I prefer calling it the House of Commons. Well, they met in there, and a man who was just engaged for that business prayed. He incidentally mentioned the crown more than he did the subjects. That struck me as kinder odd, because from what I had seen of the royal family and the house they lived in, and what I had seen of the subjects, I thought the royal family was doing pretty well and didn't particularly need any help.

At least to be fair, I thought the subjects should have had an even break.

★

These Englishmen are just about the smartest folks there is. It's one place where fascism, communism, or nudism will never get anywhere. They got a park here in London—Hyde Park—that's all built for folks that are *agin* something.

Yesterday I saw it at its best. There was the Fascists holding a meeting and two hundred yards away the Communists was holding another one and in between was all of London laughin' at both sides.

★

The Tower of London's reputation was built on obituary notices of people who had displeased princes and kings.

★

We wanted to fly to Paris, so we drove out to the edge of London, and when you drive out to the edge of London, why, you have drove out to the edge of something. It began to look from the taximeter like London didn't have any edges.

HUNTING FOR GERMANS IN BERLIN WITH WILL ROGERS

Pathé Ind., Inc., Copyright May 10, 1927, MU 4019; renewed April 1, 1955, R 147182; b&w; silent; 1 reel, 20 prints. Release: May 29, 1927. Extant. Distributed by Pathé Exchange, Inc.

Production Staff: Producer and director: Carl Stearns Clancy; author and titles: Will Rogers.

Germany has the most beautiful forests, all out in rows. Every time they cut down a tree, it looks like they planted two in its place. Every time we cut one down, the fellow that cuts it down sets down to have a smoke and celebrate. He throws his cigarette away and burns up the rest of the forest.

★

Germany has banned that splendid film *All Quiet on the Western Front,* on account of it showing Germany losing the war. I guess Hollywood is going to take it back and make it with a different ending.

★

Kaiser Wilhelm's slogan was "Germany Uber Alles!" I don't know what the *Uber* means, but whatever it means, he was wrong, and it's too late to look it up now.

★

Germany has some sort of a custom where they allow you to commit suicide in case you have been found to be against the government. In America we just let you go on making speeches, and it amounts to about the same in the end.

★

A German outrun the great Finnish runner Nurmi. This has been three great days for Germany. They won a foot race and got into the League of Nations. They feel that these two events will just set them in right for the next war.

Yours, for *ein Dunkel und ein Helles* (a dark and a light [beer]).

PROWLING AROUND FRANCE WITH WILL ROGERS

Pathé Ind., Inc., Copyright July 19, 1927, MU 4176; renewed July 11, 1955, R 152891; b&w; silent; 1 reel, 20 prints. Release: September 18, 1927. Extant. Distributed by Pathé Exchange, Inc.

Production Staff: Producer and director: Carl Stearns Clancy; author and titles: Will Rogers.

Synopsis: French Senate (Chamber of Deputies); Ritz Hotel; Claridge Hotel; The Carlton; Les Halles (food center); Bois de Boulogne; Longchamp Racetrack; Saint-Germaine; Arc de Triomphe; Fontainebleau; Victor Hugo's house; Cathedral of Notre Dame; Folies-Bergère; Le Rat Mort; Moulin Rouge; Paris by night.

We're just off the coast of France. I hear a noise. I think it's the franc dropping.

★

France says that this year's harvest crop of American tourists has not reached the expected yield. The number has been beyond expectation, but the shakedown per person has been very low. Where tourists used to carry a letter of credit when leaving America, they are now carrying lunch boxes. Americans are going there nowadays to look, and France can't find any way to keep 'em from looking without paying.

I would suggest that they put in hot dog stands.

Coney Island got rich on 'em out of the same kind of people.

★

Nice, France, is pronounced "neece," not "nice"! They have no word for *nice* in French.

★

In France, they ask: "Rogers, why is it nobody seems to like America?" I had to admit that we was in kinda bad. We wasn't hardly what you would call the world's sweetheart.

But after they kept this up for quite a while, I used to casually ask them—be it Frenchman, Englishman, or whatever—well, we are in bad, but will you just kinda offhand, just casually, name me a list of your bosom friends among other nations?

I tell you, they can't hate us as bad as they hate each other.

★

France and England think just as much of each other as two rival bands of Chicago gangsters. A Frenchman and an Italian love each other like Minneapolis and Saint Paul. Spain and France have the same regard for each other as Fort Worth and Dallas; and Russia hates everybody so bad it would take her a week to pick out the one she hates most.

★

There really ain't anywhere where you can put your hand on a country. Its heart is not at its capital, as some think. It's not in its biggest cities. It's not in the country.

It's a great kick to sit and hear somebody say: "Well, I lived in France for years, I know what France will do! I know the heart of the real France."

Sightseeing with Will as tour guide; *Prowling Around France;* Le Château de Saint-Germain-en-Laye. (*The Penguin Collection*)

Well, the poor fellow is not purposely lying. He really thinks he knows.

WINGING 'ROUND EUROPE WITH WILL ROGERS

Pathé Ind., Inc., Copyright November 15, 1927, MP 4454; renewed October 7, 1955, R 157172; b&w; silent; 1 reel; tinted. Release: November 20, 1927. Extant. Distributed by Pathé Exchange, Inc.

Production Staff: Producer and director: Carl Stearns Clancy; author and titles: Will Rogers.

Synopsis: Air trip, Imperial Airways, Croydon Field, London: cliffs of Dover, crossing the Channel, Oostende, Belgium; Amsterdam; Berlin; lake at Zurich, Switzerland. Side air trip over the Alps; Paris, flying over Arc de Triomphe; le Bourget airfield.

There ought to be a law against anybody going to Europe till they had seen the things we have in this country.

★

Well, I felt I had a right to go to Europe because I am one of the few Americans that have seen America first. I haven't seen near all of it, and when I get back, I'm going to look over some more. I have been over to Europe two or three times, years ago, but I thought, well, I will go and see if the boys have scared up anything new. They haven't anything new, except the prices.

★

You can't find a piece of ground in Europe that hasn't been taken at least a dozen times from somebody or other that really think they have an original claim to it.

★

Headline in paper says: EUROPE CRITICIZES UNITED STATES! If memory serves me right, we haven't complimented them lately ourselves.

★

It will take America fifteen years steady taking care of our own business and letting everybody else's

93

alone to get us back to where everybody speaks to us again.

★

I would like to stay in Europe long enough to find some country that don't blame America for everything in the world that's happened to 'em in the last fifteen years. Debt, recession, disarmament, disease, fog, famine, or frostbite. If the dog had two pups, and they were expecting more, they will show in some way that we was directly responsible for the canine delinquency.

Now the birth rate is falling off, so I am going to get out of here before we get blamed.

★

Europe must sit up nights just thinking of ways to get us in worse than we are, if possible.

★

Some Americans in Europe are traveling incognito. They are not bragging on where they come from and nobody knows they are Americans.

★

Passports, that's one thing you want to carry in your hand anywhere in Europe. They just seem to get a pleasure out of having you dig for it.

★

I had to get a passport. They told me to produce a birth certificate or somebody who knew of my birth.

I told her: "Lady, I have no birth certificate. Where I come from, you being there was certificate enough that you had been born. And as for somebody who was present at my birth, you know, the old-time lady of which I am a direct descendant was of a rather modest and retiring nature, and being born was a rather private affair, and not a public function."

★

In Europe, public men do resign. But here it's a lost art. You have to impeach 'em.

★

There is one good thing about European nations. They can't hate you so badly they wouldn't use you.

★

You know, Louisiana has more water in their cellars than the whole Adriatic Sea.

★

It's open season now in Europe for grouse and Americans. They shoot the grouse and put them out of their miseries.

★

I see where they are forming in Europe a new organization called "the United States of Europe," or something. Nobody knows what it is or what its aims are, but we ought to be for it if only for one reason, and that is, it's the first thing been formed since the war that we haven't been asked to go over and join.

EXPLORING ENGLAND WITH WILL ROGERS

Pathé Ind., Inc.,   Copyright November 28, 1927, MP 4475; renewed October 7, 1955, R 157173; b&w; silent; 1 reel. Release: December 18, 1927. Extant. Distributed by Pathé Exchange, Inc.

Production Staff: Producer and director: Carl Stearns Clancy; author and titles: Will Rogers.

Synopsis: Windsor Castle; the king's Life Guards; the dungeon; Eaton College; king's riding park; the castle grounds; motoring through England; the churchyard made famous in Thomas Gray's poem, *Elegy;* Ascot Racetrack; the Hampton Court palace of Henry VIII and grounds; boat ride down the Thames.

Daily Channel swimming catastrophy: A German swam in here today, got one look at England, turned around, and is swimming back.

★

All the Channel swimming was called off today on account of rain and a wet track.

★

England has the best statesmen and the rottenest coffee of any country in the world. I just hate to see morning come, because I have to get up and drink this coffee.

★

Poor coffee and no bathtubs have drove more Americans out of England than unfamiliarity with their language has.

★

I pulled a thing that is an unforgivable sin in England, or Europe. I asked for water. They have everything else, but nothing disrupts a well-organized dinner outside of America as much as to have some bonehead ask for a glass of water. It is just used for raining purposes every day here in England.

★

I told you how bad it's getting with the tourists over here. Some of them are getting almost what they deserve.

★

Well, you know England has been the daddy of the diplomat, the one with the smooth manners. But still going after what he wants, but always a gentleman.

You know, that's one thing about an Englishman: He can insult you, but he can do it so slick and polite that he will have you guessing until away after he leaves you just whether he was friend or foe.

★

You see, "Sir" is about the lowest form of title there is; it's the Ford of titles.

★

There is a cricket match going on here that has been for three months—one game! England had an earthquake yesterday, and it didn't even wake up the spectators.

★

The same cricket match that I told you about before is still going on. One man has been batting three days. Come over and see it. If the tea holds out, it will run till winter.

I have been thrown out of the grounds twice for applauding. They contend I was a boisterous element.

Yours, for long, lingering sportsmanship.

REELING DOWN THE RHINE WITH WILL ROGERS

Pathé Ind., Inc., Copyright December 28, 1927; MP 4563; b&w; silent; 1 reel. Release: January 15, 1928. Extant. Distributed by Pathé Exchange, Inc.

Production Staff: Producer and director: Carl Stearns Clancy; author and titles: Will Rogers.

Synopsis: Trip from Mainz to Cologne; vineyards, Mäuse Tower; Schloss Ehrenfels (castle), Pfalz Castle, Die Katz Castle, Die Maus Castle, and others; Drachenfels (where Siegfried killed the dragon); Lorelei Rock; Bacharach wine distilleries; Ehrenbreitstein (old military fort); kaiser's statue at Koblenz; Cologne, the city hall, streets and houses, the marketplace, and the cathedral.

I am going into Germany. I want to see what reason they had wanting to try and get into the next war by way of the League of Nations.

★

France says that her and Germany were old pals again. I guess they are; floated down the Rhine in Germany all day yesterday and there was so many French soldiers in the way, I couldn't see the castles.

★

I want to tell you tourists are taking this sightseeing serious. It's no pleasure; it's a business.

They go in great for ruins. Now a ruin don't exactly spellbind me. I don't care how long it has been in process of ruination. I kept trying to get them to show me something that hadn't started to ruin yet.

★

England, France, and Germany have diplomats that have had the honor of starting every war they have ever had in their lifetime. Ours are not so good—they are amateurs—they have only talked us into one. Yet diplomacy was invented by a man named Webster, to use up all the words in his dictionary that didn't mean anything.

OVER THE BOUNDING BLUE WITH WILL ROGERS

Pathé Ind., Inc.,   Copyright January 17, 1928, MP 4631; renewed January 16, 1956, R 162706; b&w; silent; 1 reel. Release: February 12, 1928. Extant. Distributed by Pathé Exchange, Inc.

Production Staff: Producer and director: Carl Stearns Clancy; author and titles: Will Rogers.

Synopsis: U.S. *Leviathan* is leaving Southampton. Will Rogers introduces Captain Hartley, William Phillips, the U.S. ambassador to Canada, all the dogs on board, passengers playing deck golf, a lady boxing a man, the interior swimming pool, girls diving in slow motion, the lounge; while arriving in New York Harbor, Rogers introduces Charles Evans Hughes, Jimmy Gleason, the actor, Ethelind Terry, star of *Rio Rita*. The ship docks, luggage is carried off.

Will you kindly find out for me through our intelligence department who the fellow is that said a big boat didn't rock? Hold him till I return.

★

My remaining days are dedicated to annihilate the author of the slogan Big Boats Don't Rock. Say, the higher they are the further they rock. They tailspin, sideslip, ground loop. It's taken a good man to stay tied in bed today. Well, here's how bad it is: There is not one American in the barroom!

★

You know I am the champion of the world getting seasick, and I know that it is just lack of nerve. If you will just keep up there and battle with it, and keep going, why you are okay. But I am kinder yellow, anyhow, and when I feel a little squirmish, why, I start hitting for the hay, and when once I get down on the bunk, why, I am a dead dog from then on, no matter if we are out for a week or a month.

★

One time I was supposed to make a one-night trip by a small boat. Well, the train I was on pulled up beside the boat, and I knowing that I was going to be sick, rushed aboard right away, and I says to myself I will get in the bunk and maybe that will help me from being too sick. Well, it's the paint and that smell of varnish that does it. Well, I got a whiff of it going down, and I crawled right into my bunk, which was in among a lot of other men's bunks. This old sniff of paint had got me, and sure enough I started in being sick. I had the old lunch basket tied on right to the edge of the bed. (They have lovely little cuspidors of a thing for birds like me.) Well, I sure was going strong. I thought, well, I haven't got long to be sick, for we will be there before long, and finally some fellow come in and asked another fellow: "What's the matter with this boat, ain't it ever going to pull out?"

Here I was practically dying and the boat was still tied to the dock.

★

There ought to be a law about making an ocean this wide. That's something Congress can take up at the next session, as they won't have anything to settle much, outside of unemployment, billions in deficit, arrange extra taxes where they will do the least harm at the next election, and think up something new to promise the farmers.

Narrowing an ocean will be just a small chore for this Congress.

WELL, I MADE 'EM A GOOD MAYOR FOR A WHILE

On December 21, 1926, I arrived back home amid big demonstrations, as honorary mayor of Beverly Hills. I thought they mistook me.

Honest, they gave me a great welcome and I thanked everybody from the bottom of my heart and President Coolidge for a lovely wire; also Al Smith and my opposition, Jimmy Walker, the mayor of New York.

So I was the only mayor that hadn't made a mistake, His Honor the mayor of Beverly Hills, the best town west of Nantucket Lightship. I made 'em a little speech. I told 'em that it didn't speak well for their town when this many hadn't anything to do but come to meet me. Now this town had everything to make a good town—burglars, poor parking regulations, shortage of water in the summer, poor telephone service, luncheon clubs, Chamber of Commerce, and everything that goes to handicap 99 percent of the towns. I said: "I want to introduce a law to make real estate men and moving-picture people as good as any other citizens—there shall be no discrimination against them."

I am sorry somebody referred to movies as an art—the success of the movies have been the animal trainers, more than the directors. The minute directors can train actors to act as natural as a dog or a horse, then they will have accomplished something. We have more swimming pools and less Bibles in Beverly Hills than any town in the world. We love to bathe collectively, but individually we are pretty dirty.

I know you will ask, "Well, Will, how are you going to run the town if you are away so much?" Say, I can run this town by telegraph. So there I was, their new mayor, God's gift to the people who hadn't seen Romania's Queen Marie.

Now let's see what else is news. Well, there is little else but Charlie Chaplin and his wife Lita Grey's divorce action. Course, if Charlie and Lita start in telling names like they keep claiming they are, that will be about news enough. Hollywood wishes they would either name them or quit talking about naming them. For just about everybody is afraid they won't be among those named.

Charlie says he will name two men, and Lita says she will send him the two and raise him five. She says she will name seven prominent film actresses. The producers are laughing up their sleeves at that. For they say there is not seven prominent actresses here. They say they have paid good money to find out just how prominent they were, and that they know.

Mayor Rogers of Beverly Hills addresses reception crowd, 1926.

The new mayor of Beverly Hills with Douglas Fairbanks, Sr. (*left*), and Tom Mix.

Mayor Rogers inspects "forces" under his command.

But I don't like to butt in. It's right here in my town of Beverly Hills. But as long as they keep their paving and water tax paid, why, I don't worry much about how my constituents live. I just sit at my desk day in and day out taking care of the worthwhile things that come up for a mayor of a thriving and growing town to attend to. I have found out that it don't pay to interfere officially with any kind of sex problem. I just figure if both sides was not slick enough not to get caught, they are too commonplace for me to waste my official time on.

My constituents, I don't claim that they are all good, but most of them is at least slick.

Now the state legislature of California passed a law saying that no one not a politician could hold office. I hereby notify the world that Beverly Hills has left my bed and board and I will not be responsible for any debts contracted by said municipality.

You see, a few months ago I read in the papers that the legislature of the state of California had passed a bill where if a town was governed by trustees, that the chairman of the board of the trustees had to be known as the mayor. That was applicable to cities of the sixth class.

Well, I never paid much attention when I read it, knowing it as one of those things they do during the sessions to try and make it look like they are doing

something. It was just in among a list of jokes that they had passed.

Well, the first thing I knew, people got to calling me up and saying, "I see where you are going to lose your job as mayor." I never paid much attention to that for about two thirds of the talk in Hollywood or Beverly Hills can't be depended on.

Then I commenced to hear what it was all about. It looked like a direct dig from the legislature. You see, a few months ago I played on my tour of enlightenment in the city of Sacramento, and I was asked to speak to them in joint session.

Well, when I addressed them I didn't want to appear critical, but I told them a few things about how their joke foundry was operating. Well, the truth hurts, I don't care how thick the hide is; even a rhinoceros can't shed off true facts, so I just figured that after I had left town they cooked up this bill to knock me out of a position that I had filled with honor and high-mindedness.

There is only one thing that makes me sore about the whole thing and that is this. This new law applies to cities of the sixth class only. My Lord, if I had known that I was ruling in a city of the sixth class, I would never have taken the thing in the first place. Mayor of a sixth-class city—why, I will be years living that down.

7

"AUDIABLES," BY FOX FILM CORPORATION

WILL ROGERS' CONTRACT WITH FOX FILM CORPORATION

On March 22, 1929, Will Rogers signed a letter of agreement, which was countersigned for Fox Film Corporation by W. R. Sheehan, vice-president. The original agreement still exists, but the present owner does not wish us to quote it in its entirety; we will therefore touch only the high points.

The agreement was for a period of sixteen months, starting June 1, 1929, terminating September 30, 1930. During this period Will Rogers was to perform and assist in the production of four talking motion pictures—all to be made in the Los Angeles studios. In addition to acting, Will Rogers was expected to perform, speak, and sing; assist in creating and writing original matter, such as dialogue of dramatic and comedy lines; assist in the selection and construction of stories and continuity thereof, and the selection of cast; edit, criticize, revise, adapt, compose, and create scenarios, titles, and write the text thereof.

The full payment for these four films was to be six hundred thousand dollars.

THE "AUDIABLES" (1929–1935)

Our old friend Tom Mix had a little local upheaval lately. Some actor said that anyway, Tony, Tom's horse, would be good in the "Talkies." He could at least snort. Well, that kinder got Tom's nanny, and he just snorted all over that person and it took a day to wind on the adhesive tape.

These actors out here are kinder sensitive about this "Talkie" business. I went to see one of the new "Squawkies" the other night. It was billed as "Metro Goldwyn's first sound picture," and the only sound in it was Monte Blue whistling. It never reproduced a word he said. It didn't even whistle the same tune he whistled, but it did whistle when he did. Well, that wasn't bad, for he had done his whistling in the South Seas, and this whistling was done in the studio, so you couldn't expect them to remember what he had whistled three months before. But that's what they was selling as a sound picture was Monte's whistling.

Now, I like Monte, he is a dandy actor, but I don't like to be hornswoggled into going in to just hear him whistle. For he is not what I would call an A-number-one good whistler. I paid to see a "Talkie" and all I got was a "Whistlie."

Anyhow, what do you say we have a little chat on the movies? Haven't dished out any movie scandal to you in a long time. Actually, it's just kinder the off-season. Spring marrying is about over, and summer divorces haven't quite got going good. But here is something that might be a lot of news to you. I was just talking to some of the biggest men in the whole industry and they told me that the business is undergoing a great change. That in four or five years you will look back and laugh at yourself for ever having sat for hours and just looked at pictures with no voice

A thoughtful moment. (*The Penguin Collection*)

or sound. I am not very much of a movie fan and don't get around much, but these men told me of the millions and millions of dollars that they are spending in talking equipment. All the big companies have made contracts with the General Electric (I think that's the one that holds most of the patents on the sound), and they all are going in for it heavy. These men said that the movies are as much in their infancy as when years ago we got all excited over *The Great Train Robbery* in some nickelodeon. They say that the talk and sounds have just begun to develop. That the ones you hear now are very crude in comparison to the ones you will get in a year or so. Every picture will bring new developments.

The whole business out here is scared cuckoo. The girl that left a ribbon counter and won a beauty contest and then was made a "star" overnight just because somebody told her every move to make and when to smile, she can just see her finish. Everybody that can't sing has a double that can, and everybody that can't talk is going right on and proving it. You meet an actor or girl and in the old days where they would have just nodded and passed by, now they stop and start chattering like a parrot. Weather, politics, Babe Ruth, anything just to practice talking, and they are so busy enunciating that they pay no attention to what they are saying. Everything is "enunciation." I was on the stage twenty-three years and never heard the word or knew what it was.

It looks like it is getting into the days of the actor. That's one thing where the stage always had it on the movies. You got to do something beside being photographed on the old stage.

Each big company is putting in studios in Los Angeles and New York, too. They also have the sound-recording apparatus so arranged that they have them on trucks and they can haul them easily anywhere and record speech or event at its original place, the same as they can take the pictures there with a camera.

Say, did you ever see a picture company on location? With all that sound equipment and men—why, it looks like Barnum's circus coming. I bet there is about fifty of us. It takes lots of folks to make these things, even when you sometimes think they ain't so hot. And the funny part about it is that a bad one takes just as much work as a good one, for we have never found anyone that can tell when it's going to be bad. You see, bad pictures are not made with a premeditated design. It looks to you sometimes like we must have made 'em that way on purpose, but honest, we don't. A bad picture is an accident, and a good one is a miracle. We do our best all the time, and all the crew, the cameramen, the carpenters, property men, sound technicians, and dozens of other expert men in their lines, they all do good work on all of 'em, but it's us actors and writers and directors that just don't click in some of 'em.

But the actor ain't the most important part in a picture by any means, and those that think he is, are coming a-cropper. I'd say a good picture is 50 percent

Roping and writing on movie set, c. 1933.

With Dorothy Stone, in Broadway show *Three Cheers*, 1928–29.

With good friend Fred Stone.

story, 40 percent directing, and 10 percent acting. Now you take *Jubilo*, the film I made for Mr. Goldwyn. *Jubilo* was a good story, it had good direction—anyone could have played in it and it would still have been a good picture.

But I must get back to what I was talking about, the "Noisies." There is about a thousand theaters equipped now with the means of showing sound pictures, and they are equipping others just as fast as possible.

You will see some great improvements.

Yes, it's going to make pictures about twice as human.

BOX-OFFICE FAVORITES

1930 Joan Crawford, Clara Bow, William Haines, Janet Gaynor, Colleen Moore, Greta Garbo, Al Jolson, Richard Barthelmess, Rin Tin Tin, Tom Mix

1931 Janet Gaynor, Charles Farrell, Joan Crawford, Norma Shearer, Marie Dressler, Wallace Beery, Clara Bow, Al Jolson, Colleen Moore, Greta Garbo

1932 Marie Dressler, Janet Gaynor, Joan Crawford, Charles Farrell, Greta Garbo, Norma Shearer, Wallace Beery, Clark Gable, *Will Rogers*, Joe E. Brown

1933 Marie Dressler, *Will Rogers*, Janet Gaynor, Eddie Cantor, Wallace Beery, Jean Harlow, Clark Gable, Mae West, Norma Shearer, Joan Crawford

1934 *Will Rogers*, Clark Gable, Janet Gaynor, Wallace Beery, Mae West, Joan Crawford, Bing Crosby, Shirley Temple, Marie Dressler, Norma Shearer

1935 Shirley Temple, *Will Rogers*, Clark Gable, Fred Astaire and Ginger Rogers, Joan Crawford, Claudette Colbert, Dick Powell, Wallace Beery, Joe E. Brown, James Cagney

★

From the list of the top money-making stars, compiled by *Motion Picture Herald*, based on reports from over two hundred thousand exhibitor reports.

Top three stars on the Fox lot: Janet Gaynor, Will, and Shirley Temple. (*Academy of Motion Picture Arts and Sciences*)

THEY HAD TO SEE PARIS

A Fox Movietone Production, Copyright September 11, 1929, LP 675; renewed November 5, 1956; b&w; sound and silent versions; 10 reels, 8,620 ft.; running time 96 minutes; no script available. World premiere: September 18, 1929, Fox-Carthay Theatre, L.A.; October 11, 1929, Roxy Theatre, NYC. Review in *New York Times*, October 12, 1929. Extant.

Production Staff: Presented by William Fox; director: Frank Borzage; assistant director: Lew Borzage; cameramen: Chester Lyons, Al Brick; based on novel (c. 1926) of same name, by Homer Croy; screenplay by Sonya Levien; dialogue: Owen Davis, Sr.; music: Con Conrad, Sidney Mitchell, Archie Gottler; song: "I Could Do It for You"; staged by Bernard Steele; editor: Margaret V. Clancey; recording engineer: George P. Costello; art director: Harry Oliver; costumes: Sophie Wachner; titles for silent version: Wilbur J. Morse, Jr.

Play: *They Had To See Paris,* by May Savell Croy, comedy in three acts, same cast of characters, except these changes: Grand Duke *Mikkail, Edd* Eggers.

Cast:

Will Rogers	Pike Peters	Bob Kerr	Tupper
Irene Rich	Mrs. Pike Peters	Christiane Yves	Fleurie
Marguerite Churchill	Opal Peters	Marcelle Corday	Marquise de Brissac
Owen Davis, Jr.	Ross Peters	Theodore Lodi	Grand Duke Makiall
Fifi D'Orsay	Claudine	Marcia Manon	Miss Mason
Rex Bell	Clark McCurdy	Andre Cheron	Valet
Ivan Lebedeff	Marquis de Brissac	Gregory Gaye	Prince Ordinsky
Edgar Kennedy	Ed Eggers	Mr. Persian Pussy	Claudine's kitty

Synopsis: Pike Peters, happy just to be a garage owner in Claremore, Oklahoma, suddenly finds himself rich when his oil well begins to produce at the rate of one thousand dollars a day. Mrs. Peters immediately sets out to plan their future life in Paris, and find a French nobleman as a husband for her daughter. Against his will and judgment, Pike bows to the pressures of his socially ambitious wife and his adventuresome daughter and son. Only when it seems that Pike is overly enjoying his alliance with Claudine, a gold-digging French-woman whom he met, does the rest of the family finally decide that it is high time to return home.

Reviews:
★ "Mr. Rogers is capital."
New York Times, October 12, 1929

★ "Cowboy Comedian Has Best Screen Role in New Audible Feature."
New York Times, October 20, 1929

Recognitions:
★ Will Rogers, Best Performance of the Month, *Photoplay Magazine*, November 1929

★ #7 among 10 Best Films of 1929, *New York Times*, January 5, 1930

★ #4 on Roll of Honor, Best of 1929, *The Film Daily*

★ #6 among Top Films of 1929, Frank T. Daugherty, *The Film Spectator*, January 4, 1930

Location Shots: Since the Peters family home was to have been Claremore, Oklahoma, the adopted home-town of Will Rogers, a film crew actually shot background material there.

Advertising poster for Will's first all-talking film, *They Had to See Paris*, 1929.

Some cast and crew members of *They Had to See Paris*. *Center:* Will's right hand rests on Marguerite Churchill, his left on director Frank Borzage. Seated next to Mr. Borzage is Irene Rich. On Miss Churchill's right is scenario writer Sonya Levien. *Rear row, far right:* Owen Davis, Jr.

With playful Fifi D'Orsay, in *They Had to See Paris*, 1929.

A nap on the set of *They Had to See Paris*, 1929.

Will Rogers Said

I was sitting around home after finishing an "audiable," and as it was to appear with a sort of ballyhoo opening, why, I figured I better kinder take to the woods till the effects kinder blew over. I wanted 'em to kinder fumigate around before I appeared in person back home.

Syndicated column, October 6, 1929

★

Breakfast this morning at Beverly Hills, and dinner tonight in Wichita. They was opening my first talking picture in Los Angeles and charging those poor people five dollars, and I just couldn't stand by and be a party to such brigandage. First-night audiences pay their money to look at each other, so if they get stuck tomorrow night, they can't blame me. It will be because they don't look good to each other.

Daily Telegram, September 16, 1929

A Word from the Director

We had many amusing experiences while making the picture. It was really more of a vacation, for working with Mr. Rogers is a refreshing adventure. He has many singular characteristics, among these is one of shyness. He hates to hog the camera, and during the

photographing of the action, whenever he was able, he stayed as far from the lens as possible. When we had rushes ready at the end of a day, or the week, and tried to get him into the projection room, it was almost an impossible task. His reticence is amazing. But finally, after much coaxing, I got him into the sound room to view some work we had made a few

104

days before. He sat silently, regarding the fleeting shadows for a few moments, and then he got up to go out. "What's the matter, Will?" I asked him.

"Oh, I dunno," he replied. "Except that maybe I don't quite think that that face on the screen looks like me. The others appear natural enough, but not mine. And that voice is not mine. It can't be. Not that voice."

I assured him that he was quite natural in the film, but he couldn't see it and walked out. After that he wouldn't go near a projection room.

When we were shooting the picture, he would change the lines to conform with what he thought they should be, and his version was usually better than the original script. I really never enjoyed making a picture as much before as I did this last one with Rogers.

Visitors Frank Borzage and Ethel Barrymore.

Will Rogers Tells Trade Secret

The talkies has made a new style of titles possible. The old titles were always subject to change. The film would be taken out and tried on an audience and if a laugh wasn't forthcoming, a new set of wisecracks was prepared. Often as not they would have no relation to the action. In the talkies conversation is adapted to the actor's personality and the lines stay as they were spoken. You don't see one picture in the projection room and another in the theater.

Interview with Louella O. Parsons, 1929

Censorship

(The following eliminations were ordered)

Pennsylvania, September 23, 1929

Reel 7: Eliminate insert of postcard reading: "Dear Pike—I wish I was in your place. Have you parley vooed them yet? Ed Eggers."

Reel 9: Eliminate underlined words from speech by Fifi: "I wish I was in your place. Have you *parley vooed them yet?*"

Views of Fifi lying back on couch with her leg in the air.

British Columbia, October 28, 1929

Reel 2: Where girl is preparing to sit on chair.

Australia, April 26, 1930

Reel 2: Shot of dancer in café throwing up clothes to sit down.

★

BROAD SCREEN BEATS TALKIES

I got home a week ago from prowling around in the various states visiting relatives and old friends, and what had been going on in Hollywood during my absence? My picture had opened amid no casualties and I had been practically forgiven for it; wasn't bad enough to shoot, or good enough to cheer. Went over to the studio and our general manager showed me the new "Grandeur"* screen.

That is, you can't take one old bed sheet and tack it up on the wall and throw some movies on it. This is a great big thing as broad as a Gettysburg painting that covers the whole of the opening of the theater. It has to be taken with a different camera and it has to be projected with a different projecting machine, and

*The Grandeur screen was forty-two feet wide and eighteen feet high; the actual size of the Grandeur picture on the film was twice the width of the old film and a trifle higher.

the width of the film is just about twice what the other was.

They say it will speed up the movies as it will take in so much territory that it will do away with the old idea of continually cutting to a close-up. That when a scene is being played and there is a bunch of people, that you will have to get over your "emotions" all at once and in the same picture, that they won't cut to each of you in a close-up.

I sho will be glad of that for I sho do hate those close-ups. When those old wrinkles commence coming and the old mane is turning snowy, why, we don't want either cameras or people to commence to crowd us.

Then the color thing is coming along fine, where they are going to get our natural complexion right in the camera, without artificial coloring after the film is taken.

Oh, we are just getting so many new things that you almost have to go every night to get 'em. A theater no more than gets in one type of apparatus than it has to start installing another one. They have more workmen in the theaters now than they have audiences. Everybody that can speak above a whisper is out here to have their voice invoiced.

Syndicated column, October 13, 1929

HAPPY DAYS

A Fox Grandeur Production, Copyright December 23, 1929, LP 1009; renewed February 1, 1957, R 185777; b&w; sound; 9 reels, 7,526 ft.; 81 minutes; no shooting script available. Release: February 13, 1930, Roxy Theatre, NYC. Review in *New York Times*, February 14, 1930. Working title: *New Orleans Frolic*. Extant.

Production Staff: Producer: William Fox; director: Benjamin Stoloff; assistant directors: Ad Schaumer, Michael Farley, Lew Breslow; staged by Walter Catlett; cameramen: Lucien Andriot, John Schmitz; for Grandeur camera: J. O. Taylor; original story and dialogue: Sidney Lanfield and Edwin Burke; dances staged by Earl Lindsay; editor: Clyde Carruth; recording engineer: Samuel Waite; art director: Jack Schultze; costumes: Sophie Wachner; music: George Olsen and his orchestra.

Cast (story line):

Charles E. Evans	Col. Billy Batcher	Stuart Erwin	Jig
Marjorie White	Margie	Martha Lee Sparks	Nancy Lee
Richard Keene	Dick	Clifford Dempsey	Sheriff Benton

Cast (principals, in alphabetical order): *

Frank Albertson	Sharon Lynn
Warner Baxter	Farrell MacDonald
Rex Bell	George MacFarlane (interlocutor)
Flo Bert	Victor McLaglen
El Brendel	J. Harold Murray
Lew Brice	Paul Page
Walter Catlett	Tom Patricola
William Collier, Sr.	Ann Pennington
James J. Corbett (interlocutor)	Frank Richardson
Charles Farrell	Will Rogers
Janet Gaynor	David Rollins
George Jessel	The Slate Brothers
Dixie Lee	"Whispering" Jack Smith
Edmund Lowe	Nick Stuart

*The world premiere program announces a "Dancing Ensemble of 100 Steppers." Listed just four names before the end appears the name Betty Grable.

Synopsis: Margie, a singer on the Mississippi River showboat managed by Col. Billy Batcher, is in love with Dick. But she is ambitious and wants to tackle Broadway. When it seems that the showboat is about to be taken by creditors, and Col. Batcher faces bankruptcy, Margie gathers all the stars who started their careers under the colonel, and they agree to stage a benefit performance in Memphis. There Margie is reunited with Dick.

Will Rogers appears in a segment with Walter Catlett, William Collier, Sr., and George Jessel.

Musical Numbers

"We'll Build a Little World of Our Own," by James F. Hanley and James Brockman, performed by Janet Gaynor and Charles Farrell;

"Minstrel Memories," by L. Wolfe Gilbert and Abel Baer, performed by George MacFarlane;

"Mona," by Con Conrad, Sidney Mitchell, and Archie Gottler, performed by Frank Richardson;

"Snake Hips," by Con Conrad, Sidney Mitchell, and Archie Gottler, performed by Sharon Lynn and Ann Pennington;

"Crazy Feet," by Con Conrad, Sidney Mitchell, and Archie Gottler, performed by Dixie Lee;

"I'm on a Diet of Love," by L. Wolfe Gilbert and Abel Baer, performed by Marjorie White and Richard Keene;

"Vic and Eddie," by Harry Stoddard and Marcy Klauber, performed by Victor McLaglen and Edmund Lowe;

"A Toast to the Girl I Love," by James F. Hanley and James Brockman, performed by J. Harold Murray;

"Happy Days," by Joseph McCarthy and James F. Hanley, performed by "Whispering" Jack Smith.

From *Happy Days* (*left to right*): Willie Collier, Will, George Jessel, and Walter Catlett, 1929. (*Academy of Motion Picture Arts and Sciences*)

SO THIS IS LONDON

A Fox Movietone Production, Copyright May 6, 1930, LP 1328; renewed July 10, 1957; R 195354; b&w; sound; 9 reels, 7,975 ft.; 90 minutes. Shooting script at AMPAS. Release: May 23, 1930, Roxy Theatre, NYC; June 19, 1930, Fox-Carthay Circle Theatre, L.A. Extant.

Production Staff: Director: John G. Blystone: assistant director: Jasper Blystone; cameraman: Charles G. Clarke; George M. Cohan's international stage hit by Arthur F. Goodrich (c. 1926); adapted by Owen Davis, Sr.; screenplay by Sonya Levien; music and lyrics: James F. Hanley and Joseph McCarthy; editor: Jack Dennis; recording engineer: Frank MacKenzie; art director: Jack Schultze.

Cast:

Will Rogers	Hiram Draper	Mary Forbes	Lady Worthing
Irene Rich	Mrs. Hiram Draper	Bramwell Fletcher	Alfred Honeycutt
Frank Albertson	Junior Draper	Dorothy Christie	Lady Amy Ducksworth
Maureen O'Sullivan	Elinor Worthing	Martha Lee Sparks	Martha
Lumsden Hare	Lord Percy Worthing	Ellen Woodston	Nurse

Synopsis: Rich Texas cotton mill owner, Hiram Draper, detests anything British. He is greatly disturbed, therefore, when his business demands that he travel to England. Accompanied by his wife and son, Hiram, Jr., the Anglophobe sets out to the land of the "marmalade eaters." After the famous scene of trying to obtain a passport without a birth certificate (the elder Draper, like Rogers, was born in the Indian Territory and has his American citizenship questioned), the ordeal of the ocean voyage begins. While Father Hiram suffers through a severe session of *mal de mer*, Son Hiram meets and falls in love with Elinor, daughter of Lord and Lady Worthing. Through several adventures in England, the two families begin to understand each other better, and all ends on notes of harmony—not too close, but harmony—when Lord Percy and Hiram, Sr., sing the same tune—"My Country 'Tis of Thee" and "God Save the King," but with vastly differing lyrics. While the Texan sings "Land of my father's pride . . . ," the man from Mayfair is heard singing "Frustrate their knavish tricks . . . " Despite those differences, the young lovers are joined in matrimony.

Reviews: ★ "Mr. Rogers is inimitable in this role."

New York Times, June 1, 1930

★ "The dry, genial Will Rogers, exponent of homely, humorous profundities, again plays a patriot abroad. This time he appears in *So This Is London*, adapted from George M. Cohan's stage success—but the film isn't up to the homespun standard of humor set by his first talkie, *They Had to See Paris*.

"In crossing the Channel to London some of the freshness of Mr. Rogers' lines and mannerisms were lost.

"You will find several genial, likeable *stretchers* [sic] in *So This Is London*, but in a session filled with movies and plays stemming from 'The Man from Home' you must accept the Westerner in Paris or London—the Westerner with all of his or her aggressively homespun bewilderment, all of his or her comic ignorance and out-of-placeness as your favorite after-dinner topic, to believe that *So This Is London* is anything but a fair follow-up to *So This Is Paris* [sic].

"Mr. Rogers is still a humorous, refreshing person but he is becoming a bit self-conscious in his projection of homely bewilderment.

"The production is handsome. But *So This Is London* is not up to the standard of humor set by the Rogers group in Paris."

New York Sun, May 24, 1930

★ "Will Rogers, wise-cracking in England, can be seen this week in an amusing travelogue-sketch entitled *So This Is London*. It has more story interest than his preceding picture, *They Had to See Paris*, and manages to be sharply satirical in its earlier reels. Mr. Rogers also seemed more at ease as the oafish American husband than he did in his former film, though there still were too many stilted scenes between him and his wife, Abbey, which had little conviction.

"The story is at its best when Rogers is clowning, and the scene where he and Worthing go shooting is as comical as 'movie' humor ever comes."

Herald Tribune, May 24, 1930

★ "Will Rogers ad-libs his way through a screen version of the George M. Cohan stage play, *So This Is London*, at the Roxy. The result is a worthy, if less hilarious successor to *They Had to See Paris*. The ball of merriment is started on its way in the initial sequences and manages to roll along throughout the film. Occasionally it encounters an impediment and things slow up for a while. But these arid stretches are forgotten with the next giggle at Will Rogers's drollness.

"Will Rogers is the whole show. In his inimitable manner he carries the audience along with a succession of dry wise-cracks and comments that were certainly never written in the script. Will introduces topics ranging from Henry Ford to Montgomery-Ward, not forgetting a plug for that beloved Claremore, Oklahoma.

"The rest of the cast is merely background for the grand show Mr. Rogers puts on. And this time there is no Fifi D'Orsay to lend that background color. Irene Rich is good, of course. She has seldom been otherwise."

New York American, May 24, 1930

LIGHTNIN'

A Fox Movietone Production, Copyright October 31, 1930, LP 1729; renewed October 31, 1957, R 201148; b&w; sound; 10 reels, 8,500 ft.; 96 minutes; final shooting script at USC. World premiere: November 28, 1930, Roxy Theatre, NYC. Review in *New York Times*, November 29, 1930, 21:4. Extant. Location shots: Cal-Neva, near border between California and Nevada, also at Tahoe Tavern, California, and at Camp Richardson, California.

Production Staff: Presented by William Fox; a Henry King Production; director: Henry King; assistant director: Frank Dettman; cameraman: Chester Lyons; based on play by Winchell Smith and Frank Bacon, produced by John Golden; opened August 26, 1918 at Gaiety Theatre, NYC—closed August 1921; screenplay by S. N. Behrman and Sonya Levien; music and lyrics: Joseph McCarthy and James F. Hanley; song "Reno Blues" sung by Goodee Montgomery; editor: Louis Loeffler; recording engineer: George P. Costello; art director: Harry Oliver; costumes: Sophie Wachner.

Cast:

Will Rogers	"Lightnin' " Bill Jones	Walter Percival	Everett Hammond
Louise Dresser	Mrs. Mary Jones	Charlotte Walker	Mrs. Thatcher
Joel McCrea	John Marvin	Blanche Le Clair	Mrs. Leonard
Helen Cohan*	Milly Jones	Bruce Warren	Mr. Leonard
Jason Robards	Raymond Thomas	Antica Nast	Mrs. Lord
Luke Cosgrave	Zeb	Moon Carroll	Mrs. Blue
J. M. Kerrigan	Judge Lem Townsend	Bess Flowers	Mrs. Weeks
Ruth Warren	Margaret Davis	Gwendolyn Faye	Mrs. Starr
Sharon Lynn	Mrs. Lower	Eva Dennison	Mrs. George
Joyce Compton	Diana	Betty Alden	Mrs. Graham
Rex Bell	Ronald	Lucille Young	Mrs. Young
Frank Campeau	Mr. Brooks, the sheriff	Betty Sinclair	Mrs. Bigg
Goodee Montgomery	Mrs. Brooks	Roxanne Curtis	Flapper divorcée
Philip Tead	Monte Winslow	Thomas Jefferson	Walter Lannon

*George M. Cohan's daughter; this seems to be her only motion-picture appearance.

Synopsis: "Lightnin' " Bill Jones, so nicknamed for his total lack of speed when asked to perform physical labor, is a Spanish-American War veteran, with a decided flair for inventive prevarication, humorous comments, and a decided partiality to hard liquor "in order to ward off a possible attack of malaria." Mary Jones is the owner of the Calivada Hotel, which sits astride the state line, half in California, half in Nevada. Because of its location, the hotel is frequented by divorce-seeking wives, who can give a California address, pretending to be on vacation, while actually living in the Nevada section, thus fulfilling the three-month residency requirement before a Nevada divorce can be granted.

Fraudulent speculators wishing to acquire the hotel and its land in exchange for worthless stock certificates persuade hardworking Mrs. Jones and daughter Milly to sell the property. This transaction is blocked when Lightnin' refuses to co-sign the deed, on advice of law student John Marvin. John is taking refuge in the California part of the hotel, avoiding arrest by a Nevada sheriff on a charge arising out of another fraudulent deal pulled by the same crooks, but charged against John. Since Lightnin' refuses to co-sign the deed, Mrs. Jones is persuaded to sue for divorce, so that her signature alone will legalize the transaction.

But in court Lightnin' and Mary Jones are reunited, and Milly and John admit their love for each other.

Review: ★ "A happy hour or so awaits those who visit the Roxy this week, for at that theatre Will Rogers gives a delightful interpretation of the tippling, good-natured and understanding "Lightnin' " Bill Jones. His acting is if anything superior to that of his previous characterization in "They Had to See Paris" and "So This Is London," pictures that have brought him a tremendous following, which was attested to by the crowds that filed into the big house for the first performance and by the fact that in spite of the wintry blasts, a line of patrons was waiting outside."

New York Times, November 29, 1930

Recognitions: ★ Will Rogers, Best Actor of the Month, *Photoplay Magazine*, January 1931

★ #4 on list of 10 Best Films of 1930, *New York Times*, January 4, 1931

★ #40 on list of Best Films of 1931, *Photoplay Magazine*

Censorship

Massachusetts Board of Censors, December 10, 1930

Order to eliminate dialogue in Part III: "Of all the damn fool things."

Will Rogers Said

We are up here at this beautiful Lake [Tahoe] near Reno, Nevada, working on a picture, and today a fellow come up and wanted me to help get him into some soft job in the movies. I asked him what he was doing and he said he was "house detective in the big hotel in Reno where all the divorcées live."

I said: "Brother, you must be hard to please. John Barrymore is not doing as well as you. Why, you got a better job than Coolidge writing a gag a day."

I told him to go back to work, and don't even envy Hoover. "But, if you are going to give the job up, consult me. I'll change with you."

Syndicated column, August 21, 1930

★

We got a funny situation here. We brought up about a dozen girls to play the divorcées in the hotel scene in

With Joel McCrea, in *Lightnin'*, 1930.

Lightnin', and here every day watching us shoot is a hundred real "divorcées" from Reno—and around the lake here—all dying to get into pictures while they are serving their [residency] time.

If any woman is missing from your community and you don't know where she is, she is here.

Syndicated column, September 10, 1930

Interview with Joel McCrea, May 24, 1970

S: Didn't you first meet Will Rogers on the California-Nevada border?

JMC: It was on the California side, at Lake Tahoe. He was Fox's biggest star, and he was doing a picture called *Lightnin'*. I was cast as his son-in-law, the juvenile lead. I met Will sitting in a buggy. The director, Henry King, asked me whether I had met Mr. Rogers, and when I said no, he introduced me. That was 1930, and it was the beginning of a friendship which you kind of felt the moment I got there.

Our first scene was on that buggy. Will was supposed to talk quite a bit, then I had a line, and then he talked on quite a bit longer. He improved it as he went along, and everybody got to laughing, but when the time came for me to talk, there was no cue. So the director said, "What's the matter, McCrea, isn't it your turn?" I said it was, but that I had not received my cue. So Will just said to me, "Joe"—he always would call me "Joe"—"Joe, you ain't like these other actors; you're kinder like me. You ain't very good looking, and you ain't a very good actor. You're just a cowboy and I'm going to help you. You see, what I do, I change the dialogue. I write a great deal of it myself. Sometimes I improve it, sometimes I don't, but I go along with it. And when I think I've said enough, I'll stop, and then I'll poke you and then you talk. I'm not going to do it for the other actors, but I'll do it for you." That was the beginning.

S: Did you ever see him just relax?

JMC: This was a man that would never have time to drink, or smoke, or anything because that would take time. It would take time to go and buy cigarettes or to clean a pipe. He had no time for that. He was always going fast; his mind was clear and fast; he rode a horse fast; he was on fire the whole time.

S: Did Mr. Rogers talk at any time about his retirement?

JMC: No! He never wanted to retire. He never had in mind cutting down on what he was doing. Really, if he had had his way, he would have gone the way he did, rather than to ever get to the point where he would have to cut down. He was a man of such enormous energy, and he wanted to do everything to the fullest—always.

A CONNECTICUT YANKEE

A Fox Production,   Copyright February 25, 1931, LP 2048; renewed March 7, 1958, R 210360; b&w; sound; 11 reels, 8,700 ft. Release: April 6, 1931, Roxy Theatre, NYC. Reviewed in *New York Times*, April 11, 1931. Final shooting script at USC; press book at AMPAS. Extant.

Production Staff: Director: David Butler; assistant director: Ad Schaumer; cameraman: Ernest Palmer; based on story "A Connecticut Yankee at King Arthur's Court" (1889), by Mark Twain; screenplay by William M. Conselman; editor: Irene Morra; recording engineer: Joseph E. Aiken; special effects: Fred Sersen, Ralph Hammeras; art director: William Darling; costumes: Sophie Wachner.

Cast:

Will Rogers	Hank Martin (Sir Boss)	Brandon Hurst	Merlin
William Farnum	King Arthur	Myrna Loy	Queen Morgan Le Fay
Frank Albertson	Clarence	Mitchell Harris	Sir Sagramor
Maureen O'Sullivan	Alisande		

Synopsis: In this famous fantasy, a story within a story, Hank, a Connecticut radio expert, is called out one stormy night to repair a faulty set. At the eerie mansion, he is knocked unconscious by a falling suit of armor just as the master of the house thinks he has discovered an ancient wavelength that allows him to listen in on King Arthur and his Knights of the Round Table.

Awakening, Hank finds that he is now in England, the date being June 21, 528. Taken prisoner, he reads in his diary that a total eclipse is to occur on this date. Condemned to be burned at the stake, he threatens perpetual darkness just as the eclipse is about to begin. Implored by the king, Hank eventually "restores" full sunlight.

Dubbed "Sir Boss" by a grateful monarch, Hank effects a vast number of changes in the realm, ranging from telephone service to a messenger service of roller-skating couriers, to armor-cleaning and -oiling establishments.

A jousting affair matches Sir Sagramor in armor against Hank dressed as a cowboy, complete with chaps and lariat. This event, of course, is broadcast—sponsored by the "Camelot Iron Works—Builders of Lance-proof Armor."

Queen Morgan Le Fay becomes enamored of Sir Boss and, demonstrating her affection, causes Hank to blush a brilliant red.

Clarence, a young page, is in love with the maiden Alisande, now held prisoner by Queen Morgan in her castle. The girl is rescued by an army equipped with tanks and helicopters and armored knights in more than fifty small automobiles. The bombing from the helicopters reduces the queen's castle to ruins and knocks out Hank, who then awakens in the present; there a real live Clarence and Alisande need help to elope. Hank gladly assists young love.

Review: ★ "Will Rogers suits the title role of the film of Mark Twain's *A Connecticut Yankee at the Court of King Arthur* [*sic*] so well that when one picks up the book one instantly visualizes this recruit from the saddle and the plains. This film, the title of which is abbreviated to *A Connecticut Yankee*, is another tribute to vocal films. And as most of it is a dream, there is nothing one can quarrel with, even if one desired to. It is a decided pity that the Roxy management did not see their way clear to hold this film over for another week, for it is done so splendidly, and is such a glorious relief from those violent gangster yarns."

New York Times, April 19, 1931

Recognitions: ★ Will Rogers, Actor of the Month, *Photoplay Magazine,* April 1931

★ #12 on Honor Roll of Films for 1931, *Photoplay Magazine*

★ #10 of the Year's Best Films, *New York Times*

---

*On August 15, 1919, *Variety* reported that Fox Film Corporation had purchased the rights to the Mark Twain story "A Connecticut Yankee at King Arthur's Court" and would present it in "screen form," and that Tom Mix would be the star of the production. The film was eventually produced in 1921, with Harry Myers playing Sir Boss.

Will Rogers Said

All I know is just what I read in the moving-picture ads, and say, boy, what an education it is! I thought underwear ads in the magazines were about the limit in presenting an eyeful, but these movie ads give you the same thing without the underwear. Even I, myself, appear in a nightgown in *The Connecticut Yankee,* so on the billboards it would add a touch of romantic glamour, to say nothing of a smattering of sex appeal.

Mind you, you mustn't let the ad have anything to do with what you see on the insides. You are liable to see the wildest stuff facing you on the billboards, and then go inside and everybody is dressed as Eskimos all through the picture. In other words, the big trouble is getting pictures that will live up to the pictures on the ads.

★

Dave Butler did *A Connecticut Yankee.* Dave is a great sportsman, and he helps the football players that are going through college by using them in all the scenes he can. It ain't anything to have a bunch of big gorillas in armor come up and grab you and take you away, and it will be the whole USC (the great University of Southern California) line and backfield. They are plenty rough, and a nice bunch of boys.

"Sir Boss" Rogers, with Brandon Hurst and William Farnum (the king) in *A Connecticut Yankee,* 1931.

Russian poster, advertising *A Connecticut Yankee*.

Interview with Myrna Loy, April 6, 1971

ML: I remember him on the set, in the commissary. I remember him outside, in his automobile, when he would whistle as I went by. He was a shy man; his head was down; I think he was especially shy with women. Of course I was pretty young in those days, scared and very shy myself. I remember that he used to like to tease me about my freckles and red hair. I remember once hearing that sharp whistle, and then a "Yahooo!" and I looked around, and there he was, passing in the car. Then, of course, I remember distinctly one of the scenes we were playing. I don't recall exactly what I was supposed to be up to, but apparently I was trying to lead him astray. That's where they used the "blushing." The film was in black and white, but they decided to tint his face, so obviously I was making passes at him. But he was charming, an attractive man, really wonderful.

Interview with David Butler, January 6, 1972

S: You directed five pictures with Will Rogers.
DB: That's right. *Business and Pleasure, Down to Earth, A Connecticut Yankee, Handy Andy,* and *Doubting Thomas.*
S: You must know his working habits pretty well.
DB: He would usually peck out his column before lunch, then come on the set and read it to everybody. Before noon he would concentrate a little more on the column than on the work. He had quite a time with his lines. You see, he learned them, but they weren't written in his language. He improved his lines. He was remarkable that way. He never liked retakes. He just wanted to do the scene, and that was that. He wanted to get back home again. He was a peculiar guy that way. He always wanted to get off at four-thirty, but if I'd ask him to stay longer, he would. He was a nice guy and would do anything to help. We always made the picture on time with him; we never went over. I never saw him moody. Some days he would clown a lot, and other days he would just go about his business. His pictures always made money, and they didn't cost too much to make. The film *Connecticut Yankee* did, because it was a costume picture, but that made a lot of money. They played that in every language—Japanese, Chinese, and everything else. In fact we saw the rushes of Will speaking Japanese. They'd get a company speaking Japanese, a company speaking Spanish, a German company, and they would dub it right here. It was very funny. Will and I saw the Japanese version while the company was doing it. Will nearly died laughing—it made everybody laugh.
S: Miss Myrna Loy mentioned that you tinted part of *Connecticut Yankee.*
DB: That was my idea. You see, they had no color, and she kissed Will, and he had to blush. The only way they could do it was to have a little Japanese girl tint every single frame progressively darker pink. This little girl had to do that on every print we sent out.

YOUNG AS YOU FEEL

A Fox Production,   Copyright April 14, 1931, LP 2355; renewed June 4, 1958, R 215879; b&w; sound; 9 reels, 7,000 ft. Release: August 7, 1931, Roxy Theatre, NYC. Review in *New York Times*, August 8, 1931. Working title: *Cure for the Blues*. Extant.

Production Staff: Director: Frank Borzage; assistant director: Lew Borzage; camerman: Chester Lyons; based on the play *Father and the Boys*, by George Ade; screenplay by Edwin Burke; music and lyrics for "The

Cute Little Things You Do," by James F. Hanley; editor: Margaret V. Clancey; recording engineer: George P. Costello; art director: Jack Schultze.

Cast:

Will Rogers	Lemuel Morehouse
Fifi D'Orsay	Fleurette
Lucien Littlefield	Mr. Marley
Donald Dillaway	Billy Morehouse
Terrance Ray	Tom Morehouse
Lucille Browne	Dorothy Gregson
Rosalie Roy	Rose Gregson
C. Henry Gordon	Lamson
John T. Murray	Col. Stanhope
Brandon Hurst	Robbins
Marcia Harris	Mrs. Denton
Otto Hoffman	Secretary
Joan Standing	Lemuel's secretary
Gregory Gaye	Pierre

Synopsis: Dyspeptic Lemuel Morehouse has built up his substantial meat-packing business by punctiliously adhering to his scheduled routine at his office desk and taking his medication precisely at the very minute prescribed by his doctor. Painfully aware of his two playboy sons, Lemuel carries the weight of the business on his shoulders, until Fleurette changes him.

Forgotten are age and digestion, and Lemuel now steps out, spending afternoons at the racetrack—sporting the latest gray suit and top hat—and evenings at nightclubs, attired in a faultlessly cut evening suit and silk hat.

Lemuel's platonic friendship with Fleurette not only helps to save her proceeds from her Colorado estate, but manages to put swindler Stanhope out of business.

Review: ★ "Will Rogers arrived, was seen and triumphed in his latest comedy, 'Young as You Feel.' It pleased youngsters, and as for elderly males in the Roxy audience, it sent them away with broad smiles of satisfaction on their countenances.

"This vehicle is spendidly suited to the versatile Mr. Rogers, who appears to have as much fun as the audience, both out of wearing his various suits of fashionable clothes, and in taking a fling at Greenwich Village types."

New York Times, August 16, 1931

Recognition: ★ Will Rogers, Best Performance of the Month, *Photoplay*, July 1931.

Will Rogers Said

With Clara Bow on her best behavior, and me behaving myself, why, there just is not much scandal out here at all. Doug Fairbanks is over in India getting even with some India royalty that visited him some time. He is supposed to be shooting tigers, but anybody that knows Doug knows that he never hunted in his life, he never shot anything, but if he can come back with some pictures with the right foot up on the neck of a dead tiger or elephant, why, it will be all right.

Every time I get a new picture finished, why, I kinder feel the itch to get out to some new place or make some sort of a little trip. Well, away a couple of weeks ago, we had finished *As Young as You Feel*, based on George Ade's old play *Father and the Boys*.

I was going to take a little trip off down in Central America, and then they kept me at home for fear there might be some retakes on it.

Well, we took the thing out and tried it in San Bernardino, California, and the customers giggled quite a bit. They said that they didn't think we could make it any worse if we tried, so I jumped on the old aerial rattler, and left from there.

AMBASSADOR BILL

A Fox Production, Copyright October 13, 1931, LP 2591; renewed January 15, 1959, R 229210; b&w; sound; 8 reels, 6,300 ft. Production started: August 17, 1931. Release: November 13, 1931, Roxy Theatre, NYC★. Review in *New York Times*, November, 14, 1931, 15:3. Working title: *Dollar Bill*. Extant.

Production Staff: Director: Sam Taylor; assistant director: Walter Mayo; cameraman: John Mescall; based on book *Ambassador from the United States*, by Vincent Sheean; screenplay and dialogue by Guy Bolton; editor: Harold Schuster; recording engineer: Al Bruzlin; art director: Duncan Cramer; costumes: Guy Duty; business manager: O. O. Dull.

Cast:

Will Rogers	Ambassador Bill Harper	Edwin Maxwell	Monte
Marguerite Churchill	The queen	Ernest Wood	Northfield Slater
Greta Nissen	Ilka	Tom Ricketts	Littleton
Tad Alexander	King Paul	Theodore Lodi	French ambassador
Gustav von Seyffertitz	Prince de Polikoff	Herbert Bunston	British ambassador
Ray Milland	Lothar	Ben Turpin	The butcher
Arnold Korff	The general		
Ferdinand Munier	Senator Pillsbury		

Synopsis: Bill Harper, Oklahoman and obviously not a U.S. State Department career man, has been appointed ambassador to Sylvania, a country somewhere in Europe.

Arriving at his post during one of the weekly revolutions, he is quite alarmed. With the king of Sylvania a fugitive, his very young son has been crowned, but the actual power is in the hands of evil Prince de Polikoff.

Bill Harper, innocent of any and all court etiquette, nevertheless makes friends with the boy king, gives him a pair of chaps, teaches him roping and even baseball.

The new ambassador has frequent disagreements with the stolid and stuffy embassy personnel, and he especially has problems with pompous U.S. Senator Pillsbury, who comes visiting on a "governmental junket."

During another revolution, Ambassador Harper and Senator Pillsbury find themselves handcuffed together. Help to cut the cuffs arrives at last, but unfortunately in the form of an inebriated man swinging an ax. The ambassador insists that someone else be called, and this time it is cross-eyed Ben Turpin—complete with ax.

Review: ★ "This amusing contribution was penned by Guy Bolton and directed by Sam Taylor, who is rather hurried where he might give more time to his episodes, and just the reverse with others that need little more than a flash. The humor here is rather more subdued than in Mr. Rogers' other vehicles, but it is a good sketch with funny lines and ludicrous situations.

"Mr. Rogers, as usual, never fails his audience. What with lines written by Mr. Bolton, and others he has perhaps made up on the spur of the moment, he elicits plenty of chuckles."

New York Times, November 14, 1931, 15:3

★This film, *Ambassador Bill*, though released November 13, 1931, was actually made *after* the film that follows, *Business and Pleasure*, which was released February 12, 1932.

Will Rogers Said

If you have lost anybody anywhere in the world, and don't know where they are, they are in Hollywood, trying to get in the movies.

Syndicated column, September 13, 1931

Ambassador Bill, 1931, with Will (*from left*): Marguerite Churchill, Ray Milland, Tad Alexander. (*Academy of Motion Picture Arts and Sciences*)

With movie czar Will Hays.

BUSINESS AND PLEASURE

A Fox Production, Copyright November 30, 1931, LP 2829; renewed January 15, 1959, R 229214; b&w; sound; 8 reels, 6,975 ft. Release: February 12, 1932, Roxy Theatre, NYC.* Review in *New York Times*, February 13, 1932, 23:4. Shooting scripts at USC, AMPAS. Working title: *The Plutocrat*. Extant.

Production Staff: Associate producer: A. L. Rockett; director: David Butler; assistant director: Ad Schaumer; cameraman: Ernest Palmer; based on the stage version (by Arthur F. Goodrich, NYC run—one week) of *The Plutocrat*, a novel by Booth Tarkington; screenplay by William M. Conselman and Gene Towne; editor: Irene Morra; recording engineer: Joseph E. Aiken: art director: Joseph Wright; costumes: Dolly Tree; business manager: E. Berry.

Cast:

Will Rogers	Earl Tinker	Jed Prouty	Ben Wackstle
Jetta Goudal	Madame Momora	Mitchell Lewis	Hadj Ali
Joel McCrea	Lawrence Ogle	Boris Karloff	Sheik
Dorothy Peterson	Mrs. Tinker	Oscar Apfel	P. D. Weatheright
Peggy Ross	Olivia Tinker	Vernon Dent	Charles Turner
Cyril Ring	Arthur Jones		

CONTRACTUAL NOTE: "Joel McCrea not to be preceded in the billing by the names of more than two other members of the cast, in type as large as that used for any other member of the cast, except Will Rogers."

Synopsis: Earl Tinker, razor-blade king from Oklahoma, is on his way to Syria to buy the secret of Damascus steel. With him—on this business trip disguised as a pleasure tour—are Mrs. Tinker and daughter Olivia. Crossing the Atlantic, Olivia meets Lawrence Ogle, a budding playwright, and a romance develops. Madame Momora, a mysterious and scheming foreigner, attaches herself to Earl, who does not realize that the madame is really working for his archrival razor-blade manufacturer. It is her assignment to find out just what the Oklaho-

116

man intends to do, to report it to her employer, and to foil any of Tinker's plans. So successful is Madame Momora that the Tinker family eventually gets nearer to being executed by Damascus steel than to obtaining the secret of its manufacture.

Disguising himself as an ancient mystic—complete with gray beard and moustache—Tinker ad-libs Madame Momora's future and collects one hundred dollars as his fee. Through a clever ruse, Tinker finally exposes the devious madame to the desert sheik and is allowed to buy the secret steel process.

Reviews: ★ "Mr. Rogers does the most to make the film likable. He hasn't gone cute on us again. Instead, he plays simply, dryly and remains steadfastly at the top of his form. I am at a loss to describe him further. Never having considered him one of the first wits of our time, save when he utters his remarks himself, I can only repeat again that he is ever so much more pungent in the talkies than he ever was in silent pictures."

New York Sun, February 13, 1932

★ " 'Business and Pleasure' taxes the most Job-like patience up to and beyond the snapping point and is unquestionably one of the dullest comedies the screen has presented in some time."

New York World-Telegram, February 1932

★ "Will Rogers has a lot of fun in 'Business and Pleasure' at the Roxy. And you're bound to laugh with him loud and heartily, every now and then. These moments are highly hilarious, even if the picture doesn't strike you as Rogers' best."

New York Daily News, February 1932

★ "Will Rogers, who never fails to give motion picture audiences their full money's worth of laughter, is as successful as ever in his latest venture, 'Business and Pleasure,' an adaptation of Booth Tarkington's story, 'The Plutocrat.' "

New York Times, February 13, 1932

Recognitions: ★ Will Rogers, Best Performance of the Month, *Photoplay Magazine*, October 1931
★ #13 in notable films of 1932, *New York Times*, January 1, 1933

*This film, *Business and Pleasure*, though released in February 1932 and reviewed in New York City on February 13; Chicago, February 21; and in Los Angeles on February 26; was actually made in 1931. It was shot ahead of *Ambassador Bill*, but released after it.

Will Rogers Said

Well, all I know is just what I read in the papers, or what I see as I mess around. We was making a movie here the other week of Booth Tarkington's book and play *Plutocrat*. That's what it was called. But it's liable to be released under the title *Riches Traded for Virtue* or *The Gangster's Lost Moll*. Well, in the picture my family and I are on one of these Mediterranean cruises and we got to Morocco, or some country down there where it's hot and full of Arabs and camels and Riffs.

Well, I will say one thing for Hollywood. If you want a couple of hundred real "Arabs" in a scene, you just let the casting department let it be known that you do and you get that many real Arabs. Anything under the sun, it's in Hollywood. I believe you could round up a hundred Eskimos.

Syndicated column, June 28, 1931

Will, hidden behind beard, with Jetta Goudal, in *Business and Pleasure*, 1931.

HOLLYWOOD PREMIERE (1932)

I am listening in on a radio that the kids put in my room here. I never was much of a radio hound. I get my Amos and Andy, and that's it, but I got it going. Hollywood is having one of its "openings." That's one of those things where there is a new movie opening at some theater.

Well, for sameness I don't suppose two Airedale pups are any more alike than all "openings." They have a microphone out in the lobby of the theater and an announcer, and he tells you who is coming in. He says: "Here comes Mr. Who, or Mr. Jasbo, we will have 'em step over to the microphone and say a few words to you." The ones that they do get to come over and say, "Hello, everybody, wish you were here," why, it's someone that works for the company that is putting on the picture.

It's got so that every studio almost sandbags its own people to make 'em go and make up the crowd. They don't attract the crowds like they used to do, and most of the companies have done away with 'em. After all, a picture does nowadays just what it deserves. You can open one down a dark alley and not let anyone know it and if it's any good, in a few days you can't get near the thing. It's like a good restaurant—you can't hide it.

That is a thankless job that announcer has. Poor fellow, he can't dig up a soul. He'll be glad when that Chevrolet thing comes.

Yep, at last, here comes the Chevrolet announcement: "We are back in the studio. Have you compared Chevrolet quality and prices with other cars? If you haven't, get up in the morning and do it."

Now we are at a Culver City nightclub. I worked at the old Goldwyn studio for three years, back in '19, '20, and '21, and I never thought Culver City would ever have a nightclub, so you can never tell what a town will turn out to be.

You remember one time when I was on the radio and did a little imitation of Mr. Coolidge? Well, some of 'em raised Cain; said I shouldn't have done it. I even went so far as to ask Mr. Coolidge if it had offended him and he replied: "Why, I didn't even pay any attention to it."

Well, one time I was asked to be master of ceremonies at the opening of that great, big picture *Grand Hotel*. Syd Grauman, the manager of the Chinese Theatre in Hollywood, is the producer, and he's not only a great showman but a fine fellow. Then Mr. Louis B. Mayer asked me, and I was tickled to do it. I had never been around any of these "openings"; in fact, I had always kidded about 'em, for the whole thing is a great "yokel" show. This was an especially big one, for it was the biggest cast picture ever made. Think of Greta Garbo, John and Lionel Barrymore, Joan Crawford, Wally Beery, Jean Hersholt, Tully

118

Marshall, and about half the other payroll of Hollywood. Well, it was a bear of a night, judging by people standing on soapboxes and folks inside with old, overhauled ermines.

Now they have an intermission, and everybody goes out and looks at each other and you can't get 'em back in again. They would rather look at each other than the show. But it was what the society reporter would call "The Elite," what the film fan reporters call "Aristocracy of Filmdom," and what the poor folks on the street would call "The Nuts."

Well, this fellow Grauman had a wonderful prologue. He put on a two-dollar vaudeville show; there was a bunch of clever acts on that program.

My job was to introduce the cast that was in the picture. Now, of course, you all know about Greta Garbo. She don't go anywhere, or she may go everywhere, for no one gets to her home to see if she has gone anywhere or not, but she really, I guess, don't get round people at all.

The studio that she worked for have to go see her in the picture when they want to see her. She is just like a hermit, and these writers that write stories about her, they never even get to a see a photograph of her.

But that night, after I had introduced all the principals of the cast except John Barrymore, who was not there, I announced that on account of the importance of the occasion, and the prominence that this particular picture had received, that Miss Garbo would break her rule and that immediately after the picture was over she consented to come on the stage and take a bow.

Well, Mr. Grauman starts his show. He thinks the later they are started, the better they are. Syd don't know, or has perhaps forgot, that all the big first nights in New York are started on time, anyhow, no matter when they are finished. Well, this one didn't start till nine-thirty, and was over—the picture—at one-fifteen. Now, that's pretty good for a country town, and in all, we are a country town. It's a big one, but it's country.

Well, I had framed up a gag with Wally Beery, who I knew would be a big hit in the picture that they had just seen, and he got some "dame" clothes. And he was my Greta Garbo. Sounds kinder funny, don't it? Well, it wasn't to them.

Wally did it fine. He even looked like her—but not enough to satisfy that crowd. Now, they should have known that Garbo wasn't going to be there any more than Coolidge, but they go and believe it and then they get sore at themselves for believing it. I didn't mean any harm. Gosh, us comedians must get laughs. But these first-nighters don't want us to get 'em at their expense. They want to be the ones that do all the laughing. I think they got their waiting's worth by seeing Wally Beery in skirts. What did they want?

Now, about the only way I got making good is to produce Garbo sometime. Course I can't do it, but it's a good idea. I got to do something to get back into the good graces of my Hollywood. Maybe I can show 'em Al Capone sometime. They all want to see him, but I will never fool the old hometown again.

Reviews of *Grand Hotel* Premiere, April 29, 1932

As can be seen, the press either did not mention the Greta Garbo gag or did not blame Will Rogers for it.

"Will Rogers in his best form, and you know what that is, made a master of ceremonies who could talk on and on and keep everybody in his seat."
Los Angeles Examiner, April 30, 1932

★

"Chinese Theatre, Scene of Gala Event. . . . Add to this the fact that Will Rogers—no less—made the introductions of the cast. Hence 'twas an evening!"
Los Angeles Times, April 30, 1932

★

"Because Greta Garbo is about to leave the country, opening night audience for 'Grand Hotel' gave credence to the announcement that she would take a bow from the stage after the picture. However this proved to be a misguided joke in very bad taste when a stage-hand, in burlesque attire, took the spotlight. Incident constituted shocking anti-climax to the classiest opening Hollywood has seen in two years."
Variety, May 3, 1932, 28:1

DOWN TO EARTH

A Fox Production,   Copyright July 11, 1932, LP 3220; renewed November 6, 1959, R 245710; b&w; sound; 9 reels, 7,150 ft. Release: September 1, 1932, Roxy Theatre, NYC. Review in *New York Times*, September 2, 1932; Los Angeles, August 27; Chicago, September 3, 1932. Shooting script at AMPAS. Extant.

Production Staff: Director: David Butler; assistant director: Ad Schaumer; cameraman: Ernest Palmer; based on story by Homer Croy; screenplay and dialogue by Edwin Burke; music: George Lipschultz; editor: Irene Morra; recording engineer: George Leverett; art director: William Darling; wardrobe: Earl Luick.

Cast:

Will Rogers	Pike Peters	Clarence Wilson	Ed Eggers
Dorothy Jordan	Julia Pearson	Harvey Clark	Cameron
Irene Rich	Idy Peters	Henry Kolker	Randolph
Matty Kemp	Ross Peters	Theodore Lodi	Grand Duke Michael
Mary Carlisle	Jackie Harper	Luise Mackintosh	Mrs. Phillips
Brandon Hurst	Jeffrey, the butler		

Synopsis: *Down to Earth* is the sequel to *They Had to See Paris*. Times have changed drastically for the worse. The Grand Duke Michael has been forced by reverses to accept the position of a Chicago hotel door-man—and is now called "Mike."

Pike Peters, still plagued by a socially ambitious, ostentatious wife—Idy—and a gambling, spendthrift son—Ross—at last issues instructions that all but two of the servants must go. Idy retains the butler, just to make an impression on visitors.

On a business trip to Chicago to raise more cash, Peters meets the former grand duke opening car doors. When Peters informs his wife that he will return from Chicago, bringing the grand duke along, Idy arranges an extravagant Louis XV costume ball. Pike Peters now realizes that it is up to him to bring his family "down to earth."

Robed as Louis XV, the king, Pike gathers the guests around him and candidly tells them that he is broke, that "the circus is over," and that they better go home.

Pike—now without a staff of servants—is seen happily cooking his own meal, freed at last from the critical, supercilious gaze of the butler.

Review:　★ " 'Down to Earth' was written by Homer Croy, who was also responsible for 'They Had to See Paris,' and the dialogue was contributed by Edwin Burke, who did his share toward making 'Bad Girl' amusing. In this present picture, however, Mr. Burke's lines lack the keenness of Mr. Rogers' other productions, but on the whole the picture succeeds in being a mildly merry hot-weather entertainment."

New York Times, September 2, 1932, 19:2

Against his will at fancy-dress party, in *Down to Earth*, 1932.

A family spat, with Irene Rich, in *Down to Earth*, 1932.

Interview with Irene Rich, January 3, 1971

S:　Let's talk about your sound films with Will Rogers.

IR:　The first one was *They Had to See Paris*. Do you know what date that was? June 1929. Frank Borzage was the director. You see, let me look in my little black diary. Here! In May 1929, I was in vaudeville, and after that I jumped out to the coast and did this film with Will Rogers. That ran, let's see, through June, July, and into August. Then I went back and picked up my vaudeville tour. Then look! In February, I stopped the tour again and did *So This Is London*. Let's see, it lasted all through February, March, April, up to the twenty-seventh of April. By this time I was getting thirty-five hundred dollars a week; that was a lot better than the five dollars per day I got as an extra when I first started.

S:　Your next picture with Will Rogers was *Down to Earth*.

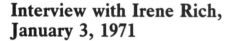

Will, now "down to earth," cooks his own meal.

IR: That started in April 1932—April fourteenth. Isn't this little book wonderful? You know I played Will's wife so often that some people thought we were really married. One time, crossing the Atlantic, Will was asked to make a little speech, and after he had addressed the passengers, he was asked questions. One woman asked him to tell about Irene Rich. And Will quipped, "Oh, you mean my reel wife?"

The woman that asked the question later wrote me about it, and I thought it cute.

WILL ROGERS LOOKS BEHIND THE MOVIE SCREEN

The other day at the studio, they were talking about a story. They said it had to be changed a lot, that the old idea of a mortgage on the old farm was all out of date, that the villains robbing a train was all the hooey. They claim that all stories had to be made modern and up to date. So I told 'em, say, listen, there is no new situation. Wives are leaving husbands, husbands are leaving wives; robberies, where they used to take your horse, and if they was caught, they got hung for it; now they take your car, and if they are caught, it's a miracle. They will perhaps have the inconvenience of having to go to court and explain it. So your movies won't be changed, any more than your morals, or your taxes, or any of the other things that you think should be remodeled.

Did you ever read those moving-picture ads? The big problem of the movies now is to deliver up to what the lithograph makers and the ad writers have shown on the outside. In other words, that branch of the industry has "outstripped" the production end.

And, too, the off-color or risqué pictures haven't been going so good as they used to. It isn't that tastes are improving, it is that there is nothing new they could shock folks with.

Movies is really the only business in the world that nobody knows anything about. Being in them don't give you any more of an inkling about them than being out of them.

The exhibitor says he wants better pictures for less money.

The producer (that's the fellow that spends a lot of somebody else's money making pictures that somebody else wrote, somebody else directed, and a lot of others acted in) says he wants better stories and better directors and better actors for less money.

The actor says: "You are not giving me a fair share of what I draw at the box office!"

The Code people say: "They got to be cleaner!"

The exhibitor says: "If you get 'em too clean, nobody is interested in 'em."

The novelist says: "What's the use of selling them a story, they don't make the story they buy!"

The scenario staff says: "It reads good, but it won't photograph!"

The exchange salesman says: "The exhibitors are a dumb lot, they don't know what their audiences want."

The exhibitors say: "We may be dumb, but we know how to count up. Give us pictures where there is something to count up."

The so-called intellectual keeps saying: "Why don't they give us something worthwhile in the movies that we can think about?"

The regular movie fan says: "Give us something to see, never mind think about. If we wanted to think, we wouldn't come here!"

The old married folks say: "Give us something besides all this love-sick junk, and the fade-out behind the willow tree!"

The young folks that pay the rent on these temples of uplift say: "Give us some love and romance. What do we care about these pictures with a lot of old folks trying to show what they do in life. We will get old soon enough without having to see it now!"

Wall Street says: "We want more interest on our money!"

The producers say: "Look at the fun you are having by being in the business. Didn't we give you a pass through the studio? What do you want for your money?"

The actors that aren't working say: "They don't want actors any more, they only want types!"

The actors that are working say: "Thank god, they are beginning to realize it's us actors they want, and not just somebody that looks like the part."

It's kind of a cuckoo business, but trains have been full for twenty years of so-called smart people that were coming out here to fix the movies, and they have all gone back. There are things that look like they ought to be changed, but the wise ones can't seem to be able to think of anything to improve 'em.

Anyhow, the whole motion-picture industry is flourishing and weddings were never more at a premium. Divorces permeate the air. High-powered road-

121

sters are skitting here and yon. So let's everybody connected with this business, and everybody that loves to go see movies, as we go to our beds at night, pray to our Supreme Being, that He don't allow it to be found out what is the matter with the movies.

For if He ever does, we will all be out of a job.

TOO BUSY TO WORK

A Fox Production, Copyright October 15, 1932, LP 3370; renewed January 13, 1960, R 250202; b&w; sound; 8 reels, 6,900 ft. Release: December 2, 1932, Roxy Theatre, NYC. Review in *New York Times*, December 3, 1932; Los Angeles, November 4, 1932; press book available. Extant.

Production Staff: Director: John G. Blystone; assistant director: Jasper Blystone; cameraman: Charles G. Clarke; based on *Saturday Evening Post* story "Jubilo," by Ben Ames Williams; screenplay and adaptation by Barry Conners and Philip Klein; editor: Alexander Troffey; recording engineer: Eugene F. Grossman; art director: Max Parker; wardrobe: Earl Luick.

Cast:

Will Rogers	Jubilo	Douglas Cosgrove	Sheriff
Marion Nixon	Rose	Louise Beavers	Mammy
Dick Powell	Dan Hardy	Jack O'Hara	Undersheriff
Frederick Burton	Judge Hardy	Charles B. Middleton	Chief of police
Constantine Romanoff	Axel	Bert Hanlon	Pete

Synopsis: *Too Busy to Work* is the story of a man's search for his wife and daughter. While the man—Jubilo—was away at war, the wife took the infant and ran away with another man. Before the war ends, she dies, leaving the baby girl to be brought up by the foster father, who loves the child as if she were his own.

Returning from the war, Jubilo becomes a vagabond, searching for his family. Eventually he discovers the truth of his wife's death, finds his daughter, and learns of the wholesome way she has been raised in a fine family. Helping her to clear Dan, the man she loves, Jubilo leaves without revealing his relationship.

Reviews:

★ "It seems to me that 'Too Busy to Work' at the Roxy is the weakest of the Will Rogers talkies. Certainly it is the most obvious and the slowest.

"One of our foremost and ablest types [Will Rogers], he is becoming limited or else he has played the same role once too often."

New York Sun, December 3, 1932

★ "Just chuck-full of whimsy and heavy-laden with hokum, this talkie version of 'Jubilo' makes pretty dull entertainment for us city slickers. Out in the great open spaces it may find more appreciative audiences."

New York American, December 3, 1932

★ "In no previous picture in which he has starred, has Will Rogers been so delightfully humorous as he is in 'Too Busy to Work,' the Fox production in which he plays the role of a whimsical and kindly tramp. . . . The story holds interest from beginning to end and it is splendidly done. . . . "

Tulsa Daily World, March 19, 1933

From Columns:

★ "Will Rogers is going to sing. His next picture will have dancing and singing numbers and Will is going to get a chance and warble. In his 'Follies' days he always had a secret yen to sing, but circumstances continually thwarted that ambition. Always when the show went to Atlantic City for its break-in there was a song for Will. Invariably it was discovered the show ran too long and drastic cutting was necessary. Will, who always had the lion's share of the 'Follies' anyway, would regretfully consent to sacrifice his song. There will be no need for this magnanimous gesture in 'Jubilo.' "

Tulsa Daily World, July 25, 1932

With Dick Powell, in *Too Busy to Work,* 1932.

Catching up on reading, between scenes of *Too Busy to Work,* 1932.

Will Rogers Said

Been prowling around quite a bit lately away up in the mountains working on a movie. It's the first time we have been on location since we made "Lightnin'." Well, this time we are making the old silent picture that I made twelve years ago, called "Jubilo." It is a tramp picture and everyone that sees me in my street clothes says that I excel in tramp parts.

Syndicated column, September 11, 1932

Did I ever tell you about the time a year, or so, ago I made a "tramp" picture, and used a big Saint Bernard dog in it? We were for a couple of weeks up in the Sierra Nevada Mountains, and I become very attached to this old dog. I was playing with a rope and I would rope him by the hour, and he never minded it.

Well, I finally decided to try and buy him. The trainer with him wasn't the owner, but knowing nothing about what in the world the dog might cost, or any other dog, I finally worked up courage and generosity enough to say to him, "Say, tell your boss I will give him one hundred dollars for this old dog."

Well, I just figured that I had the dog and had just thrown in fifty or seventy-five dollars for good measure. The trainer kinder grinned and said, "Well, I doubt if you get him, Will. The dog gets one hundred and fifty a week."

Well, I knew I couldn't afford to pay him that if I had him, especially just to walk around and be roped at.

Syndicated column, July 8, 1934

BASH AT FOX (DECEMBER 1932)

We had a big time out at our studio the other day. The Fox Studios where I labor is the only studio that has been built entirely since the talkies come in. It's all new and all talkie. Well, in most studios they have little cubbyholes or places for writers. Well, Mr. Winfield Sheehan conceived the idea of building them a real building all to themselves, nothing in it but writers, and we had a big dedication of it the other day. Mr. Rupert Hughes, the eminent author, come over and spoke in behalf of the authors. He is part and parcel of our industry. We hate to call it that, it sounds so sordid. He is really a co-artist with us in this constructive photography we carry on.

It is a beautiful building, and when you tourists come to the coast, you must see it. It's more French than Shakespeare, as the French plays rather lend themselves to "Box Office" more than the Bard's stuff. Lots of people like to read Shakespeare, but that's the trouble: He appeals to the people who can read and not the ones who want it read to 'em by an actor, either on or off the screen. The successful author is the one who can write for the ones who can't read.

Little Miss Janet Gaynor did the unveiling, and while she didn't lay the cornerstone, she did unveil it. In fact, two—we had two cornerstones. That was in case you was standing where you couldn't see 'em unveil one, you could see the other. She did a gracious and dignified act with it.

Naturally I had to blather too, and this is what I said, as best as I can remember:

We are gathered here today, we are gathered here today . . . Have the Research Department look up and see why we are gathered here today. I will have the answer back in a week or so. Every department at Fox's functions.

Well, while the Research Department is finding out, I tell you, we are gathered here principally because Mr. Sheehan and Mr. Wurtzel told us to.

We are gathered here today to do honor to the author. He has had everything else done to him but honor. That's about the last misfortune that can hit him. We are going to do honor to the author if, when the picture is finished, we can find out who the author is.

Fox has built this house for 'em. They used to just run around on the streets here like wild urchins do in Russia.

They never had a home before, not only never had a home at the studio, but never had one after they left the studio. The trouble is going to be getting 'em out of here at nights. Some of 'em instead of bringing typewriters will bring a bed. The rooms are not only equipped for light comedy, but light housekeeping.

In case any of 'em want to write, there is a set of O'Henry and a set of Zane Grey and a lavatory.

Every town in the early days had its Red Light District. That is, sin was segregated. Fox is the first to segregate it in the movies. This is the Red Light District of Movietone City.

There are rules for the house. No casting for pictures is allowed in the rooms. When a writer turns in a script, don't leave the premises, for it will be back as soon as it is read. Don't use all of your best lines. The actor will forget 'em anyhow.

Rupert Hughes is here representing the authors; Conrad Nagel is here representing the actors; and there is a guy here who means more than all of you, yet he won't be introduced or you won't know him. He is the guy representing the Chase National Bank.

The writer works on three or four scripts at once. Don't let 'em get mixed up with each other, or maybe you might. That might be the making of a story.

They have a room in here called the "violent" cell, where the writer of an original story is confined for one week after he has seen the finished picture.

This is a unique building, since it is for certain people to be confined in. Sing Sing is brick. You are sent there for various deeds. Here we specialize. It's only for those who have been found guilty of writing.

They have a vault here which is supposed to contain all the old manuscripts by old authors. Some say they are going to get 'em out and do 'em as the authors wrote 'em.

An author's writing hours are from nine to five, whether he can think of anything or not. There is no visiting allowed among the rooms, even if the authors are speaking to each other or not.

Writers with secretaries are supposed to do all their dictating off the lot. The Morality Clause covers the entire 140 acres of Fox Hills.

Writers should write their dialogue so that it can easily be rubbed out.

This will be a great asset for the studio visitors. The guides can take 'em and show 'em forty authors thinking at once. Did you ever see forty authors thinking at once? Did you ever see forty authors think? Did you ever see one think? Well, if you have seen one, you have seen forty.

They built the building near the gate so an author after receiving his notice won't have to walk far or be humiliated by having to pass anyone. An author leaving this studio for another one is not allowed to take any plots or towels with him.

If you have to turn in a script by Monday and haven't got it, use one you turned in on the last picture. They didn't read it either.

The authors are here for a trial. If they don't produce anything in the next two months, they are going to turn 'em back to where they came from.

As soon as Prohibition is repealed, this place was built so there can be a bar here. I have the empty-bottle privilege.

When an author is thinking, don't anybody bother him but his secretary. She knows what he is thinking about.

When a new German picture comes out with a new idea, meet and decide on which writer will do a copy of it. Don't all write it at once.

STATE FAIR

A Fox Production,   Copyright January 22, 1933, LP 3634; renewed April 15, 1960, R 255642; b&w; sound; 10 reels, 8,894 ft. World premiere: January 26, 1933, Radio City Music Hall, NYC. Review in *New York Times,* January 27, 1933. Shooting scripts at AMPAS, USC. Extant. Location shots: Corona, Calif.; background shots at Iowa State Fair.

Production Staff: Producer: Winfield R. Sheehan; director: Henry King; assistant director: Ray Flynn; cameraman: Hal Mohr; adapted from the novel by Philip Stong; screenplay and dialogue by Paul Green and Sonya Levien; music director: Louis DeFrancesco; editor: R. W. Bischoff; recording engineer: A. L. von Kirbach; art director: Duncan Cramer; wardrobe: Rita Kaufman; business manager: B. McEveety.

Cast:

Janet Gaynor	Margy Frake, daughter
Will Rogers	Abel Frake, farmer and hog raiser
Lew Ayres	Pat Gilbert, newspaper reporter
Sally Eilers	Emily Joyce, a girl at the fair
Norman Foster	Wayne Frake, a son
Louise Dresser	Melissa Frake, wife
Victor Jory	Barker of the Hoopla stand
Frank Craven	Storekeeper, a dour country philosopher
Frank Melton	Harry Ware, a neighboring young farmer
Blue Boy	Himself

Synopsis: It is State Fair time and the Frake family looks forward to the trip to the state capital. Abel Frake, the father, will enter Blue Boy, his prize Hampshire boar, for the grand championship; Melissa, the mother, will match her pickles and mincemeat in competition; Margy and Wayne, their children, hope for adventures.

The fair will last a week, and camp is pitched on the grounds. While Abel fusses with an apathetic and listless Blue Boy, and Melissa worries through preliminary judging, Margy and Wayne are on their own. Wayne meets and falls in love with Emily Joyce, a seductive little trapeze artist working at the fair, while Margy meets Pat Gilbert, a newspaper reporter.

Wayne spends a night with Emily and wants to marry her, but she is wiser and persuades him to go home and marry the girl he left there. Margy and Pat, too, have fallen in love and Pat wants to get married, but Margy has heard of Pat's reputation as a lady's man, and she wants to go home and think it over.

Abel is worried over Blue Boy's failure to impress the judges. But when Esmeralda, a frisky, redheaded sow, is moved into the pen next to Abel's boar, Blue Boy is stirred at last into strutting and showing off, catches the attention of the judges, and wins the championship.

Melissa's pickles and her mincemeat—doubly fortified with brandy, first by a concerned Abel and, unaware of the earlier spicing, by Melissa—both win first prize.

Now homeward bound, Abel and Melissa have their victories; Wayne has his memories of his first adventure; and Margy has a heartache, until—arriving home—she receives a telephone call from Pat that he cannot live without her and that he is on his way to the farm to ask Abel for her hand.

Review:

★ "Watching this film is almost as interesting as going to a State Fair, for nothing seems to be neglected during the week in which it is supposed to take place. It is a homey tale, with many an intriguing bit. . . . Miss Gaynor here gives her best performance in talking pictures . . . Mr. Rogers is excellent in his role."

New York Times, January 27, 1933, 13:2,3

From Columns:

★ "While scenes were being filmed in the pen, the hog refused to budge so that the right angle might be obtained for the cameramen. Mr. Rogers ventured a suggestion.

" 'You're probably lining up on the wrong side of his profile. Tell you what, I'll switch over to the right side. It does't make any difference with my face. After all, it is his pen.' "

★ "Work has started on 'State Fair' this week when Henry King took a technical crew to Iowa to make scenes of the State Fair there. These scenes will be used as process shots and atmospheric bits in the picture. Accompanying Mr. King was Phil Stong, author of the prize winner."

New York Times, August 28, 1932, Sect. 8, 3:7

After the completion of the film, when the last scene had been shot, a studio official suggested that Rogers buy Blue Boy, as there was quite a lot of meat there for the Rogers household. Thinking it over, Rogers turned down the offer. "No," he said, "I just couldn't do it. I wouldn't feel right eating a fellow actor."

★

"I lost old 'Blue Boy,' he retired, said the work was too tame. Going to miss him, for I got along with him better than any actor I ever played with. He was just nine hundred pounds of harmony. Me losing him would be just like Laurel and Hardy splitting."

Syndicated column, June 25, 1933

★

"The only movie news I know is—and you saw it in *Time* this week, if you read *Time*—that Blue Boy died, and his death was in among the deaths of prominent men in *Time*—among those big bankers and politicians. I'm not joking about that—it really was. He just passed out. Hollywood life was too fast for him.

"But he comes as near being a real star as anyone—old Blue Boy. He would never hog a scene at all—oh, Lord, that was a bum pun. Wouldn't Eddie Cantor love to have that pun. Well, anyhow, I ain't kidding, old Blue Boy passed out, and like all Hollywood actors, he left several wives. The only ones at the funeral was the three little pigs."

Broadcast, January 28, 1934

Recognitions: ★ Will Rogers, Best Performance of the Month, *Photoplay Magazine*, April 1933
★ #4 of Year's Best, New York Times
★ #5 of Year's Best, National Board of Review, 384 critics voting

Censorship

"Certificate of Approval withheld pending elimination of bedroom scene and dialogue between Norman Foster and Sally Eilers." Classified as "Sex Picture" by Women's Clubs.

Territory: Ohio

The eliminations listed below . . . must not be included in any prints exhibited in the state of Ohio:

With Janet Gaynor and Lew Ayres, in *State Fair*, 1933.

Reel 8: Wayne is telling his parents that he is going to be gone all night, eliminate remark by Ma: "I bet you boys just fool around and don't get a wink of sleep."

Reel 9: Eliminate all views showing interior of Emily's bedroom where bed, ceiling, and windows of room are shown and voices are heard offscene.

With Blue Boy, in *State Fair*, 1933.

Eliminate accompanying dialogue as follows:

EMILY: Wayne, darling, I couldn't milk a cow.
WAYNE: The hired man milks the cow.
EMILY: What you expect of your wife is something I could never be. Do I look like a farm girl, Wayne? It's simply impossible.
WAYNE: You don't love me, then?
EMILY: I'm not the girl for you to marry, Wayne. The girl you told me about back home—she's the one. I'm sure of it.
WAYNE: But I don't love her as I do you. I can't leave you now.
EMILY: I'll be the one to leave.
WAYNE: Oh, we don't leave the ones we really love.
EMILY: Yes, we do, darling—my boy. Listen, Wayne, to one who's much older in the heart and try to believe it. You came to the State Fair, you found a girl who at least did you no harm. Can't you let it go at that?
WAYNE: You talk like the sort of woman I'd kill any man for thinking you.
EMILY: If I were the sort of woman you think I am, we should never have met in the first place. Wayne,

dear, why should you try to make something more out of this than there really is in it? We have been happy and no one is ever sorry when there's a little bit more happiness in the world.

With Henry King, who directed *Lightnin'* and *State Fair*. (*The Penguin Collection*)

Will Rogers Wrote

Well, sir, you get pretty interesting letters from folks sometimes. Here is one from a farmer from Yakima, Washington:

Saw "State Fair" last night, the wife and I. It was pretty good. Lot of these movie shows we see we don't understand, or they don't seem real to us, and we kinder come away feeling we missed something, but this one we kinder felt like we was right in the hog pen with you and Blue Boy, and camped with you at the fairgrounds. I thought perhaps if it wasen't too much trouble would you send two complimentary tickets to this friend of mine —— at Miller, South Dakota. He could take Mother and see this picture when it gets there. He don't have much to go to shows on.

Now I think that was nice sentiment and the friend gets the passes. But let him go on with the letter:

I am still wondering why that Hampshire boar didn't get up in the pen when you prodded him. I sort of know Hampshire hogs. Now you take a Duroc or Chester White or a Poland China, when they get fat they are just like most human beings, plain downright lazy, but not a Hampshire. They are quick to be on their feet, and I have yet to see a Hampshire when he was prodded that diden't get right up. Back in South Dakota I had a big rangy Hampshire boar.

He was the orneriest thing you ever saw. He would jump a forty-inch woven wire fence like a coyote, and go miles to pick a fight with another boar. I used to go after him horseback and with a blacksnake whip and chase him home. My mother is a widow woman, has been since I was six years old. She lives back in Dakota, and this fellow I want you to send the passes to is her neighbor. He can take her to the show. He is a bachelor, and is so homely he says no one would every marry him. He farms next to our old place. He has done a lot for us. He would come with his horses and

help me put in our crop, then hire me to come and help him put in his. That away when I was six years old. Hard times never did mean much to him. He kept right on raising hogs, Hampshire hogs, by the way. He started me up in the hog business by giving me a few runts now and again.

People around there used to make a lot of fun of him because he listed his corn instead of plowing the ground and planting it. When all the neighbors bought tractors he stuck to the horses and said, "Them durn fool tractors won't eat grass."

You could always depend on him. One time my hogs all got the Cholera. A couple of fat ones were already dead, and the rest were awful sick. About sundown I went over to his house and told him about it. He tied his team at once to the fence, unhitched one horse and rode back with me, took one look and said, "Why, that's Cholera." The roads were terrible, but he rode 20 miles bareback to the nearest town he could find that had some Cholera medicine and a vaccinating syringe, came back that night and helped me and my mother by lantern light vaccinate them hogs. It was several months before we had enough to pay him for the medicine. Several years later it was him who told me, "I can get you a pass on a hog train to the coast. You might get something a little better out there. Your kid brother is growing up and I will kinder help him out if him and your mother need any help."

He took me to the train and as I went to leave I tried to thank him, but he wouldn't let me. Said, "Aw, shucks, I will never be good for anything but a plug farmer." Then he passed something into my hand, and turned around with a "Well, so long." He had left in my hand two $20 bills.

I guess he knew I only had $3 with me. In the six years I have been gone I have never heard from him but once, but every time mother writes she mentions that —— was over today and helped bring in a load of hay, patch up some harness, and grease the wagon.

I have never written to any movie actors before and I don't know whether they care to read such letters as this. The theater was packed the night I went, and everybody enjoyed the whole show. Them other actors and actresses in there with you was good too, but I sure did enjoy that hog. But I don't know why he didn't get up when you poked him.

Now I call that a wonderful love story, that devo-tion of that homely bachelor to that neighbor widow. That would make a movie, and I would like to play the hog man. Nothing appeals in a story like simplicity. Well, I wrote this old boy why the old boar didn't get up when I poked him, but that's a secret among us actors. We don't tell everybody how we do things, and old Blue Boy was the best actor of the two of us.

Syndicated column, April 23, 1933

Rogers Writes a Column

Well, all I know is just what I read in the papers, and as there hasn't been much in the papers, why, I am kinder stuck on something to write. I got it! I will do like those New York columnists do.

Here goes on my first lap of trying to be a columnist.

Up betimes and at my stint. My first stint is a lot of sliced fresh peaches, then some ham and then some eggs washed down with about a dozen saucers of coffee. I lay late, almost till 6:30. The papers came, but having nothing but politics, I cared not one whit for 'em. It does seem that our country could be run better by someone, if we could only think who. Mrs. Rogers came down and we had the usual argument as to how late the boys stayed out. They have to drive over a cattle guard coming in and it's as good as an alarm clock as it rattles under the car wheels.

There was a big opening in Hollywood last night, but as I had nothing to wear, or say, I didn't go. Son Jimmy came down at last to breakfast and said he had to drive half the night to find some movie house where they were showing a double feature.

Came by Clara Bow's ranch up in the desert in Nevada the other day. She's got a Hollywood home right in the heart of the desert. Got cattle on it, not a California ranch with rabbits or avocados. I love my navy beans better than any other dish, or half dozen dishes. Just old plain white navies, cooked in plenty of ham or fat meat, with plenty of soup among 'em. Not catsup or any of that stuff. Just beans and corn bread, old corn pone (white, with no eggs), with the salt and water it's cooked with, and raw onions. Those three things are all I want.

I was the first fellow in Cooweescoowee District, Cherokee Nation, Indian Territory, that ever did the "cake walk." Who does the Kingfish and who does Van Porter—Amos or Andy? Greta Garbo is high hat-tin' Sweden more than she did Hollyhockville. I love to stroll down in the old part of Beverly Hills, places that have been built for four or five years. Marie Dressler is my pet actress. Charlie Chaplin is my pet actor. I got two teeth out away back, but they did adjoin, and it shows when I laugh too much in the movies.

I have about quit trying to play polo; depression and old age hit me the same summer. Dick Powell, master of ceremonies in one theater in Pittsburgh for three years, made good in a big Hollywood studio. He come from Little Rock. His father sold harvesters, since wheat used to be worth cutting. I used to have two ingrowing toenails. Every time I shoot a pistol I shut my eyes.

I was never in a nightclub; not morals, just never had a card. Mrs. Ziegfeld spent the evening with us yesterday, as lovely and bright a person as one could meet. Jim Rogers burned his hand roping a calf. I didn't; I missed mine.

Why, my article is finished already. This kind of stuff is a cinch. I must get a little more scandal in the next one, and I know a lot.

Syndicated column, September 25, 1932

Interview with Hal E. Roach, Sr., January 2, 1971

HR: Will loved brown Mexican beans. One day he told Betty, "Betty, I want those Mexican beans every night." So the first night Betty had a rather modest little dish of beans prepared, and Will said, "Betty, that's not what I want. I love them, I want a lot of these beans." Well, the next day, there was a bowl containing at least four quarts of beans sitting in front of Will. And for the next month, a bowl with four quarts of beans was in front of Will every night until he got so damn sick and tired of Mexican beans that he had to call it quits.

Interview with Lew Ayres, December 31, 1970

S: I have heard many a time that Mr. Rogers didn't learn his lines at all, and that as far as dialogue was concerned, he would rewrite his own.

LA: I think that was generally true, and some of us reacted with grave concern at any thought of working with someone like this. We were more or less bound by our limited capacity, not only to the sense of the scene, but, truthfully, to the dialogue itself. It sometimes made it difficult on actors who worked with him. It took a particular kind of personality to respond to this loosely arranged manner of carrying on dialogue with him. Maybe his years in vaudeville were responsible. At that time we didn't have the real respect that came about later. That is an interesting point. In a sense, he was far ahead of his time. Not only as a human being, but as an actor, too. You see, we are talking about something that took place in my life thirty-seven years ago, and I am looking at it from another perspective. One of the reasons I didn't know him too well was, of course, the big age difference. I am now sixty-two, so nearly forty years ago would put me in my mid-twenties. He was considerably older, and a most eminent man, so well known everywhere. Most of us stood in awe of him, but not as an actor. We stood in awe of him as a person of affluence and influence in the world. We recognized what he stood for—though not as much as history has proved. But in the acting sense, while I don't say that today's dramatization moves as far away from the actually written dialogue as Will Rogers was able to carry it, his relaxed attitude when you watch him today in those old films is like the most modern New York laboratory theater performance. There is nothing stilted, static about Will Rogers. He was alive and real. I wish today I had just his talent as a performer.

S: Will Rogers, oddly enough, did not consider himself to be an actor. He would say that as long as a part fitted him, he could play it, but he didn't want any part where he would have to "act."

LA: As time has gone on, many of us view acting differently. In older times, an actor was considered only such when he could portray many kinds of characterizations that were not necessarily like himself. That a man could assume the garb of a soldier of the king, next time play a beggar, or a young man, or an old man—that was more before motion pictures, which came up with the big close-up and revealing us to be what we really are. But in the theater, with makeup and lighting, we had a greater range. I now find that many of the so-called great personalities that had been recognized as "personality actors"—when we did not believe them to be great actors—I now maintain that that is good acting. The capacity of a man to communicate his personality—and we thought of Will Rogers as a personality—to communicate that to an audience is an art. It is an artist who does that. My evaluation of Will Rogers as an artist is that he was able, and willing, to reveal that within himself which he really was. So I consider him a fine actor, though apparently he would never have admitted it.

He was unique. Will Rogers had a way of slapping you down while he picked you up. That is a great art, and Rogers certainly was great. And it is all the more remarkable—a curious fact—that these rare gems of personality are so few and far between. Our population has almost doubled since then, and out of this vast number wouldn't you think some similar personality would have emerged? But of the really great, and Rogers is certainly among them, there are so few.

Interview with Henry King, January 14, 1972

HK: In July 1930, I went with Fox, and the first assignment I had before signing a full contract was a special contract just to do a picture with Will Rogers. That was the Frank Bacon show *Lightnin'*.

S: You also directed Mr. Rogers in *State Fair*.

HK: I went to Des Moines, Iowa, to the State Fair to buy three hogs. One that won first prize, called "Blue Boy" in the film, and I bought two understudies—just in case anything happened to Blue Boy.

S: These hogs were obviously not specially trained, not like the usual film animals. Weren't you worried about having Will Rogers handle such animals?

HK: Of course you'd never know what to expect of any of these boars, but the thing that relieved me was an incident I observed. Rogers didn't go to lunch at noon one day, when we stopped. I went to the restaurant and did the things a director has to do, you know, a lot of little details, preparing for the afternoon's work. Well, when I came back onto the

set, looking for Will, I passed Blue Boy's pen, and there he was. Blue Boy was asleep, and so was Will—sound asleep, using Blue Boy for a pillow. From that time on I never worried about Blue Boy hurting Will. When we woke Will, he said, "I think Blue Boy likes me." Now I would never have done that, but Rogers would slap him on the back, and rub him, and sit on him, or lean against him or walk around him. He had absolutely no fear of animals.

S: Was Will Rogers usually on time in the mornings?

HK: In the morning the son of a gun would always meet you on the set. He'd be there ahead of you, walking around, snooping around the set for props. He loved props. If there was a scene he had, sometimes he would say, "This darn script! You don't expect me to take these words too serious, do you?" "No," I'd tell him, "they are all in fun." But if he could find a pair of scissors, he could find more things to do with them. He used his props like all good actors. And I tell you, whether he was a good actor or not, he sure knew how to use props.

STARS' SALARIES (1933)

I read some blab about somebody telling how overpaid the movie stars are. In the first place our salaries are always overestimated, but a movie star is one person that can't be overpaid, that is, not for long. There is no other business in the world where the company you work for knows to a penny just what you are worth to them.

Is there any way checking up on a bank president or vice-president to see what he can actually by his own efforts draw into his bank? Is there any other business you can think of outside of stage or screen where they know just exactly how good you are to them in dollars and cents? Greta Garbo don't get that dough because she is a long tall Swede; she drags it into a box office and they know just how much she dragged in. They can tell you to a dime what Dietrich with her breeches on or off can draw into a box office. So they are all worth what they can get, and they can only get what they can draw. There comes a time soon enough in their lives when they don't get it. And then you must remember that at the present income-tax rate, the government takes fifty-five cents of every dollar from any of the high-priced stars. You see that hires many a politician, and that gives some of us a little license to holler how the government is run, even if it's only a holler.

Now get this in our laws. A movie star getting $300,000 a year would be taxed over half of it, while a financier receiving $300,000 a year interest from tax-exempt government bonds wouldn't pay a cent to the upkeep of his government from which he not only received protection for himself and family, but also his government guarantees him his original investment! And it gives him in addition $300,000 for which he does nothing. Now think that over a bit!

So don't begrudge the movie folks that are lucky enough to get some money for a little while. It's not a business where you can charge off depreciation for your buildings or equipment every year. No matter what age might be doing to talent, there is nothing you can charge off on it. There is many an ex-star broke today that have in their short careers paid the government more money than a half dozen successful businessmen will in a lifetime. Mind you, this is not a wail about taking it away from any of us, but make the thing fair—take it away from all alike!

So instead of writing a scenario, write to your congressman and tell him to do away with tax-exempt bonds. Then you will get some money in circulation.

Remember, write to your congressman. Even if he can't read, write to him.

DOCTOR BULL

A Fox Production, Copyright August 31, 1933, LP 4091; renewed October 20, 1960, R 264436; b&w; sound; 8 reels, 7,000 ft. Release: October 5, 1933, Radio City Music Hall, NYC. Review in *New York Times*, October 6, 1933. Shooting scripts: USC, AMPAS. Working title: *Life's Worth Living*. Extant.

Production Staff: Director: John Ford; assistant director: E. O'Fearna; cameraman: George Schneiderman; based on the novel *The Last Adam,* by James Gould Cozzens; screenplay by Paul Green; continuity: Jane Storm; music director: Samuel Kaylin; recording engineer: E. F. Grossman; art director: William Darling; wardrobe: Rita Kaufman; unit manager: B. F. McEveety.

Cast:

	Will Rogers	Dr. Bull, village physician and health officer
	Vera Allen	Janet Cardmaker, a widow, sister-in-law of the aristocratic Mrs. Banning
	Marian Nixon	May Tupping, telephone operator

Howard Lally	May's husband
Helen Freeman	Helen Upjohn, post mistress
Effie Ellsler	Aunt Myra Cole, Dr. Bull's aunt and housekeeper
Andy Devine	A drug clerk
Berton Churchill	Herbert Banning, the town capitalist
Louise Dresser	Mrs. Rita Banning, Herbert's wife
Rochelle Hudson	Virginia Banning, their daughter
Ralph Morgan	Dr. Verney, specialist in nearby town
Tempe Pigott	Grandma Banning
Elizabeth Patterson	Aunt Patricia Banning
Nora Cecil	Aunt Emily Banning
Patsy O'Byrne	Susan, Dr. Bull's cook
Vera Buckland	Mary, Janet Cardmaker's cook
with Robert Parish	

Synopsis: Dr. Bull is the general practitioner in New Winton, Connecticut. For more years than most can remember, he brought babies into the world and set broken bones; he dispensed medicine and sage advice; he experimented with medication for a paralyzed patient who was given up as hopeless by Dr. Verney, a specialist. Dr. Bull has also helped arrange romances, assisted a pregnant girl get her reluctant beau, and is not above giving occasional aid to ailing cows. In short, he is medic and confidant for all who call on him, whether they can pay him or not.

But town gossips carry tales about Dr. Bull and the widow Cardmaker. People say they spend so much time together after a hard day's work that they are really married—or ought to be.

Janet Cardmaker, widow, is the sister of the richest and, naturally, most important and most influential man in town, Herbert Banning. The Banning family looks upon the country doctor with disrespect and declares him a disgrace; they also question his competence, especially when a typhoid epidemic breaks out.

As the town's health officer, Dr. Bull is held responsible by the Banning family, and he is charged with incompetence and neglect. A town meeting is called and the town votes that Dr. Bull be dismissed. Eventually the doctor proves that the cause for the epidemic is Herbert Banning's construction camp, which has been polluting the town's water supply.

And when the paralyzed youth regains full use of his legs, Dr. Bull is completely vindicated.

Reviews: ★ "Mr. Rogers is admirable and ingratiating, and the production is, as previously stated, Hollywood at its best. But, in its return to sweetness and light as a part of its program, it had best take along its ability to plot tales."

New York Sun, October 6, 1933

★ " 'Doctor Bull' is a leisured tale, toned down in pace to the tempo of New England life, and as such, it suffers seriously as a motion picture. There is no drive or coherence in the story, and its interest is therefore centered almost entirely on Will Rogers' characterization. It is a part which he plays with an unerring sense of its values, but his very dominance leaves the rest of the picture rather flat."

New York Evening Post, October 6, 1933

Recognition: ★ #25 on list of Year's Best Films, *Photoplay Magazine,* 1933

Will Rogers Said

We been kicking along out here in the movies. I been working on a country doctor story, handed out enough pills and castor oil to do something to the whole world.

Syndicated column, July 2, 1933

At soda fountain with Andy Devine, in *Doctor Bull*, 1933.

Mike Donlin's Exit

One of the pleasant things connected with working in the movies is that you are all the time running into actors and friends, folks that you used to know and play on the bill with in vaudeville, or in a show.

In my last released picture, called *Doctor Bull*, worked with me an old-timer, one of the unique characters of not only one amusement line, but two. He was not of the stage, he was drafted from another line of recreation. He had become the best-known baseball player of his generation; he it was, who really introduced so-called *color* into our national pastime. When Mike Donlin joined the Giants away along about 1904, or thereabouts, he was the Babe Ruth of his time. He couldn't knock as many balls out of the park as Babe, but he could knock more men out of it. He could take a short arm jab, and bunt some boisterous spectator from the front row to the last.

In those days of the McGraw team, you played one inning and fought two. When you slid into a base, you slid into a fight. An umpire waved you out with one hand and warded off a swinging bat with the other. When an umpire yelled you are out, he had to look quick to tell who was out, him or the player.

College degrees hadn't entered baseball then, but degrees in language had. Well, that was when Mike Donlin was supreme. He was a quiet, orderly fellow, but he has licked more men than the First Division.

We had a great stage comedienne in those days, Mabel Hite. I think Mabel was from Kansas City originally. Well, there is very few funny women. Come to think about it, there is few funny men, but there has always been a scarcity of women comediennes. Mabel was a big favorite, in musical comedy, the greatest of her time. She fell in love with Mike at the height of his wonderful career. She had a sketch in vaudeville with Walter Jones, a splendid comedian. I played on the bill with them with my old pony and Buck McKee.

I hadn't married Mrs. Rogers then. She was still a girl of sound mind, in Rogers, Arkansas. Mike and Mabel married. America's most popular comedienne, to America's most popular ball player. It was the most popular wedding New York ever had. She put him on the stage in a vaudeville act. I saw their opening at Hammerstein's on a Monday afternoon. In my thirty years in all branches of show business I never heard such a reception. It's always lingered in my memory, and when dear old Mike was playing with me in my last picture, *Doctor Bull*, I used to tell him about it.

Along about that time Betty Blake down in Rogers, Arkansas, had a mental relapse and said yes after several solid years of no's. She threw her lot with Buck and I, and the pony "Teddy." From cheap hotels to dark stage-door entrances, she trudged her way. We met Mabel and Mike. We played on the bill with 'em—they the big headliners and drawing cards, my act put in just to make it so it read "Ten Acts of Vaudeville."

Now my wife reminded me of this the other night. They invited us up to their apartment in New York. It was the first time we had ever been in a swell apartment. It was the first time big actors had ever invited us out. We went up on the streetcar. This was in the winter of 1908. We had just been married. It was a fairyland night for the rope-throwing Rogers.

Mabel is dead, died just a few years after that, at the height of her career, but my wife will never forget her kindness to us, for you must remember there was "Class" in vaudeville, as well as in society, and for an "Act" to visit a headliner was an event.

Mike carried on as best he could. Bad health, bad luck, but always that something that made him the real fighter. He was tremendously fortunate in his next marriage. A girl much younger, beautiful girl. She stuck with Mike through many ups and downs, and an awful lot of downs among the few ups. He did some splendid things on the stage. He was always natural in anything he did.

He has been out here in pictures for years. Everybody liked him. Everybody used him when they had the chance. Everything he did was okay. Here was sometimes, maybe, a hundred people there with him, all kinds and all types of folks on a movie "Set," yet there he sat, joking and laughing. Health very bad. Maybe in actual pain. There was out of that hundred perhaps ninety or more people that never heard one speck of applause (for them personally) in their lives, yet here sat this fellow who maybe meant nothing to them, who had day after day, year after year, had thousands rise when he came to bat, had had audiences cheer for actual minutes when he come onstage. Here he was, looking for no sympathy, offering no alibis, not sore at the world, not sore at anybody, just a kindly soul who hadn't raised his hands in combat in thirty years. "Peace on Earth," Mike Donlin, that was your motto. You lived game, and you died game.

Syndicated column, October 8, 1933

Will Rogers Has the Last Word

Once again, Will Rogers' humor prevailed and changed minds after decisions had been made. It had happened before at Fox, and this time it was a telegram that changed the title of Rogers' latest film. The executives were determined, the title had been decided on. James Gould Cozzens' novel The Last Adam *was going to be a motion picture named* Life's Worth Living. *A meeting of sales and studio executives, taking place in Atlantic City, New Jersey, received the following telegram, signed by Will Rogers; Will had been asked to send greetings to the group from Movietone City, but this is what he wired:*

I HEAR YOU ARE HAVING A CONVENTION BACK THERE. I THOUGHT CONVENTIONS PASSED OUT WITH THE REPUBLICANS. THERE IS NOTHING AS USELESS OUTSIDE OF A ROGERS CLOSE-UP, AS A CONVENTION. BUT AS YOU ARE GATHERED TO DO SOME GOOD, ANYHOW, PUT THE NAME "DR. BULL" ON OUR NEXT PICTURE. SOME HALFWIT SUGGESTED "LIFE'S WORTH LIVING." NOW WE FIND THAT THEY HAVE TRIED TO HANG THAT TITLE ON EVERY FOX PICTURE SINCE "OVER THE HILL," SO THEY FINALLY SAID: GIVE IT TO ROGERS. SOMEBODY MUST BE WINNING A BET IF HE GETS THAT TITLE ON SOME PICTURE, WHETHER IT FITS OR NOT, SO YOU HYENAS HAVE A CHANCE TO HELP PASS IT ALONG TO SOME OTHER POOR DEVIL TO USE.

"LIFE'S WORTH LIVING" SOUNDS LIKE A GRADUATION ESSAY. AS A MATTER OF FACT, IF YOU DON'T MAKE SOME BETTER PICTURES, LIFE WON'T BE WORTH LIVING AND IT WILL COME TO THE POINT WHERE THE EXHIBITOR IS AS BAD OFF AS HE SAYS HE IS. I REALLY WANT TO CALL IT "OL' DR. BULL," BUT THEY SAY YOU CAN'T USE THE WORD "OLD" IN A TITLE, THAT PEOPLE MIGHT THINK YOU WERE OLD AND THAT OTHERWISE THEY WON'T FIND IT OUT. THEY GOT SOME GREAT ANSWERS. WHAT HAPPENED TO "OLD KENTUCKY," "OLD HOMESTEAD," "OLD MAN RIVER," "AULD LANG SYNE"? "OLD" DIDN'T DO THEM MUCH HARM.

Obviously Mr. Rogers made his point.

HOLLYWOOD

Today is the anniversary when California entered the Union. We took it away from Mexico the next year after we found it had gold. When the gold was gone, we tried to give it back, but Mexico was too foxy for us. In '49 the wayward sons of ten thousand families crossed the country, and the roads was so rough they couldn't get back.

Just when the mining had petered out, somebody discovered a moving-picture camera, and the old days of '49 were on again. Now child prodigies come by the busloads. Fords are packed with literary geniuses. My pictures alone have been the means of bringing every hard-looking old "bird" in the world out here.

It's a great old state. We furnish the amusement to the world—sometimes consciously, sometimes unconsciously; sometimes by our films, sometimes by our politicians, but you can't beat it.

Winter is coming and tourists will soon be looking for a place to mate. Now let's get this Florida versus California argument settled. I can afford to be fair, I can't sell my lots out here, anyhow.

Florida excels in fish and Democrats. So, if you like to fish and look at Democrats, Florida is your onion.

But you got to come to California to see Janet Gaynor, Sally Eilers, Clara Bow, and the great Garbo.

Yes, old Hollywood is just like a desert water hole in Africa. Hang around long enough and every kind of animal in the world will drift in for refreshments.

Los Angeles used to be considered by her critics as just a great big overgrown town with none of the big cities business methods like Chicago and New York.

But they can't say that anymore. We are a modern American city at last. Yes, sir, in Hollywood you will see things at night that are fast enough to be in the Olympics in the daytime. When Judge Ben Lindsey was in Hollywood, his "companionable marriage" idea created no stir here at all. The idea is as old and commonplace out here as traffic lights.

The other night at a benefit, backstage, I introduced a dozen screen friends to each other, and then had them say: "Why, Will, we used to be married to each other." Well, I just got discouraged. Why only yesterday the headlines in all the Los Angeles papers said: AUTHORITIES HAVING TROUBLE ROUNDING UP TWELVE ESCAPED LUNATICS! I guess the main trouble is recognizing 'em. I bet they get a different twelve back in.

Say, did you know we have a discoverer out here in California, a Dr. House? He has invented a serum called scopolamine, a thing that when injected into you will make you tell the truth—at least for a while, anyway.

They started it by trying it on some male movie star in Hollywood and he told his right salary and his press agent quit him. They then tried it on a female movie staress, and she recalled things back as far as her first husband's name and remembered her real maiden name.

It really is a wonderful thing, and if it could be brought into general use, it would no doubt be a big aid to humanity. But it will never be, for already the politicians are up in arms against it. It would ruin the very foundation on which our political government is run.

If you ever injected truth into politics, you'd have no politics.

MR. SKITCH

A Fox Production, Copyright December 6, 1933, LP 4342; renewed January 24, 1961, R 270116; b&w; sound; 7 reels, 6,150 ft. Release: December 22, 1933, Roxy Theatre, NYC. Review in *New York Times,* December 23, 1935. Shooting script at AMPAS. Working title: *See America First.* Extant.

Production Staff: Director: James Cruze; cameraman: John Seitz; based on *Saturday Evening Post* story "Green Dice," by Anne Cameron; screenplay by Ralph Spence and Sonya Levien; music director: Louis DeFrancesco; recording engineer: W. D. Flick; art director: William Darling; wardrobe: Rita Kaufman.

Cast:

Will Rogers	Mr. Skitch	Harry Green	Cohen
Zasu Pitts	Mrs. Skitch	Charles Starrett	Harvey Denby
Rochelle Hudson	Emily Skitch	Eugene Pallette	Cliff Merriweather
Florence Desmond	Flo		

Synopsis: Mr. Skitch, as the head of a family of six, starts off on an auto tour with the hope of regaining the family fortune, lost in a bank failure. He finally manages to find a job in a gambling casino, and gambles with the first dollar he earns. He wins three thousand dollars, only to have his wife lose it in an auto camp. Penniless once more, Mr. Skitch and his brood set out for Hollywood, with the hope of capitalizing on the talents of a movie-star impersonator by becoming his manager. Mr. Skitch finally extricates himself from the financial difficulties in Hollywood.

Review: ★ "Will Rogers, champion of comedians, is taking audiences at the Orpheum Theatre on a grand tour of laughter, in his latest Fox release which proves to be even more amusing than the story that was so popular several years ago.

"Rogers has ample opportunities to display his quick wit, and it goes without saying that he takes full advantage of this chance, in a role that is perfectly suited to his talents."

Tulsa World, December 24, 1935

POSTSCRIPT: *It was Will Rogers' persistence that made Fox finally change the name of this film from* See America First, *and/or* Green Dice, *to* Mr. Skitch.

Censorship

"Deletion recommended under *vulgarity clause*": scene of Ford car carrying sign: "My Essex—does yours?"

On the way to the sound stage, filming *Mr. Skitch*, 1933.

With Zasu Pitts, in *Mr. Skitch*, 1933.

PICTURES VERSUS STATECRAFT

Brother, have I lately prowled. I just flew back here to California from one of these cross-continent escapades. I finished a picture one night, and the studio told me that it would take them about a week before they would have it all assembled and be ready to preview.

Here is the way we work it with these pictures. When the picture is finished they take it out to some suburban theater of Los Angeles, and run it. It's advertised in front of the theater that there is a preview of a new picture that night, but it does not say what one it is, or whose.

A few of the main studio people connected with the making of it and the principals go, and it's run. Then they see how it goes, and try to see what is the matter with it. Course we don't always see, and then, too, sometimes we know the main thing that's the matter with it, and that is that it should never have been made, but as it is made and lots of money is invested in it, why, they take it back and work on it, maybe retake scenes.

Then maybe they will take it out and try it again on some other defenseless audience. I made one, one time, that we previewed so many times, and so many places, that the last couple of weeks we had to take it away up around San Francisco. All southern California rebelled and said, "We have seen this thing enough!" You see, we try to make them as good as we can. Bad pictures are not made with a premeditated design. It looks to you sometimes like we must have purposely made 'em that way, but honest, we don't. A bad picture is an accident, and a good one is a miracle.

But this is not what I started in to tell you at all. I was going to tell you how I got away.

You see, I have to go to Washington every so often to see what the senators are doing. I can't just leave 'em; they wouldn't do a thing, or if they did, it would be the wrong thing. I got to go there and kinder prod 'em up every once in a while, same as Mr. Roosevelt has to bring 'em in and pat 'em on the back every so often.

You see, that's the way he works 'em, he never scolds 'em. He knows they are just like children at heart, and when he wants something done, he just coaxes 'em, brags on 'em, and first thing you know they have voted yes.

Well, I can't do that; in fact, there is few that can. I am not that even-tempered. Our president is almost a freak in that respect; he seems to know just where their back itches and there is where he scratches. But I can't do it, I have to cuss 'em a little sometimes. I like 'em, maybe at heart as much as Roosevelt, maybe more, but they do vex the very old devil out of me, and all of us at times.

Well, as I say, the studio said I could go, but when they showed the picture that if there was any—what we call—retakes, that I was to be back there at a certain date to make 'em.

Well, I had just got settled down good in the Senate Gallery, when the news come that they had showed the picture, and that there was practically nothing wrong with it but the last five reels (they must have skipped the first one). So right in the middle of a Huey Long oration, I had to grab a plane and hike back to California.

So if the Senate gums everything up it will really be my fault, for I was not there to guide 'em.

Syndicated column, February 11, 1934

DAVID HARUM

A Fox Production, Copyright February 27, 1934, LP 4513; renewed March 14, 1961, R 272271; b&w; sound; 9 reels, 7,525 ft. Release: March 1, 1934, Radio City Music Hall, NYC. Review in *New York Times*, March 2, 1934, 23:2. Reviewed in Chicago, March 12, 1934. Shooting script at USC; assigned to National Telefilm Association, March 19, 1975. Extant. Location shots: Riverside and Inglewood, Calif. Sound system: Western Electric Noiseless Recording.

Production Staff: Producer: Winfield R. Sheehan; director: James Cruze; assistant director: Eli Dunn; cameraman: Hal Mohr; from novel by Edward Noyes Westcott; screenplay by Walter Woods; additional dialogue: Homer Croy; music director: Louis DeFrancesco; editor: Jack Murray; recording engineer: W. D. Flick; art director: William Darling; wardrobe: Russell Patterson; unit manager: B. McEveety.

Cast (Fox Movietone Studio, Call Bureau Cast Service, February 1, 1934):

Will Rogers	David Harum	Irene Bentley	Mary
Kent Taylor	John Lennox	Charles B. Middleton	Deacon Perkins
Evelyn Venable	Ann Madison	Sarah Padden	Widow Cullon
Louise Dresser	Polly Harum	Roger Imhof	Hotel proprietor
Lillian D. Stuart	Sairy Harum	Noah Beery, Sr.	General Woolsey
Stepin Fetchit	Sylvester		

Bits

Charles Coleman	Flowers, the butler	John Westervelt	Singer
Jane Darwell	Mrs. Woolsey	Spec O'Donnell	Tim, office boy
Frank Melton	Caruthers Elwin	Ky Robinson	Steve Willis
Connie Baker	} Guests	Edward Gargan	Bill Montague
Wally Dean		Jerry Stewart	Chet Timson
Jack Mower		Larry Fisher	
Mary Blackwood		Luke Cosgrove	} Bits
Frank Rice	Robinson	Ned Norton	
Clifford Carling	Steve	Harry Dunkinson	
Harry Todd	Elmer	Harrison Greene	Barber

136

Frank La Rue	Politician	Gus Reed		
High Boswell	Businessman	Walter McGrail		Bits
Thomas Curran	Banker	William Arnold		
Jack Clark	Traveler	William Norton Bailey		
Morgan Wallace	Mr. Blake	Eric Mayne		Doctor
Arthur Belasco	Crocker	George Irving		Father
Ruth Gillette	Lillian Russell	Harold Nelson		Jeff

Synopsis: The time is before the turn of the century. David Harum is a shrewd, homely, philosophical banker in a small town in upper New York State. After business hours he carries on a long-standing contest to best Deacon Perkins in the age-old pastime of horsetrading. Their feud dates from the time the Deacon was able to sell Harum a blind horse. Again the Deacon seems to have outwitted Harum, when the banker finds himself the owner of a particularly balky horse. While furthering the romance between his teller, John Lennox, and beautiful Ann Madison, Harum discovers accidentally that his horse has unexpected powers as a trotter, when sung to.

With this knowledge, Harum enters his new acquisition in a race and beats the Deacon's best horse.

Reviews: ★ "Will Rogers has an extraordinary facility for getting under the skin of the characters he plays without make-up or actually submerging his own personality. As the Connecticut Yankee, he looked as though he had stepped out of Mark Twain's book, and he was precisely the man for Bill Jones in *Lightnin'*.

"Now he is to be seen as the leading light in that genial old favorite David Harum, and one thinks of the former cowpuncher, not as Will Rogers, but most decidedly as David Harum.

"Even though the film occasionally overemphasizes the natures of some of the persons involved, Mr. Rogers gives to his part exactly what is wanted.

"*David Harum* is another of those welcome, refreshing pictures which, judging by the constant outbursts of laughter, was enjoyed greatly by an audience at its first exhibition.

"Mr. Rogers is at the height of his form here."

New York Times, March 2, 1934, 23:2/3

★ "It is quite evident that *David Harum* was selected to be made into a picture because of its homely qualities, homeliness now being on the upgrade as screen fare. Certainly there does not seem any other reason that would justify the exhumation of Edward Noyes Westcott's leisurely study of small-town characters of the early nineties.

"Though we have not read the book, its presentation on the screen does not suggest that whatever virtues it may have are susceptible to dramatic treatment. It may be that a spirited production and a more alert company of actors might have brought a degree of life to the picture; as it is, the current offering leans heavily on Will Rogers, and Mr. Rogers seems inclined to let the whole thing slide off his shoulders. We can hardly imagine any material less inspiring to work with than the skimpy story of David Harum, small-town banker and gentleman horse trader."

New York Evening Post, March 2, 1934

Recognition: ★ #8 on Honor Roll of Best Pictures for 1934, 424 ballots cast by nation's film reviewers

Preview

A few nights ago we previewed a picture David Harum, at one of Beverly Hills' big movie houses. We generally take 'em out to some little out-of-the-way town, but everybody was too lazy to drive anywhere, so they just tried it on the home folks. The picture had been going only a short ways and the leading lady, Miss Evelyn Venerable [Will Rogers' nickname for Miss Venable]—from the Shakespearean stage and this is her third picture—appeared; well, somebody in the dark whispered over my shoulder from the row behind and asked who the girl was. Well, you know who it was who asked? It was Jean Harlow and Mr. Rosson, her husband, and they were very interested in the girl, also the boy, Kent Taylor. Well, I felt proud that they would turn out to see my little picture, and every once in a while I would peek back and they would be holding hands. Now that is mighty big news for a Hollywood couple that are really married.

"Then of course, outside the theater was the usual autograph pests. They don't any more want your autograph, but they just seem to act like they had a bet on with each other. Half the time they don't even know who it is they have asked to write. I don't know, but that strikes me as being the dumbest fad that's been invented. My Lord, what could a lot of us movie folks mean? I can see somebody wanting Presi-dent Roosevelt's, or Chief Justice Hughes', or Col. and Anne Lindbergh's. But the crazy way they are running after names now, their list would read like a petition for someone to get the Post Office.

Syndicated column, February 25, 1934

Making the Picture

I am away, making a movie of old David Harum. I prove to be a better horse trader in the picture than I am in real life. They come from miles around out here in California to hook me in a horse trade. When we do David Harum, we're going to have an illustration at the first of the picture, explaining to the young folks what a horse is. Of course, old David Harum, you know, he was a banker, too, and we'll have to go kinder easy on that. While the audiences won't know what a horse is, they unfortunately do know what a banker is. We may have to change him from a banker into something else, in order to get sympathy for him.

Radio broadcast, November 26, 1933

★

David Harum, they claim that's the most widely read book over the course of years, that is in the library.

I will be a terrible guy to play it, for I am the world's worst horse trader. But you know the old horse is coming back faster than he left? This racing all over the country is going to help a lot to popularize the horse.

You know when you see a horse race, the horse that's in front is the winner, but when you see a fifty-, one-hundred, or five-hundred-mile automobile race, why, the fellow that is in front may be thirty laps behind. You don't look at the race, you look at a big scoreboard to see who is ahead. No, sir, there is no kick in the world like a nose-and-nose finish of the old bang tails.

Yes, the horse is coming back.

Oh by the way, I don't by any means want this to be taken as an advertisement, but I have got some mighty good "all-purpose" horses that can be bought, worth the money.

Syndicated column, September 24, 1933

★

Had an interesting little four days stay in Riverside, California. We were out there filming the trotting scenes in *David Harum*.

Well, sir, there is nothing any more interesting to talk to than an old horse man, and there is nothing any older than a trotting horse man. I never saw a man in the trotting horse business under eighty.

The only thing I had to recommend me was that I looked as old as a driver. I used to be a pretty good just-old-common-horse driver as a young fellow back home, but I never made the tracks. My father was the best driver I ever saw, though. Well, he had quite a little training in his young days. He used to haul freight from Saint Joe, Missouri, to Dallas, Texas. Lord, his son hasn't got hardly enough endurance to make the same trip in a plane.

So, if I show any driving ability in this my first real effort, it is inherited. It's not from hard work, perseverance, and taking advantage of my opportunities.

Syndicated column, January 21, 1934

With Evelyn Venable, in *David Harum*, 1934.

With Stepin Fetchit and Evelyn Venable, in *David Harum*, 1934.

The big race, in *David Harum*, 1934.

Interview with Evelyn Venable Mohr and Hal Mohr, January 4, 1971

S: Miss Venable, you appeared in two Will Rogers films.

EVM: Yes. *David Harum* and *County Chairman*.

S: Mr. Mohr, you were the director of cinematography on three Will Rogers films.

HM: That's right, *David Harum*—that's the one Evelyn and I met on—*State Fair*, and *County Chairman*.

S: In those days life was easier in the studios, wasn't it?

EVM: It was an awful lot of fun. There wasn't the terrible pressure of schedules. And, of course, Will always took his time, whenever he wanted to.

HM: There was an expression I remember very well, that Will always used around four o'clock in the afternoon. He would say, "Mr. Cameraman, what time is it?" And when he was told that it was around four o'clock, he would shout out "Santa Monica Canyon!" and off he'd be.

S: Didn't he also write his column on the set?

HM: He had a roadster that he drove—I don't remember what it was—and he took that car wherever he went, even on location. He had his little typewriter in the back of it, and between takes and setups, he would sit there and peck at that typewriter, writing his daily column.

S: I have heard that in the mornings he was quite preoccupied, until the column had been sent off.

HM: That's right; he'd do scenes, of course, but the moment the take was finished, he was off to his little roadster, which was parked nearby, and he'd get to work on the column again.

S: What would he do in the afternoon between takes?

HM: Oh, he would kid around and egg us on so we'd get through, so he could get back to Santa Monica

Canyon. I think he just lived to get back to that canyon.

EVM: I don't blame him.

S: *County Chairman* was just recently on TV. Mickey Rooney was in it, he was then a small boy.

HM: The only two people for me that were in those films were Evelyn Venable and Will Rogers. You know, I remember we were on location up at Sonora. Naturally, everywhere Rogers would go, the chambers of commerce, the boards of education, the various women's clubs would descend on him, trying to prevail upon him to come and speak to their organizations. So he finally said, "I'll put on a show for you. I'll do it at the auditorium of the high school, and you can all come to that." So Evelyn and I went with him, as well as a couple of other people from the cast. And he was up there, on the stage, for about two and a half hours, a steady solo show, except that he introduced the cast. It was a free show, but he worked just as hard as he ever did in the *Follies;* he was just magnificent.

Will did everything in good taste. It seems a shame that a man like Will couldn't be perpetuated forever. He would have been terrific medicine for this period. I think today's kids would have listened to him. I think everybody would have listened.

EVM: He had some answers to offer, instead of just criticisms. He would have been just as great today.

HM: Will could get along with anybody. I remember driving out on location with him. It must have been for *State Fair*. We drove out to the Mojave Desert, and we stopped for breakfast at Mojave—the entire motorcade stopped. Mojave was a rail junction with a large complement of hoboes. As we were stopped, Will wandered over to the freight yards, and there were a bunch of 'boes. And he just sat down with them and talked with these fellows for over an hour, while the whole motorcade waited to proceed on location.

S: How was he to work with?

EVM: Just darling! Just one thing—and I am sure you have heard this from other actors—he didn't follow the script. You had to be on your toes. You had to dovetail what you were supposed to say into what he actually had said. You had to do that to make sense and follow the story line. It was fun, because it gave a good deal of freshness to the scenes. But it was a little bit nerve-racking, too.

S: Did he ever break you up?

EVM: Many times! But he broke himself up, too. Sometimes he would say something totally irrelevant, something funny that had just occurred to him. But that was what was nice about pictures then; there wasn't the horrible pressure because of costs.

S: Did Mr. Rogers have any idiosyncrasies?

HM: I do remember Will doing things like knocking on wood when he went into a scene or when he came out of a scene he thought was okay.

EVM: I remember when he liked a scene as it was

played, he'd yell "Print it!" and he wouldn't do it again. He liked it just as it had been played.

S: You have an autographed picture of Will Rogers hanging on the wall. What is the inscription?

EVM: It says, "From the old matchmaker, with affection and good wishes to Evelyn and Hal, from Will Rogers." He was kind of interested in the fact that we met on *David Harum,* and then a year later, we did *County Chairman* just immediately before we were married.

HM: Of course, Will was not actually the matchmaker. He liked to call himself that; he felt responsible in a way, but I think it was chemistry beyond Rogers or anybody else. But something of Will Rogers rubbed off on everybody. Most of the people who were around Will were pretty decent people, but some of his philosophy would rub off on you. Now Will and I didn't agree politically, but there was so much about this man that you had to admire, that you unconsciously tried to emulate a lot of his thinking.

ACADEMY AWARDS

On March 18, 1934, Will Rogers was the master of ceremonies at the Academy of Motion Picture Arts and Sciences Awards. Where heretofore such affairs had been just a stream of long-winded, dull speeches, Will Rogers changed all that, and ever since producers of the event have tried to inject entertainment into it. Incomplete notes of what Will Rogers said that evening have survived.

I was always a little leery of this organization. The name Arts and Sciences—I think that name has bluffed out more people than it has attracted. This is the highest sounding named organization I ever attended. If I didn't know so many of the people who belonged to it personally, I would have taken that name serious. Call them "Arts and Sciences," but do so with your tongue in your cheek. Everything that makes money and gives pleasure is not "art." If it was, bootlegging would have been the highest form of artistic endeavor.

This is rather an unusual dinner this year. In looking over the possible winners, this is not a Metro-Goldwyn-Mayer dinner. Heretofore if you worked for Metro, when you signed your contract, you could, if you insisted, have a clause inserted in there where you was to receive an Academy statue. Louis B. Mayer, always a generous fellow, he would furnish the accountants that counted the votes.

And those little statues they hand out; they are lovely things. We may run out of these things and have to send down to Frank Borzage and get another dozen. He was using 'em for tenpins one night I was there. They are lovely things. They were originally designed for prizes at a nudist's colony bazaar, but they didn't take 'em. It must be terrible artistic, for nobody has any idea what it is. It represents the triumph of nothingness over the stupendousness of zero.

I will tell you what gave me the courage to come here tonight among this galaxy of feminine loveliness and masculine intellect. Looking over the backs of chairs, it looks like Ermine's last roundup. But when I heard that Sam Goldwyn had just lectured at Harvard, I says, brother, Hollywood's highbrows can't scare me. Yes, sir, Sam lectured to the professors, in person, without the voice being dubbed in by somebody else. Now they have asked him to come again and bring the English version.

It takes great restraint to stand here and hand out tokens of merit to inferior actors. There is great acting in this room tonight, greater than you will see on the screen. We all cheer when somebody gets a prize that every one of us in the house knows should be ours. Yet we smile and take it. Boy, that's acting!

It burns me up to have to publicly admit that Leslie Howard has anything histrionically on me. But everything equals up in the long run. I bawl him out something terrible when I get him on my side playing polo.

Adapters, commonly known among authors as "book murderers." They are the people that show you how the book should have been written in the first place. If given the Bible to adapt, they would claim that it started too slow, that the love interest should start in Genesis, and not Leviticus, and that the real kick of the story was Noah trying to have each animal find its mate. They would play that for suspense. There has always been a suspicion whether an adapter don't help more books than he hurts. You know, all books are not so hot, either.

If he is adapting a play, all an adapter has to do is to take out the second act, all but 10 percent of the adultery, and a few other things. An adapter is one who wants to bet you you won't recognize your own story. Original writers are men who have had good enough lawyers to protect them from plagiarism. They cuss the movies, unless some adapter happens to have made their story worth looking at.

Actors, Laughton is the first actor to put sex-appeal in whiskers. Muni played "The Chain Gang" picture. Now he can't go south of the Mason-Dixon line. He liked the part of a prisoner so well that he will never be satisfied till he is one. And if he stays with Jack Warner in some of his escapades, he will get there.

I have never seen any of these pictures. They don't look at mine and why should I go see theirs?

The best cameraman is the one with the best assistant.

Sound—this goes to you for bringing up the good lines and drowning out the bad ones.

Directing—I have always had the greatest regard for directing.

Photography is an art where if you shoot enough weird shots that you get the audience's mind off the actors, you will get a medal, not only by the academy, but by the audience.

Cameramen have ridden a dolly so much lately till they are putting sleepers on 'em.

Art director—he must make it look like a room, but not a room that anyone ever lived in.

His sets must be different. If the audience guesses what they represent, then his art has failed.

★

Review

"Will Rogers has never been known to pull his punches. At the recent Academy Awards dinner, the prophet of Fox Movietone City tossed big executives, stars, artists and whatnot on the griddle and roasted them to a turn. He even took a crack at the industry itself.

'It's a racket,' said Will; 'if it wasn't we all wouldn't be here in dress clothes.' And commenting on the fearsome sound of the Academy's full title, 'Academy of Motion Picture Arts and Sciences,' Will said: 'If the movies are an art, I kinda think it'll leak out somehow without bein' told; and if they're a science—then it's a miracle.'

Will's wit changed the big affair from the customary ceremony of long-winded speeches into a joyous riot."

Photoplay, June 1934

STAND UP AND CHEER

Will Rogers does not appear in this film. He is, however, responsible for it, as he and Philip Klein suggested the original story to Winfield Sheehan.

A Fox Production, Copyright April 25, 1934, LP 4638; renewed June 21, 1961, R 277925; b&w; sound; 9 reels, 7,300 feet. Release: April 19, 1934, Radio City Music Hall, NYC. Review in *New York Times*, April 20, 1934, 17:1. Shooting script at UCLA. Working title: *Fox Movietone Follies*. Extant.

Production Staff: Producer: Winfield R. Sheehan; associate producer: Lew Brown; director: Hamilton MacFadden; cameramen: Ernest Palmer, L. W. O'Connell; based on story suggested by Will Rogers and Philip Klein; screenplay and dialogue: Ralph Spence; music: Lew Brown and Jay Gorney; lyrics: Lew Brown; music director: Arthur Lange; dances staged by Sammy Lee; editor: Margaret V. Clancey; recording engineer: E. F. Grossman; art directors: Gordon Wiles and Russell Patterson; wardrobe: Rita Kaufman.

Cast (Fox Movietone Studio, Call Bureau Cast Service, February 9, 1934):

Warner Baxter	Lawrence Cromwell	Arthur Byron	Harley
Madge Evans	Mary Adams	James Dunn	Dugan
Nigel Bruce	Dinwiddie	Skins Miller	Comedy Hill Billy
Stepin Fetchit	George Bernard Shaw	Theresa Gardella	Aunt Jemima
Frank Melton	Fosdick	Nick Foran	
Lila Lee	Zelda	Shirley Temple	
Ralph Morgan	President's secretary	John Boles	Specialty numbers
Frank Mitchell ⎫	Senators	Sylvia Froos	
Jack Durant ⎭		Jimmy Dallas	

Bits

Frances Morris		John Davidson	Sour radio announcer
Lurene Tuttle		Harry Dunkinson	
Dorothy Gulliver	Stenographers	Gilbert Clayton	
Bess Flowers		Herbert Prior	Quartette
Lillian West		Carlton Stockdale	
Selmer Jackson ⎫	Correspondents	Lucien Littlefield	Professor Hi De Ho
Clyde Dilson ⎭		Arthur Loft	
Edward Earle	Secret Service man	Jack Richardson	Bits
Gayne Whitman	Voice for president	Joe Smith Marba	Elephant trainer
Frank Sheridan		Carleton E. Griffin	
Paul Stanton	Senators	Paul McVey	
Wellis Clark		Rolin Ray	Secretaries
Arthur Stuart Hull		Reginald Simpson	
Cy Jenks	Rube farmer	Arthur Vinton	Turner
Aggie Herring	Irish washerwoman	Sam Hayes	Radio announcer
Phil Tead	Vaudevillian	Tina Marshall	Boy's mother
Randall Sisters	Trio	Dora Clemant	
George K. Arthur	Dance director	Peggy Watt	
Baby Alice Raetz	Child bit	Dorothy Dehn	Secretaries
Ruth Beckett	Child's mother	Ruth Clifford	
Bobby Caldwell	General Lee	Dagmar Oakland	
Wilbur Mack	Beamish	Vivian Winston	Bits
Elspeth Dudgeon		Glen Walters	Hillbilly's wife
Jessie Perry	Reformers		
Harry Northrup			

Synopsis: Lawrence Cromwell, a stage producer, is called to Washington by the president, to head a newly formed department as Secretary of Amusements. His assignment is to bring smiles back to the faces of Americans, to help them overcome the effects of the economic depression.

Once established in office, Cromwell orders dozens of jazz bands, grosses of chorus girls, dozens of blues and torch singers, and "one sixth of a dozen masters of ceremonies."

Cromwell runs into severe problems with senators on Capitol Hill, as they oppose his laugh-providing plans and actually try to ruin him by spreading harmful rumors. Of course, Cromwell prevails.

There is the mandatory romance, with Cromwell falling in love with Mary Adams, who is in charge of the children's entertainment, but the film, while poking fun at the functions of government, is primarily a musical extravaganza with songs and dances, displaying a huge cast.

Reviews: ★ "The film has dash and vigor, entertainment and numerous laughs, tuneful music and bright dance numbers."

The Motion Picture Almanac

★ "With its adroit travesty on politics, its pleasant tunes and its effervescent quality, *Stand Up and Cheer* often comes to a conception of what a modern Gilbert and Sullivan opus might be."
New York Times, April 20, 1934

HANDY ANDY

A Fox Production, Copyright July 17, 1934, LP 4836; renewed May 7, 1962, R 295064; b&w; sound; 9 reels, 7,600 ft. Release: August 3, 1934, Roxy Theatre, NYC. Review in *New York Times*, August 4, 1934. Extant.

Production Staff: Producer Sol. M. Wurtzel; director: David Butler; cameraman: Arthur Miller; based on play *Merry Andrew*, by Lewis Beach; adapted: Kubec Glasmon; screenplay by William M. Conselman and Henry Johnson; music: Richard Whiting; lyrics: William M. Conselman; music director: Samuel Kaylin; sound engineer: F. C. Chapman; art director: Duncan Cramer; wardrobe: Royer.

Cast (Fox Hollywood Studio, Call Bureau Cast Service, May 21, 1934):

Will Rogers	Andrew Yates	Adrian Rosley	Armand Duval
Peggy Wood	Ernestine Yates	Conchita Montenegro	Fleurette
Mary Carlisle	Janice Yates	Helen Flint	Mrs. Beauregard
Robert Taylor	Lloyd Burmeister	Richard Tucker	Mr. Beauregard
Frank Melton	Howard Norcross	Al Logan	Williams
Roger Imhof	"Doc" Burmeister	Charles Teske	Dancer (double for
Paul Harvey	Charles Norcross		Mr. Rogers)
Grace Goodall	Mattie Norcross		
Jessie Pringle	Jennie		
Gregory Gaye	Pierre Martel		

Bits

Fred ("Snowflake")		Charles Gregg	Carpenter
Toone	Darky	Gertrude Weber	Bridge party guest
Bert Roach	Phil	Addison Richards	Golf professional
James Conlin	Henry	Patsy Lehigh	Double for Conchita
Ella McKenzie	Young mother		Montenegro
Gloria Roy }	Party guests	August Aguirre	Double for Will Rogers
Clara Fontaine }		Ann Doran	Double for Peggy Wood
Eddie Lee	Japanese cook		
William Wagner	Music teacher		

Synopsis: Andrew Yates is the owner of a small-town pharmacy, which is his joy in life. Involved in his work, he has never learned to play nor has he any hobbies. Ernestine, his wife, is socially very ambitious and she delights in giving musicales at her home, at which she sings.

To preserve domestic tranquillity, Andrew has learned over the years to give in to his wife's whims. Only rarely does he oppose her. When she insists that he sell the drugstore to a large chain, headed by the Norcross family, Andrew reluctantly agrees. But when Ernestine plans that their daughter Janice marry Howard, the dull heir to the Norcross fortune, Andrew speaks up for Lloyd Burmeister, the man Janice loves.

Having sold the drugstore, Andrew is at a loss how to occupy his time. He takes up raising pigeons, only to create chaos during one of his wife's soirees; he opens a drug counter in his own house, dispensing medication to the poor; and he even takes up golf—at Ernestine's urging—resulting in physical distortions and a barrage of uncomplimentary remarks on the game.

When Ernestine insists that they visit New Orleans for Mardi Gras, Andrew devises a plan. If his wife wants him to play, he will play so hard that she will beg him to stop. At the costume ball, Andrew appears dressed as Tarzan and performs what seems a mixture of Apache, carioca, and primitive jungle dances. His plan works and on the return trip home, the Yateses learn of their daughter's marriage to the man of her choice. And when the Norcross chain fails, Andrew buys back his old drugstore, and he is happy and busy once again.

With Mary Carlisle, in *Handy Andy,* 1934.

With Peggy Wood, in *Handy Andy*, 1934.

Frank Melton carefully keeps his distance, in *Handy Andy*, 1934.

Interview with Peggy Wood, September 10, 1970

S: Will Rogers appeared in London, in a Charles Cochran show.

PW: So was I, but not at the same time. He and Cochran were good friends.

S: The story goes that when Cochran offered him a signed, blank check, Mr. Rogers tore it up.

PW: That's quite like him! When Will Rogers and I appeared in the movie *Handy Andy*, we finished ahead of time, ahead of schedule, and that last day he stalled and stalled and stalled. In one scene he had to lie in bed, and he wouldn't get up. All because he wanted the crew to get their full accrued pay, if I may make a pun. Only when he was assured that the crew would get their full pay did he get off that bed. He was going to get them their full money—and he did.

S: Let's get back to the sound film you made with Mr. Rogers, *Handy Andy*.

PW: Neither Rogers nor I liked the film very much; I thought what I had to do was just plain silly, and he thought so too. We all went to the Mardi Gras in New Orleans and we dressed up in silly clothes.

JUDGE PRIEST

A Fox Production, Copyright September 28, 1934, LP 4979; b&w; sound; 9 reels, 7,400 ft.; running time, 79 minutes. Release: October 11, 1934, Radio City Music Hall, NYC. Review *New York Times*, October 12, 1934. Shooting scripts at AMPAS, USC. Extant.

Production Staff: Producer: Sol M. Wurtzel; director: John Ford; cameraman: George Schneiderman; based on character created in stories by Irvin S. Cobb; screenplay by Dudley Nichols and Lamar Trotti; music: Cyril J. Mockridge; lyrics: Dudley Nichols and Lamar Trotti; music director: Samuel Kaylin; recording engineer: Albert Protzman; art director: William Darling; wardrobe: Royer.

Cast (Fox Hollywood Studio, Call Bureau Cast Service, July 16, 1934):

Will Rogers	Judge William ("Billy") Priest	Henry B. Walthall	Rev. Ashby Brand
Tom Brown	Jerome Priest	Hatty McDaniels	Aunt Dilsey
Anita Louise	Ella May Gillespie	Hyman Meyer	Herman Felsberg
Brenda Fowler	Mrs. Caroline Priest	Louis Mason	Sheriff Birdsong
Stepin Fetchit	Jeff Poindexter	David Landau	Bob Gillis
Frank Melton	Flem Talley	Paul McAllister	Doc Lake
Rochelle Hudson	Virginia Maydew	Grace Goodall	Mrs. Maydew
Matt McHugh	Gabby Rives	Ernest Shields	Milan
Roger Imhof	Billy Gaynor	Vester Pegg	Herringer
Charley Grapewin	Sargeant Jimmy Bagby	Francis Ford	Juror #12
Berton Churchill	Senator Horace K. Maydew	Paul McVey	Trimble

Bits

Winter Hall	Judge Fairleigh	Harry Tenbrook	
Duke Lee	Deputy	Pat Hartigan	
Gladys Wells		Harry Wilson	Townsmen
Beulah Hall Jones		Frank Moran	in saloon
Melba Brown	Colored singers	Constantine Romanoff	
Thelma Brown		Margaret Mann	Governess
Vera Brown		George H. Reed	Colored servant
May Rousseau	Guitar player		

Synopsis: The year is 1890; the Civil War has been over for twenty-five years, but it is still very much alive in the Kentucky town where Judge Priest presides over the court. His position is coveted by State Senator Horace K. Maydew, who belligerently confronts him in open court.

But a new member of the Priest family appears; Jerome, fresh out of law school, is eager for his first paying client. He is also busy trying to escape his matchmaking mother, especially as he has his eyes on Ella May Gillespie, a maiden of unknown background. When Flem Talley makes some disparaging remarks about the girl's past, blacksmith Bob Gillis comes to her defense and beats Talley in a fight. Later, to take revenge, Talley and some friends ambush Gillis. In the struggle, Gillis stabs Talley. Charged, Bob Gillis now becomes Jerome's first client. On the stand Talley perjures himself, his friends corroborate the lies, and the case for Gillis seems lost. The trial has dragged on, until now it is the town's Confederate memorial celebration. Judge Priest, having had to disqualify himself from the case, now joins his nephew for the defense. Calling the Reverend Ashby Brand to the stand, the former Confederate officer tells how in the last days of the Confederacy he had to recruit prisoners from various jails to strengthen the ranks. One of those prisoners, Bob Gillis, then convicted to life imprisonment, performed with unequaled bravery. But because of his criminal record he had never revealed his past, nor indeed the fact that he is Ella May's father.

Touched by the heroic story, Gillis is acquitted and all now proceed to take part in the memorial parade.

Reviews:

★ "It seems pretty safe to recommend 'Judge Priest' to every moviegoer as grand, well-written, shrewdly acted comedy drama."

New York Sun, October 12, 1934

★ "Mr. Rogers outdoes himself in the characterization of the gentle, foxy old Judge, and we hope he'll stay Southern instead of Middle-West or New England. But for all his scintillance in this star-spangled part, he must take Henry B. Walthall with him for every bow."

New York American, October 12, 1934

★ "You will enjoy the weep of your life at 'Judge Priest.' It's great entertainment."

New York Daily Mirror, October 12, 1934

★ ". . . Rogers' best, a heart warming and genuinely moving story of a sleepy Southern town in the nineties."

New York Evening Journal, October 12, 1934

★ "Nothing could be much simpler than the story of 'Judge Priest.' . . . And by the same token nothing could be much more delightful and entertaining."

New York World-Telegram, October 12, 1934

★ "The photoplay which Fox has assembled around Dr. Will Rogers, the eminent newspaper columnist, presents the cowboy Nietzsche in one of the happiest roles of his screen career . . . and let it remind you that Will Rogers, although he bears the burdens of the nation on his shoulders, continues to be a remarkably heart-warming personality."

New York Times, October 12, 1934

Recognition: ★ # 12 on Honor Roll of Year's Best Films, voted on by 424 national film critics

---

With Henry B. Walthall, in *Judge Priest*, 1934.

Will with young Tom Brown and others (*from left*): Paul McAllister, Charley Grapewin, and Hyman Meyer, in *Judge Priest*, 1934.

Interview

During filming of Judge Priest, *Will Rogers also appeared in the leading role in the stage production of Eugene O'Neill's* Ah, Wilderness! *at the El Capitan Theatre, wrote a weekly and a daily syndicated newspaper column, delivered numerous radio braodcasts, as well as addressed innumerable banquets for senators, congressmen, statesmen, and film executives.*

Asked the old, familiar question, "Do you get more sat- *isfaction out of your screen or stage work?" Rogers answered: "The greatest personal satisfaction I ever got was from my 'concerts.' That was the hardest work, but it was the most gratifying. Then you are on the stage with no one to help you. The first season I used a quartet. But the second season I was alone. People said you couldn't hold an audience for two hours alone, with no material but your own. That was much more gratifying than playing in a picture—personally gratifying, I mean."*

A History Lesson

We been working for the last three or four weeks on a movie, written by Irvin Cobb. It's one (or a dozen rather), for while we bought one, Cobb says he recognizes parts of about twenty of his stories in it. You know those wonderful stories are really what made him so widely known.

He is the most interesting man I have heard in many a day. He does know his Civil War history. There was an old-time picture on the walls of my home (in the movie) and it was of Robert E. Lee and all his generals, and I would ask Cobb about any one of 'em and off he would go, just rattling off the exploits of each one.

If I ever get any time to read a book, I am going to get me one about some of these boys. My daddy

147

fought with Stand Watie in the Confederacy, but you couldn't get much war news out of Papa. If Irvin hangs around us all doing this picture of his we are making, I will be a pretty fair educated guy.

This old boy Ford is no cluck on history, either, you get a lot from him; but his stories are mostly about Irish wars. He can lick the English for you as entertainingly as Cobb can the Yankees. Funny part—Ford is a Yankee from Maine.

Syndicated column, June 24, 1934

Another Judge Priest

Tuesday afternoon

To Henry Ginsburg, Esq.

I just had Sheehan on the wire—and he's agin the notion!

He doesn't profess to have any legal claim on the character of Judge Priest, in fact agrees that the character is mine, but he raises the point that in all probability he shall want to make another picture with Rogers playing the part of the old Judge before long—indeed he says he'd like to do at least two more features within the next year or so, using the same part and so he asks as a favor to him, that we forgo for the time being any thought of my undertaking to play Judge Priest in short comedies. He can't object of course to my playing a judge modelled on the same lines, but ethically he maintains that he should have a monopoly in the name itself, at least until the present picture has been marketed to the customary limits.

In view of his attitude, which I suppose from his point of view is not too selfish, I'd advise you to notify Hal [Roach] that for the present I feel we should lay off even the tentative and sketchy suggestion that I might try to play "Judge Priest" for Roach. I'll play him, all right, if we go ahead, but I think we'd have to call him Judge Brown, or Squire Jones, or what-have-you?

I'm trying to be fair to my connection with the Roach interests and also to my ancient friendship and warm affection for Winnie Sheehan when I take this position. I'm sure you'll understand and that Hal Roach will also.

With regards, yours Faithfully,

Irvin S. Cobb

Irvin S. Cobb on the Set

I came out here to try this crazy, fascinating, maddening picture game and to watch the filming of the screenplay *Judge Priest*, as based on certain stories of mine, and when I saw the script of the adaptations I said to myself: "Well, Will is a great person, but after all he's only human, and, after all, among a dozen other things which he does superlatively well, he is in the acting business, which is a jealous business and a tricky trade. The way this piece is written, another actor gets practically all of the final scene, which is the big scene of the whole play. Surely Will will find a plan of shoving that other poor chap, whoever he is, into the shadows and steal the climax for himself, or else he'll just stand on his rights and demand that the final situation, the final lines, be switched over to him."

What happened? If you remember *Judge Priest*, you know what happened. That splendid veteran artist, Henry Walthall, carried off the last sequence with Will standing in the sidelines throwing him the cues and practically effacing himself in order to give Walthall a better opportunity to hold the center of the stage. And another result was that Walthall, who of recent years rather had faded out of prominence, was given a fat contract by somebody on the strength of his performance in *Judge Priest*.

Will Rogers Said

Well, all I know is just what I run into out in front of a movie camera. I been making a lot of faces here lately; I have used up all my expressions two or three times. You know, us actors just got certain little grimaces that we make for hate, fear, merriment, and exaltation. Scorn is one of our good ones. We can just wipe you out with a look that we label "scorn."

About the same situations come up in every picture, so it's really just like a politician's speech. If he is asked any questions from the audience, they are generally the same ones in every town, and he has the same answers—and that's the way we are. An actor is a fellow that just has a little more monkey in him than the fellow that can't act.

The old monkey has learned just about what to do under most circumstances that come up, and we got about the same looks we had when the pictures were silent, only now with the look, we got noises that go with it. You can't swear as much as you could in the old days—that is, out loud. In the old days these folks that can read your lips used to get more out of the movies than most people.

Everybody seems to be making a lot of pictures nowadays, course, not near enough to give all the folks work that deserves work. There is some awful good actors that are out of work. You know some of the smallest of parts, or bits, that you see so well done in pictures nowadays, might be some actor doing it, that if you looked up his record you would find that he was perhaps a star one time, or that he or she had played leads in some big pictures or stage plays.

They never whine, never alibi. If you don't happen to have known them in better days, you would never know a thing about it. I defy the world to show more spunk than you will find among actors that things are not breaking so well with.

I have yet to ever hear a knock. They just sit day after day and watch inferior actors like a lot of us, who have just been lucky. They watch us with never a shake of the head that might show that they could do that very same better than we are doing it.

Jack Ford is one of Hollywood's best directors, and

Marching while the band plays "Dixie" (*from left*): Paul McAllister, Will, Charley Grapewin, Henry B. Walthall, and Hyman Meyer, in *Judge Priest*, 1934.

one of the likable things about Jack is that he remembers. Jack used to direct westerns, and made some great ones with Harry Carey, the most human and natural of the western actors. Well, the other day on a big set, a jury and court room trial, Jack had all his old cowpuncher pals, I had known most of them for many years, too, and it sure was good to see 'em again.

Ah, there is a story in almost any person sitting on a movie set. There may be many a broken heart, but I have yet to see one of 'em show it.

Syndicated column, July 1, 1934

We are all sitting out here on the set, taking the parade in an old Confederate Reunion convention. I am sitting here on the running board of a car with the typewriter on my knee, trying to knock out a few "Personals." I have on the old Confederate Gray (the long gray coat). It's Irvin Cobb's story of *Judge Priest*. The parade is in a little small town of Kentucky, and it's wonderful to see all the old costumes on all the men and women and even the children. Folks often ask, "Where do you get the old clothes?"

Well, costuming is one of the biggest businesses out here. There is just one company that has a great building of their own, six or eight stories high, that

THE WHITE HOUSE
WASHINGTON

October 8, 1934.

Personal

Dear Will:

We saw "Judge Priest" last night. It is a thoroughly good job and the Civil War pictures are very true to life as I remember the battles of that period!

Also, I am very glad to see that you took my advice in regard to your leading lady---this time you have one who is good to look at and can also act.

I suppose the next thing you will be doing is making application for an appointment on the Federal Bench. I might take you up on that!

Always sincerely,

Franklin D. Roosevelt

Will Rogers, Esq.,
Beverly Hills,
California.

A comment from the White House to "Judge" Rogers.

covers half a block. You can get any suit (or hundreds of 'em) of any time period in the world. You can say I want five hundred Confederate Grays, and five hundred G.A.R.s, old period clothes for five hundred people along the street.

Then there is all the "Mother Hubbards" and old calicos for all the colored women folks and kids. Then the fife and drum corps, then the old-fashioned "buggy" and "surreys" and "hacks" and all the horses and harnesses. Then the little reviewing stand which is about the only thing that hasn't changed much. There is always just about the same amount of queer looking people in it with high hats on, looking down on the "riff raff" marching. Then the dogs, all breeds and all descriptions that would be in a parade. Well, that's another big industry. There is several men out here with as many as fifty different breeds of trained dogs to "act" better than most of us actors. Just today I see some hogs along the old wooden sidewalk. You rent them, any color and breed. They ain't trained much, only just to root and grunt and look like a hog.

There's the old Southern Court House with its big pillars, fronting out on the park, or square, with the Confederate Monument in it, and the cannon and cannon balls piled in each corner of the park. Now all this has been put there, not a speck of it is real. It's all been made just for the picture. The trees, great big ones, have been transplanted. Yet when this picture is finished and gone, this same spot may be the Bowery in New York, or the whole acres of this space may be taken up with an iceberg, or an ocean with a liner on it.

Yesterday I worked at a beautiful graveyard scene, willow trees, old untrimmed rambling rose bushes, tall uncut grass, all upon a little raised mound. And where do you think it was? All "made" on the inside of one of the great stages. And it was something that you couldn't imagine not being real when you looked at it.

These scenic artists are marvels. They and the photography are the principal advancements that this business has shown. Acting is just as bad, and so is the stories. But the mechanics have improved.

Now I have to get up and run over and march again, for we will have to take this parade scene a dozen times, and a dozen different ways, or angles. But there is something about marching to "Dixie" that you never get tired. And what wonderful characters some of these extras are, sitting around here in their uniforms. I am the least real looking one in the whole mob. Little Henry Walthall, that great actor, looks every inch the ex-chaplain. Many an ex-cowboy is marching in these uniforms and some others that are not in the scenes that brought the horses over. We lay around under the shade here when not "shooting" and talk old-time vaudeville with some of 'em, or I might roll over under the shade of the next tree and talk calf roping to some boys that made Cheyenne or Pendleton, away back when they were wild. There goes that fife and drum corps with "Dixie," you just got to get up and march even if there wasn't any camera. Picture making is a nutty business, but it's fascinating. There is Jack Ford, our genial, kidding but terribly competent director, yelling: "See if you can get Rogers on the set!"

The band is playing "Dixie."

Syndicated column, July 8, 1934

A Critic Writes

We turned out a little movie here a short time ago, and from reports it seemed to be pretty good, that is for mine. Well, just as I was sorter grinning a satisfied grin, why, I get this:

It's from a lady who signs herself ———, daughter of a Southerner, from St. Petersburg, Florida.

When one who is all Southern goes to the theater to see you play in a supposedly Southern play, a story depicting the Old South, and comes out of that theater resolved never to see you play again, what is wrong? *Judge Priest* is far, very far, from being a true picture of the South of that period that it depicts (or any other period). Our feelings are hurt. That you should be so misled as to think you were interpreting a Southern jurist.

If Mr. Irvin Cobb wrote that story as it was presented, then Mr. Cobb is not a true Southerner. The Negroes kept, and still do, their places as servants, respectful and obedient, never appearing in public except in caps and aprons (in other words, uniforms); the women with clean dresses, caps and aprons, the men wearing a white coat, all the time keeping a respectful silence. The South of that day was known for its culture, and I know not in history of a Southern jurist manifesting so great ignorance as Judge Priest manifested.

You played the part excellently but you did not understand the South and only Southern men and Southern women should play the parts portraying life in the "Old South" as they only understand the South. Judge Priest's sister-in-law was also a travesty, a woman who held the social position of the sister-in-law of Judge Priest was usually a gentle, refined woman of understanding. Even though she were haughty, she would always be gentle. It's a pity those who do not know anything about the "Old South" should assign you to a part that is destined to ruin you with the Southern people.

Should you live in the South among real genuine Southern people, you would agree with me, I know. There are many in the South who will continue to enjoy you in the pictures, who will understand that you have been misled as to the South. But something should be done to redeem that false picture of the South. I should suggest that the play be presented again—with a cast of all Southerners, then there would be a different interpretation.

We like you, Mr. Rogers, but we think you have the wrong opinion of us. Sincerely yours, ———, daughter of a Southerner, St. Petersburg, Fla.

Now there is lots of ways to treat that. I could start in by kidding about it. But it's a lovely letter, it's printed word for word for word, with the deletion of one or two rather flattering personal allusions to me. And the letter deserves, I think, an answer in the same spirit as meant. I myself would like to see it played by real Southerners. I was raised in the Indian Territory (my father fought with the famous Stand Watie Regiment for the Confederacy), and if this lady will look at her map, she will notice that Oklahoma, which was the Indian Territory, lays south of the Mason and Dixon line. So I am not the daughter of a Southerner, but I am the son of one, and I am like her, if it's to be done over again, it should be written by a man further south than Paducah, Kentucky.

There is just one little hitch about doing it all with Southerners as she suggests. You couldn't have any villains, or mean parts, for they would have to be Northerners, for no true Southerners would ever be mean, or a villain, so you would have to bring in a couple of Yankees for those. I tried to get old Stepin Fetchit to not speak in public, but we figured he wouldn't be understood anyhow, so we just let it go ahead, and that, I know, was a breach of the old Southern etiquette.

Now there is only one thing in the whole letter that I think the criticism was not justified, and that was about my sister-in-law. She said that all the Southern women would always be "gentle." Now right there, as much as I hate to enter into any controversy with someone I know is a lovely lady, but that "continually" being gentle stuff among all the women?

Now here is another way I got mixed up with the South in addition to both my parents being born and raised there, and me too. I married one of 'em. Now I wouldn't be gallant, and I wouldn't be just, and I wouldn't be a Southern gentleman if I didn't pay my wife a lovely, a deserved compliment, but I have seen her when she could have been "gentler," and then, compared to some other Southern women I have known, my wife is plum "gentle."

Women, even Southern women, are a good deal like horses, they are gentle as long as you handle one gentle. But you start roughing 'em up!

But a good dose of legitimate criticism does us

The master roper. (*The National Archives*)

good, and I want to thank this lovely lady and I will see that she gets the sister-in-law part in all Southern productions.

Syndicated column, November 11, 1934

POSTSCRIPT: Oh, yes, here is some Daughters of the Confederacy that want to make Irvin Cobb and I a couple of Honorary Daughters.

Syndicated column, November 18, 1934

Interview with John Ford, January 17, 1972

JF: He was just a small-town Oklahoma boy. That's all he talked about—well, among other things; he talked all the time, but he always brought up the topic of Claremore and Ponca City.

S: The character of Judge Priest fitted right in with that background. Was that shot on location?

JF: No, we did it right in the studio.

S: In those days, how long would it take to make a picture?

JF: On the largest pictures it would take four to five weeks. And they weren't expensive pictures at all, but they all did very well. In fact, my favorite picture of all time is *Judge Priest*.

S: Will Rogers didn't stick to the written dialogue, did he?

JF: Oh, no! Never! Nobody could write for Will. He'd read his script and say, "What does that mean?" And I'd say, "Well, that's rather a tough question. I don't know what it means exactly." Then we would finally figure out what it meant and I'd say to him, "Say it in your own words!" And he'd go away, muttering to himself, getting his lines ready, and when he came back, he'd make his speech in typical Rogers fashion, which was better than any writer could write for him. Because no writer could write for Will.

S: I understand that Mr. Rogers wouldn't even read the script or prepare himself, but would come on the set and ask you, "What's this next scene all about?"

JF: Yes. We talked it over, and he'd ask, "Do I have any lines?" and I'd say, "I'm afraid so." And he'd say, "Well, let me look at them." And I'd say, "Go out, read 'em your own way, change 'em, take a pencil, write something. This is hogwash! It's from an

151

Oxford graduate. Go on, write it your own way!" And what he came up with was so much better than what was written in the script. But I don't think he ever read a script at home. I had only one request of him. Once I said, "Look, I'm a late sleeper. I have to get up and stand in the shower bath for ten minutes, a cold shower. Then I have a cup of coffee, and dash down here, and I'm always a little late. But I'm down here at eight-thirty." Will said, "I'm an early riser.

You know my cowboy training." So I told him, "Well, will you hang out in your dressing room until I get on the set? You're making a bum out of me!" But he didn't. He wanted to visit with the grips and the cameraman and the rest of the cast, and whiz around and chat and talk, making jokes. I'd sneak on the set and he'd spot me, "Ah, there he is! The late sleeper!"

Interview with Tom Brown, January 4, 1971

S: In *Judge Priest* you had a nice job; you had Rochelle Hudson chase after you, and you ended up with Anita Louise.

TB: I think that's true. Anita, actually, is an old, old friend of mine. We went to school together in New York. We modeled for—I think it was Alcoa, or some motorboats—Anita was six and I was eight. And then we went to professional school together in New York. But I used to know the whole Rogers family. I knew both the boys and Mary. We had mutual friends; the Stones were very good friends—Fred and Dorothy, and Paula and Carla. I knew them in Forest Hills. I used to play tennis over there. You see, I come from New York; I was on the stage before I came out here.

S: You must have started as a very young child.

TB: I started in my mother and dad's vaudeville act when I was eighteen months old. I'll be fifty-six in two days, and I'll be fifty-four and a half years in show business. When I came out here I was so young—I was seventeen. I lied about my age because I didn't want to have a welfare worker on the set. You see, this law had just gone into effect at that time. Here I was doing young leading men's roles—love scenes and everything—and I just couldn't take it to make these love scenes and have a welfare worker sitting on the set because I was a minor, so I said I was nineteen!

S: There was quite an age difference between you and Will Rogers.

TB: I used to call him "Uncle Bill." To me he was

very special. He was always so busy, but he would talk to almost anybody, but he just didn't have the time to sit down and chat aimlessly. I remember he was going to do tours for some charity—was it polio? I don't recall, but he was constantly, constantly doing something, and yet I never saw the man fatigued. Oh, occasionally he would blow a line, then he'd kinder grin and go off to one side, and then come back again. I just think the whole thing amused him; I think all life amused him. Oh, I think he realized the seriousness of it, but there was always that twinkle; you felt it every time you met him. There was no heavy-handed quality to Bill at all.

S: It's said that Will Rogers would not stick to the script very much, that he would ad-lib as he went along.

TB: He had a way of expressing things in his own words. John Ford, who directed *Judge Priest*, as you know, is a very forceful man, a very forceful director, but he never questioned Bill on anything that he said. But Bill stuck to the main plot. He didn't confuse anybody, he just had his own way—and his timing was magnificent. Now you know, an awful lot of actors in those days tightened up the minute the cameras started going, but Bill was exactly the same in rehearsals as he was on the film. He never wore makeup and I don't remember ever seeing them comb his hair or doing anything to him. He'd walk on the set and he'd walk off the set; it was as though he wasn't even at work—he was the same. Even though *Judge Priest* was a costume piece, I wasn't even aware that these weren't his clothes—he was that natural.

THE COUNTY CHAIRMAN

A Fox Production,   Copyright January 11, 1935, LP 5266; renewed December 7, 1962, R 306385; b&w; sound; 9 reels, 6,950 ft. Preview: December 17, 1934; release: January 18, 1935, NYC. Reviewed in NYC, January 19, 1935; reviewed in Los Angeles, February 2, 1935; reviewed in Chicago, February 16, 1935. Assigned to National Telefilm Association, March 19, 1975. Extant. Location shots: Sonora, and Mojave Desert, Calif.

Production Staff: Producer: Edward W. Butcher; director: John G. Blystone; cameraman: Hal Mohr; based on play by George Ade (opened in NYC, 1903); screenplay by Sam Hellman and Gladys Lehman; contributor: Walter Woods; music director: Arthur Lange; recording engineer: W. D. Flick; art director: William Darling; wardrobe: William Lambert.

Cast   (Fox Movietone Studio, Call Bureau Cast Service, November 30, 1934):

Will Rogers	Jim Hackler	Erville Alderson	Wilson Prewitt
Kent Taylor	Ben Harvey	William V. Mong	Uncle Eck
Evelyn Venable	Lucy Rigby	Mickey Rooney	Freckles
Berton Churchill	Elias Rigby	Robert McWade	Tom Cruden
Louise Dresser	Mrs. Mary Rigby	Gay Seabrook	Lorna Cruden
Stepin Fetchit	Sassafras Livingstone	Russell Simpson	Vance Jimmison
Frank Melton	Henry ("Hy") Cleaver	Alfred James	Ezra Gibbon
Jan Duggan	Abigail Tewksbury		
Charles B. Middleton	Riley Cleaver		

Bits

Francis Ford	Cattle rancher	Harry Dunkinson ⎱	
Harlan Knight	Sheepherder	Walter Downing ⎰	Bits
Carl Stockdale ⎱		Eleanor Wesselhaeft	Squatter's wife
Sam Flint ⎬	Delegates	Carmencita Johnson ⎱	
Frank Austin ⎰		Frank Hammond ⎬	Bits
Paul Kruger	Bridegroom delegate	Lorraine Rivero ⎰	
Anders Van Haden	Bit man in bowling alley		
Ernie Shields	Bit		
William Burress	Doolittle		
Lew Kelly	Station agent		

Synopsis: Lawyer Jim Hackler, his party's chairman of Tomahawk County, Wyoming, is masterminding the campaign of his young law partner Ben Harvey. Ben is running for the post of county prosecutor against the leading crooked politican, Elias Rigby. Not only is this a political battle for Jim Hackler, but he has an old score to settle also, for some twenty years earlier, this same Elias Rigby stole Jim's girl, Mary, and made her his wife. There is one further complication: Jim's protégé, Ben Harvey, and his political opponent's daughter, Lucy, are sweethearts.

While Ben is a political neophyte, Jim is an old pro. Teaching Ben the basics of political life, Jim informs him that there are but two things important in political life: promises and personality. "You have the personality," he points out, "and I'll equip you with a full set of promises." Jim also alerts Ben to always remember in his campaign speeches to denounce the Turks for massacring the Armenians.

"What's that got to do with anything?" Ben wants to know.

"Why, that's good politics," explains the older man. "You see, Rigby may not mention it, and that puts him in the position of favoring the massacre!"

In the end, Jim Hackler digs up incriminating evidence against Rigby, but realizing that innocent people would also be hurt, he suppresses it. Even without it, Ben wins the election and the girl.

Reviews: ★ " 'The County Chairman' affords Mr. Rogers an opportunity to give his views on politics in general and in particular on how they should be practiced in Wyoming, as well as numerous chances to comment on world affairs and the progress of science, especially as it concerns the development of a new-fangled contraption called the automobile.

"As you must know by now, Mr. Rogers is superfine at it."

New York World-Telegram, January 19, 1935

★ "Will Rogers is having a grand time—and his audience with him. . . . As Jim Hackler, party chairman of Tomahawk County, Wyo., where the political hatchet is never buried, Mr. Rogers has abundant opportunity to indulge in the shrewd, homespun comments that have made his reputation. It is fairly safe to assume that many of his lines are not to be found in the play or in the additional dialogue contributed by its screen adapters, but stem from Mr. Rogers' private stock, based on what he 'reads in the papers.' "

New York Times, January 19, 1935, 8:1/2

Recognition: ★ #33 on Honor Roll of Best Movies of 1935, as voted on by 451 national film critics

Will Rogers Said

Well, all I know is just what I read in the papers or what I see since I got back to "Cuckooland." Well, it seems mighty good to be back and getting to work in the old movies again. We started off as soon as I got home, making George Ade's famous old story, *The County Chairman*, only we are laying the action of the story instead of Indiana, why, we are putting it in the West, as we wanted to get some western and ranch atmosphere, so we all bundled off up to Sonora, California, on what we call "location."

Syndicated column, November 4, 1934

With Mickey Rooney, in *The County Chairman*, 1935.

With Berton Churchill, Kent Taylor, and Evelyn Venable, in *The County Chairman*, 1935.

WILL ROGERS ON FAME

There ain't any unemployed in this country—what the so-called idle are doing is getting autographs, and say, they are working twenty-four hours a day. Fellow comes up and says: "I see all your pictures," and I ask him which ones, and he can't name a one.

Woman brings a little five-year-old girl up and says: "Tillie wants to meet you, she reads all your little articles in the papers and enjoys 'em." Tillie says: "Who is he, Ma?"

★

Well you actors and politicians can have all the race-horses and cigars named after you, but I got some clippings from down in South Carolina, that was mighty gratifying to me.

Will Rogers, an old pot hound, was voted the best hunting dog in the state, and he took another prize for the finest-looking dog. So my regards to the champion of South Carolina.

★

A movie actor is no better than his double.

154

LIFE BEGINS AT FORTY

A Fox Production, Copyright March 1, 1935, LP 5449; renewed December 7, 1962, R 306396; b&w; sound; 8 reels, 7,325 ft. Shooting began December 10, 1934. Preview: February 1, 1935; release: April 4, 1935, Radio City Music Hall, NYC. Review in *New York Times*, April 5, 1935. Shooting scripts at AMPAS, UCLA, USC, Lincoln Library, NYC. Assigned to National Telefilm Association, March 19, 1975. Extant.

Production Staff: Producer: Sol M. Wurtzel; director: George Marshall; cameraman: Harry Jackson; based on book by Walter B. Pitkin; screenplay by Lamar Trotti; contributors: Dudley Nichols and William M. Conselman; with additional dialogue by Robert Quillen; music director: Samuel Kaylin; dances staged by Jack Donohue; editor: Alexander Troffey; recording engineer: Bernarr Freericks; art director: Duncan Cramer; assistant art director: Albert Hogsett; wardrobe: Lillian.

Cast (Fox Hollywood Studio, Call Bureau Cast Service, January 22, 1935):

Will Rogers	Kenesaw H. Clark	Slim Summerville	T. Watterson Meriwether
Rochelle Hudson	Adele Anderson	Claire Du Brey	Mrs. T. Watterson Meriwether
Richard Cromwell	Lee Austin	Sterling Holloway	Chris
Jane Darwell	Ida Harris	Roger Imhof	"Pappy" Smithers
George Barbier	Col. Joseph Abercrombie, Sr.	Jed Prouty	Charlie Beagle
Thomas Beck	Joseph Abercrombie, Jr.	Charles Sellon	Tom Cotton
John Bradford	Wally Stevens	Ruth Gillette	Mrs. Tom Cotton

Bits

John Ince	Storekeeper	Allan Sears ⎫	
T. Roy Barnes	Simonds, salesman	Carl Miller ⎬	Townsmen
James Donlan	Farmer	Bill Baxter ⎭	
Robert Kerr	Bank teller	Kathrin Clare Ward	Housewife
Frank Darien ⎫		Crete Sipple	Townswoman
William Burress ⎬	Abercrombie's friends	Guy Usher	Sheriff
Harry Dunkinson ⎭		Watson Children	Meriwether children
Gloria Roy	Bit girl	Creighton Hale	Drug clerk
Edward Le Saint ⎫		Robert Dalton	Steven's henchman
Jac Hoffman		Barbara Barondess	Abercrombie's maid
Rhody Hathaway		Edward McWade	Doctor
Ernest Shields		John Wallace	Peg-leg man
Robert McKenzie		Herbert Hayward ⎫	
Rodney Hildebrand ⎬		W. J. Kolberg ⎬	Rural characters
Jack Walters	Townsmen	Gordon Carveth ⎫	
J. B. Kenton		William Sundholm ⎬	Stunts
Larry Fisher		Floyd Criswell ⎭	
E. W. Borman		Billy Bletcher	Hog caller
John Webb Dillion		Len Trainer	Stand-in for Rogers
Jack Henderson		Emily Baldwin	Stand-in for Hudson
James Marcus ⎭			

Synopsis: Kenesaw H. Clark is the editor of a small-town newspaper, who also writes an advice column, entitled "Life Begins at Forty." All runs smoothly until Lee Austin returns to his hometown, having served his three-year sentence for a bank theft he claims he never committed.

Editor Clark offers the young man a job on the paper, only to be pressured by Col. Joseph Abercrombie, the town banker, to dismiss the "jailbird" immediately. When Clark, who believes in Lee's innocence, refuses to fire him, Banker Abercrombie forecloses on Clark's newspaper. Unperturbed, resourceful Editor Clark opens up a rival newspaper, operating an old hand press.

Though happily in love with Adele Anderson, for Lee Austin the future looks bleak until Clark decides to be a real newspaperman. First he opposes Banker Abercrombie in the upcoming election by running T. Watterson Meriwether—the laziest man in the county—against him. Then he begins to investigate the old theft, making inquiries and interviewing people, until he finds that the banker's own son, Joseph Abercrombie, Jr., was the real thief.

Reviews:　★ "Mr. Rogers again brings the American village into the heart of Manhattan by starring in the Music Hall attraction, 'Life Begins at 40.' Will Rogers is what New Yorkers like to believe the prototype of the American small-town philosopher. They give one a comfortable feeling, these Rogers comedies, about the solidity and innate common sense of this country. They bring, in addition to unusually dependable entertainment value, a note of good cheer.

"Will Rogers, although very much himself in each scene and each film, has a curious national quality. He gives the impression somehow that this country is filled with such sages, wise with years, young in humor and love of life, shrewd yet gentle. He is what Americans think other Americans are like."

New York Sun, April 5, 1935

★ "Just about the funniest film you've seen, and the top for Will Rogers, the new one at the Music Hall is a sure cure for Spring fever, or what have you. Mr. Rogers' shafts of humor are directed straight at the heart, or the funny-bone of America and American audiences."

New York American, April 5, 1935

★ ". . . the inspiration stopped after the studio purchased Dr. Pitkin's book for the screen. The film has its moments [but] this is only average Rogers though, with a pace which is too deliberate for comfort and a general lack of inspiration. The star himself is a thorough delight regardless of what he is doing."

New York Times, April 5, 1935

Recognition:　★ # 39 on Honor Roll of Best Films of 1935, voted on by 451 national film critics

Interview with Sterling Holloway, December 31, 1971

S:　Do you recall the film *Doubting Thomas?*
SH:　That was originally *The Torch Bearers.* The strange thing about the film was that there were most-ly stage actors, people who really knew what they were doing. Of course, Will Rogers was from the stage, too, but he was not an actor, as such. And this cast just acted all around him, and it seemed that he

On location to film *Life Begins at Forty*, Will, Richard Cromwell, Rochelle Hudson, and director George Marshall, 1935.

Hatching a plan with Sterling Holloway, in *Life Begins at Forty*, 1935.

was just there. But when the film was shown on the screen, none of the others meant anything. You couldn't take your eyes off Will Rogers. He was just such a great personality, and he was a great entertainer. It really amazed me, because you thought he was just shuffling through the part, that it really wasn't going to count—but it sure did. And how!

S: You also appeared with Will Rogers in *Life Begins at Forty*.

SH: I was doing a scene with him. I had to carry a chicken down the street; it was a crowded street, and the chicken was flapping its wings and kicking hard. Will Rogers looked at me and said, "You know, you're holding it the wrong way. You know, if you hold that chicken the right way, you won't have any trouble." So I asked him, "What is the right way?" And Will Rogers said innocently, "I haven't any idea."

S: Did Will Rogers know his lines when he came on the set?

SH: No, he didn't. He would say, "What's the sense of this scene here now?" And he would just get an idea of it.

S: Then actually the lines were his own?

SH: Mostly.

S: Wasn't this hard on the other actors?

SH: It wasn't for me. It fascinated me, and I loved it and I played right along with it, which is maybe the reason I was in a few of his films. And I can guarantee that whatever he did was better, because it was strictly Will Rogers, and that's what they wanted, and everybody loved it. It was always a happy set, and actors were always trying to get on a Will Rogers picture. It was, as they say, "no sweat." I remember he would come to me and say, "Now, in this scene I will say so-and-so, and when I do, you ask me 'why?'" He would just set up a special gag in a scene. So we played the scene, and he would say what he had arranged, and I'd be surprised and say "But why?" and he would have an excellent comeback ready for it. But he wouldn't rehearse them. He didn't like to give them away. He liked to please everybody—he was strictly a showman, an entertainer. He was an intuitive performer; he knew exactly what was right. No director really ever could tell him how to do something. He knew the "how" always.

WILL ROGERS TELLS ABOUT SOME FRIENDS

Some great columnists on days when they have no gossip, why they tell you things that "perhaps you didn't know before." Well, I never did do that, for I never was in any shape to tell you anything you didn't know. In other words, I always had to write up to my readers, and not down. But I am going to have a crack at that kind of thing.

Now for instance, just the other day Harold Lloyd was up to my little ranch, and he offered me a Great Dane dog. Now did you know that he raises the finest Great Danes there is, forty or fifty of 'em? I didn't take him, for those brutes eat more than I can earn.

Did you ever read such a procession of acclaim as Charlie Chaplin is getting all over Europe?

One night a few years ago I was asked to introduce him at the Lambs Club in New York—that's the most exclusive actor organization. It was his first trip to New York in a good while and he was having some unfavorable publicity at the time. Well, I told them that in all my little years on the stage and screen that I had only met one person that I could honestly call an "artist"; every other person I ever saw, someone else could do what he was doing just as good. But that Chaplin, he writes, directs, and acts the whole thing. Anyone else making a picture there is at least a dozen people that are directly concerned in its success—Chaplin replaces all of them alone.

Now Charlie is using his sons in his films and he says he is afraid his boys will grow up and find out they were actors once. Charlie, actors are like politicians: They never grow up.

I was down one night last week with Charlie Chaplin, listening to our friend Will Durant, the philosopher, debate on world economics. Charlie, as I said, has made a study of that. He is the greatest economist in the world. Every nation has lost its export trade, yet stop and think of it, Charlie manufactures the only article in the world that hasn't depreciated. He has never let the supply equal the demand. While all the world's big industrialists were greedy, Charlie never went in for mass production. Seems odd that a comedian can do what governments are not smart enough to do.

Irene Rich and her daughters drove in. We had finished a picture lately, Irene and I. She is one that don't try to always stay eighteen and claiming the daughters are "adopted." One finished Smith College a year ago, and Irene gets up and announces it to the world.

I gave one of my little lectures here in Beverly Hills and I certainly want to thank the neighboring village of Los Angeles for turning out in such paying quantities to see a mayor who is funny purposely, and not unconsciously. Sorry that my friends Tom Mix and Doug Fairbanks couldn't be with us, but they were both running pictures of themselves at their homes and couldn't leave.

I been gnawing my way through quite a few public gatherings, one of the most satisfying was one given for Marie Dressler. It was given by her studio, Metro-Goldwyn-Mayer, and it was just about the flashiest and highest class thing you ever saw. They do things right over there.

Well, I had to drag out the old blue serge suit, double-breasted that has fooled many a one, if you don't watch it too close, into thinking maybe it's about a quarter breed tuxedo.

It was on one of their great big stages and it was all decorated for the occasion. The bunting and the flags covered up the scars of some pretty bad pictures that I made there away back in 1919, '20 and '21. You see, I used to mess 'em up there in the silent days for Sam Goldwyn.

But never mind me, it's Marie that we all want to hear about. Now you folks, you think of her that she is your ideal actress, be it male or female. Well, what you think of her is just a preliminary of what we folks that are in the business with her think of her. Do you know that there is no person in the entire moving-picture business that has served the rigid and long apprenticeship of her craft that Marie Dressler has? There is noting in the whole repertoire of the line of entertainment that she has not been in, and served it with great distinction.

Did you know she has a really fine voice, sang in light opera? Did you know she plays beautiful on the piano, and has a great appreciation and knowledge of really classical music? That she has always been a great personal friend of all the noted musical people during her long career? Although she never went to school in her life, not even a day, she is one of the best informed, finest and brightest conversationalists you ever talked to.

Did you know that she weighs 210 pounds and that 190 of it is heart? She has made the world realize that there is character in a face. She has been a great incentive to us other hard-looking old battleaxes (I know Marie will forgive me for that). It was a great treat to all of us to be invited there.

Say, did you know that Hal Roach is one of our best aviation enthusiasts?

Frank Borzage, just about one of the greatest directors we have, has just taken up flying, and his instructor said it was uncanny the way he learned. He has his own plane now; also his wife learned to fly. Henry King, who directed *Lightnin'*, is an old-time flyer.

Now I was coming home last week from Oklahoma. I have made this trip by air one hundred times, but I never saw such mobs at the fields. Rudy Vallee was on our plane. I was just as excited as they were, and, say, he is a very modest, likable fellow. I was even flattered when the folks at Amarillo thought I was his father.

Then I was trying to snooze on this airplane and what keeps me awake but some big guy snoring. I look and if it's not Wally Beery. He had climbed on somewhere during a stop. He is a good pilot himself and generally flies his own plane. He wasn't so good looking at laying there snoring, but he is by far one of the most popular persons, man or woman, on the screen.

Pola Negri, the foreign movie queen, gave a party the other night. I read about it in the papers. I didn't get to go. Well, one thing, I wasn't invited. I jump around so much I guess she didn't know where to get ahold of me.

Mrs. Franklin D. Roosevelt just finished a transcontinental flight. Now there is a real boost for aviation. But here is what she really takes the medal for—out at every stop, day or night, standing for photographs by the hour, being interviewed, talking over the radio, no sleep. And yet, they say, she never showed any sign of weariness or annoyance of any kind. No maid, no secretary, just the First Lady of the Land on a paid ticket on a regular passenger plane.

If some of our female screen stars had made that trip, they would have had one plane for secretaries, one for maids, one for chefs and chauffeurs, and a trailer for "business representatives" and "press agents."

A press agent, you know, is not to see how much they can get in the papers about their clients, but how much they could prevent from getting in the papers.

Did you see where Bernard Shaw come to town a week or so ago and threw the biggest commotion in the film colony since Marlene Dietrich traded her chemise for breeches? That old Shaw baby just had answers to all the riddles.

"When will you have your plays filmed?"

"When the movies are able to handle them as they should be."

"Which is your best play?"

"They are all good. I don't write any other kind."

My daughter graduated yesterday at a girl's preparatory school. They read off what course each girl had taken. When they said: "Mary Rogers, diploma in English," I had to laugh at that. One of my children studying English. Why, it's just inherited. You don't have to study it in our family.

Doug Fairbanks had a niece graduating, Wallace Beery had a relation, Frank Lloyd, the great director, had a daughter there, and all four of us just sat there and purred like four old tomcats basking in a little

From left: Hal Roach, Theda Bara, Will, and Charley Chase, who directed Will and others, under the pseudonym Charles Parrott, December 10, 1933.

From left: Will, Jr., Will, Billie Burke, Wiley Post, Fred Stone.

With Madeleine Carroll—not yet the great star—on studio lot. Official caption identified Miss Carroll as "new Fox Film featured player." (*The Penguin Collection*)

With Hal Roach (*left*) and Harold Lloyd.

With Tom Mix at Los Angeles Christmas Benefit, December 16, 1932.

Visiting the Children's Hospital, Boston, with newly married Babe Ruth and bride, May 25, 1929.

reflected sunshine and secretly congratulated ourselves on choosing a profession where education played no part.

Among the prominent movie visitors was Sessue Hayakawa, the Japanese screen star and his cunning little wife. After introducing them to the audience, I said that they were a movie couple who were still married to each other, which might not mean so much in their country, as perhaps it was native custom to stay married in Japan, but that in this country, it was a novelty.

I see by the Paris papers that Harry and Evelyn Nesbitt Thaw are going back together again. Well, everybody wishes them lots of happiness. That brings up a mighty good idea. Let everybody go back and start in with the original. In nine cases out of ten it will be found they were the best after all. Can you imagine the scramble in Hollywood, trying to locate the original?

Say, have you ever been to a world's championship wrestling match? Us movie actors are advised to go there by our producers, so we learn how to act. It was a fine show, everybody enjoyed it, but wrestling management are overlooking an extra big revenue, for folks would pay even more to see them rehearse with each other before the match.

Well, that's all I know.

DOUBTING THOMAS

A Fox Production,   Copyright June 7, 1935, LP 5596; renewed March 18, 1963, R 312489; b&w; sound; 8 reels, 6,500 ft. Release: July 10, 1935, Rivoli Theatre, NYC. Review in *New York Times*, July 11, 1935. Extant.

Production Staff: Producer: B. G. DeSylva; director: David Butler; cameraman: Joseph Valentine; from the play *The Torch Bearers,* by George Kelly; adapted by Bartlett Cormack; screenplay by William M. Conselman; music director: Arthur Lange; recording engineer: Joseph E. Aiken; art director: Jack Otterson; wardrobe: René Hubert.

Cast   (Fox Movietone Studio, Call Bureau Cast Service, March 20, 1935):

Will Rogers	Thomas Brown	Helen Flint	Nellie Fell
Billie Burke	Paula Brown	Johnny Arthur	Ralph Twiller
Alison Skipworth	Mrs. Pampinelli	Fred Wallace	Teddy Spearing
Sterling Holloway	Spindler	Gail Patrick	Florence McCrickett
Frank Albertson	Jimmy Brown	Ruth Warren	Jennie, the maid
Frances Grant	Peggy Burns	John M. Qualen	Von Blitzen
T. Roy Barnes	LaMaze, the director	William Benedict	Caddy
Andrew Tombes	Hossefrosse		

Bits

George Cooper	Stage manager	Ray Cook	Bit cameraman
Helen Freeman	Mrs. Sheppard	Kay Thiel	Beauty operator

Synopsis: Thomas Brown is the manufacturer of Brown's Breakfast Sausages. Years ago his fluttering wife, Paula, had toyed with the idea of becoming an actress. A determined Thomas had—so he thought all these years—dispelled that notion for ever. Now young Jimmy, heir to the Brown Breakfast Sausage fortune, has a girl friend, Peggy Burns, who has just been approached by a swindler, LaMaze, a supposed Hollywood director. Peggy is told that she is precisely the type Hollywood is looking for, and that all she really needs is a screen test. LaMaze is willing to make the test; all Peggy would have to pay is seventy-five dollars for the film.

When Jimmy recounts this to his father, the elder Brown advises his son to squash the idea at once.

Returning from a business trip, Thomas Brown finds that the local pretentious "drama teacher," Mrs.

Pampinelli, has persuaded Paula to join the town's amateur theatrical group. Further, the Browns' home has now become the group's rehearsal studio. Dreaming of stardom, the members of the group, too, have been persuaded to take screen tests—at seventy-five dollars each.

As Thomas had suspected, the amateur group's one and only performance at the country club is a disaster—obvious to all but the participants.

Thomas now hires a touring actor to pretend that he is the famous Hollywood director Von Blitzen, who wants to see all the screen tests, including Thomas Brown's. As arranged, Von Blitzen tells the stage-struck group that they are rank amateurs and offers the "surprised" Brown a contract to come to Hollywood.

Preparing to leave his business, family, and home in pursuit of fame, Thomas is implored by his wife to change his plans. He finally "makes the great sacrifice of giving up his career," having made the point.

Reviews:

★ "Rogers enters into his task with considerable gusto, and the result is some fairly funny slapstick in a moderately amusing and considerably outdated comedy.

"Mr. Rogers is about as usual, but his picture is not nearly up to the standard of his 'Judge Priest,' or 'Life Begins at 40.' "

New York Herald Tribune, July 11, 1935

★ "Retention of the Grace Moore-Columbia hit 'Love Me Forever' . . . at Radio City Music Hall, gives the Rivoli Theatre this excellent entertainment which certainly may be included among the best of Will Rogers' fun films."

New York American, July 11, 1935

★ "Mr. Rogers is too good a humorist and too valuable as a homespun philosopher to be hidden under this type of story."

New York Times, July 11, 1935

★ "It has aged not at all since it delighted Broadway theatre audiences. It has life, sparkle, wit and lusty slapstick clowning. Especially, it now has Will Rogers, who contributes to it one of his finest comedy performances."

New York Mirror, July 11, 1935

Will Pays for Peace

"Will Rogers may be rated a millionaire, but he's still an Oklahoma cowhand at heart.

"When he reported for work in *Doubting Thomas*, he discovered that his Fox bosses had engaged a valet for him.

"The unfastidious Will put up with the constant whisk-brooming and tie straightening throughout the first day with only passive resistance, but on the following morning the servant was conspicuous by his absence.

"Investigation revealed that Will was paying the fellow five extra dollars a day to make himself scarce."

Hollywood, May 1935

With Billie Burke (*seated*) and Alison Skipworth, in *Doubting Thomas*, 1935.

With "wife" Billie Burke, and "son" Frank Albertson, in *Doubting Thomas*, 1935.

Will Rogers Said

I'm back out here in old Orangejuice Land again, toiling to try and hand a fraction of the folks a laugh on the screen. When your beauty has deserted you, when you are getting old, you have to resort to pure skill or trickery. I kinder take up the trickery.

Now in the old days, just looks alone got me by. The Lord was good to me in the matter of handing out a sort of a half-breed Adonis profile (well, it was a little more than a profile that you had to get). Straight on I didn't look so good, and even sideways I wasn't too terrific, but a cross between a back and a three-quarter view, why, brothers, I was hot. The way my ear (on one side) stood out from my head was just bordering on perfect. In those old, silent-day pictures that back right ear was a byword from coast to coast. You see, all screen stars have what they call their better angles. These women have just certain cameramen to shoot them; they know which way to turn 'em and how to throw the light on 'em.

Well, they don't pay much attention to lighting with me. The more lights go out during the scene, the better. So we toil and we struggle to maintain what is left of our beauty and manliness. I doubt if women have got much on men when it comes to trying to outlook themselves.

But I got to get back to the movies and tell you what we are all doing out here. I am working on a picture they say they are going to call *Doubting Thomas*. Well, I don't know why. There is not much that I doubt either in the picture or out. I am a mighty trusting fellow and believe most everything. It's from a very successful play a few years back called *The Torch Bearers*. It was very clever, and we got us a fine cast, a lot of old friends among 'em. Mrs. Flo Ziegfeld (Billie Burke) is playing my wife. She has duplicated her stage hit in the movies.

I can remember her (Miss Burke) when she was first married to my boss, Mr. Ziegfeld. At least they hadn't been married long when I started on the Midnight Frolic Roof. How proud of her he was. They and the Barrymores, and the John Drews and parties used to come up on the roof and sit at a ringside table. Gosh, what a place that was, the first midnight show, and the greatest and most expensive.

But I am getting old and rambling, I guess. Andrew Tombes, who used to be with us in the famous 1922 *Follies* that ran two years in New York. He and I sang and burlesqued the famous Gallagher and Shean song. He was afterward with me with Dorothy Stone's show, and he is the one that sang the full-dress-suit song, only we were barefooted. (A nut idea that went over.) Well, Andy is with us in this. He is the most versatile performer in musical comedy and will be just as big on the screen.

Lord bless her, Miss Alison Skipworth, the grand old performer, she is playing her original role from the stage in this play, and Helen Flint, that was the bad girl in the saloon scene in our coast stage show of *Ah, Wilderness!*, a fine trooper. Sterling Holloway, a great comedian, oh, we got a lot of 'em. It's like a real old stage reunion.

Well, I got to close, so it's just pure strategy that keeps me in there fighting now.

STEAMBOAT ROUND THE BEND

A Twentieth Century-Fox Production, Copyright September 6, 1935, LP 5971; renewed August 21, 1963, R 320836; b&w; sound; 9 reels, 7,350 ft. Release: September 19, 1935, Radio City Music Hall, NYC. Review in Chicago, August 24, 1935; in New York City, *New York Times*, September 20, 1935, 17:2. First preview: July 22, 1935. Shooting scripts at AMPAS, UCLA, AFI. Working title: *Steamboat Bill*. Extant. Location shots: Sacramento and Stockton, California.

Production Staff: Producer: Winfield R. Sheehan; supervisor: Sol M. Wurtzel; director: John Ford; assistant director: Edward O'Fearna; cameraman: George Schneiderman; based on novel *Steamboat Round the Bend*, by Ben Lucien Burman (c. 1933); screenplay by Dudley Nichols and Lamar Trotti; music director: Samuel Kaylin; editor: Alfredo De Gaetano; recording engineer: Albert Protzman; art directors: William Darling, Albert Hogsett.

Cast (Fox Hollywood Studio, Call Bureau Cast Service, June 28, 1935):

Will Rogers	Dr. John Pearly	Francis Ford	Efe
Anne Shirley	Fleety Belle	Stepin Fetchit	Jonah
Irvin S. Cobb	Captain Eli	Raymond Hatton	Matt Abel
Eugene Pallette	Sheriff Rufe Jetters	Roger Imhof	Pappy
John McGuire	Duke	William Benedict	Breck
Berton Churchill	New Moses	Lois Verner	Addie May

Bits

John Lester Johnson	Uncle Jeff	Dell Henderson	Salesman
Pardner Jones	New Elijah	Ernie Shields	Bit
Vester Pegg		Otto Richards	Prisoner
John Tyke		Jack Pennick	Riverman
Wingate Smith	Utility characters	Heinie Conklin	Tattoo artist
Sam Baker		Captain Anderson	Jailer
Fred Kohler, Jr.	Fleety Belle's fiancé	Grace Goodall	Sheriff's wife
Charles B. Middleton	Fleety Belle's father	Ferdinand Munier	Governor
Ben Hall	Fleety Belle's brother	D'Arcy Corrigan	Hangman
Cy Jenks	Farmer	James Marcus	Warden
Louis Mason		Hobart Bosworth	Minister
Robert E. Homans	Race officials	Luke Cosgrove	Labor boss
John Wallace	Character bit		

Synopsis: "Doctor" John Pearly cures all, and everything, with his "world-famous" Pocahontas Remedies as he travels along the lower Mississippi. Those "remedies" are mostly pure alcohol—and therefore popular, even if they cure nothing. Dr. John acquires a collection of waxwork figures, which he plans to display aboard his broken-down riverboat the *Claremore Queen* (named after Mr. Rogers' adopted hometown). His crew consists of the pilot, Duke, his nephew; his engineer, Efe; and Jonah.

Duke, in self-defense and in defense of Fleety Belle, a swamp girl, kills a man. When Duke brings the girl aboard, John Pearly advises him to turn himself in and to tell the truth. The only witness to the fact that it was a case of self-defense is a revivalist who travels up and down the Mississippi River, calling himself the "New Moses."

Without a witness corroborating his claim, Duke is sentenced to death. An appeal fails. Frantically, John Pearly, now Captian Pearly, and Fleety Belle travel up and down the Mississippi searching for the New Moses. No sign of the religious man can be found. The date for Duke's execution is set, and his wish to marry Fleety Belle is carried out in jail, before he is taken to the county seat.

Involved in a Mississippi steamboat race against Captain Eli's *Pride of Paducah* (Mr. Cobb's hometown), the New Moses is spotted along the shore. To lose no time, Captain Pearly does not diminish speed but simply lassoes him in passing and brings him aboard.

Running out of fuel, and about to fall behind, Captain Pearly ropes the passing *Pride of Paducah*, and lets the other boat pull him. Approaching the finishing line, the county seat where Duke's execution is to take place, Captain Pearly orders everything burnable aboard to be sacrificed: first the wood, then the wax figures, and finally the high-proof patent medicine. Powered by almost pure alcohol, the *Claremore Queen* wins the race and arrives in time to present the eyewitness who will clear Duke; thus the execution is halted.

Reviews:

★ " 'Steamboat Round the Bend' in our estimation, is one of the finest films Will Rogers ever made. Its story is heart-warming and full of appeal, and its action contains both action and comedy.

"The star was never better than he is in the straight role of the Mississippi River captain who is faced with the absolute necessity of doing two things—winning a race and saving his nephew from being hanged.

"The picture captures your interest from the opening."

Kansas City Star, September 1935

★ "It is high among the best films ever made by Mr. Rogers, is valorous entertainment, and will arouse in audiences no emotion beyond that of admiration for the actor."

The Literary Digest, September 28, 1935

Recognition: ★ # 20 of Year's Best Films, as voted by 451 national film critics

Steamboat Round the Bend

When Will Rogers was killed on August 15, 1935, Fox had two of his films ready for release—In Old Kentucky and Steamboat Round the Bend. What to do? When a beloved star died, tradition in the past had been for the producer to be concerned about the display of poor taste by showing the still-unreleased films. The thought had been that audiences would not wish to see their favorite on screen, knowing that he, or she, had died. Thus it had been with Wallace Reid, Rudolph Valentino, Mabel Normand, and others. Yet not one single film of those stars ever went unreleased.

With the films of Will Rogers, exactly the opposite seemed true. Immediately crowds flocked to those theaters playing earlier films. People who might ordinarily not have gone, went, just to see Will Rogers one more time. There was a nationwide clamor to re-release all the earlier films. This Fox would not do at that time. A company spokesman declared that Fox would not seek to profit from the tragedy. And while Will Rogers' last two films were released, Fox wanted to play it safe. Hoping to keep the memory of its number-one box-office attraction fresh for the two yet-to-be released films, it was decided to release the stronger of the two films first. In the company's view, that was Steamboat Round the Bend, which was released a mere nine days after Will Rogers' death—first in the Mid- and Far West. Pleased with the response, it was released everywhere.

Apparently one scene—the final one—was changed. According to an unidentified newspaper clipping on hand, this is what took place:

When *Steamboat Round the Bend* was made, the closing scene showed Will Rogers waving farewell to Irvin Cobb, as Cobb's boat faded out of the picture. The last thing one saw was Will waving farewell. Had that scene been left in the picture, it seems to me, every spectator would have felt as if he saw Will waving farewell to the world, and to him. I have heard that Cobb urged the cutters to save that scene, as the most effective thing in the picture. But the final decision was that it wouldn't do, as it would send audiences away from the theater crying.

Will confers with Irvin S. Cobb (*center*) and director John Ford. The trio worked together on Cobb's stories of *Judge Priest*, 1934, and when Cobb appeared as a rival riverboat captain in *Steamboat Round the Bend*, 1935.

Hollywood, August 20, 1935

"Will Rogers' picture 'Steamboat Round the Bend' opens Saturday, the 24th, at Loew's State, L.A. and Grauman's Chinese here on a single bill. Rushing in this picture necessitates pulling 'Curly Top.' No ad campaign for Fox Westcoast on 'Steamboat' until Friday evening papers when half page splashes will be taken with regular linage thereafter. . . . 'Steamboat' also opens on the 24th at the California Theatre at Stockton, California."

Variety, August 21, 1935

Chicago, August 20, 1935

"Grosses on Will Rogers pictures zoomed into high ground throughout this territory with news of the fatal accident last Friday. 'Doubting Thomas,' current release, is now playing in a number of subsequent theaters. Theaters report that they are getting heavy play, even from that portion of the public who were never Rogers picture fans. Exhibs have been hustling over to the exchange to secure re-releases on Rogers pictures, particularly 'David Harum' and 'Judge Priest.' But all Fox exchanges received a general order from the home office, that none of the Rogers pictures are to be permitted as re-dates in any theater at this time. Fox Films prefers that the theaters first play the two as yet unreleased Rogers flicks 'Steamboat Round the Bend' and 'In Old Kentucky.'"

Variety, August 21, 1935

Full-Page Ad

"So that our position may be fully understood, we have steadfastly refused to make announcements as to our policy on the Will Rogers pictures, old or new, until everything that human mortals could do for Will Rogers had been done. That time is now past. We have been deluged with telegrams and letters. . . .

"We have refused, and will refuse, to re-issue any of the old pictures at this time, or take care of the hundreds of demands for spot bookings of the older Rogers pictures. We believe that the orderly showing of these pictures, without making any attempt to cash in on the publicity by the re-issuing of old pictures, is the only decent and proper way to handle it. And that will be our policy. It is our opinion that Will Rogers will live in the memory of the people of the world for many, many years to come and that there will be a legitimate demand to see the work of this great character from time to time. But we refuse to make any attempt to cash in on that, which would not have come to us, except in the regular, orderly way. We believe this would have been Will Rogers' wish if he were here today to express himself."

S. R. Kent
President,
Fox Film Corporation
Variety, August 28, 1935

Will Rogers Wrote

Couple of weeks ago we were up on the Sacramento River making a movie with Irvin Cobb and director Jack Ford (who directed *Judge Priest*).

Well, sir, I had a happy experience. I knew he was up there somewhere, I didn't know just where, as I hear from him every little while, but I hadn't seen him in years, that was Buck McKee. Buck McKee was the cowboy that used to work with me in a vaudeville act and rode the horse, or little cowpony rather, Teddy. He trained the pony for the stage. He wasn't any trick pony; he just worked on a smooth board stage, with felt bottom boots buckled on his feet like galoshes, and ran for my fancy roping catches. But Buck trained him to do on a slick stage what a good cowpony can do on the ground.

We started the act in the spring of 1905, just exactly thirty years to a week from when I met Buck up in Sacramento. He was with me for I think it was four or five years. We made two trips to Europe together. We went over just one year after I had opened on the stage. That was in the spring of 1906. We went to the Wintergarten Theater in Berlin, that was the premier vaudeville theater of all Europe. We played there a month. The act was quite a novelty, as it was the first one to ever use a running horse to be lassoed at on the stage.

We came back from Berlin to London and played the Palace Theatre there; then we went back to London in 1908. We also played in that very same Sacramento in the hot summer of 1907 on what was called the Sullivan and Considine Circuit. J. C. Nugent, the splendid actor and playwright, with all his talented family was on the bill and Billy Hanlon's was our hang-out. He is now the proprietor of the big and fine Senator Hotel in Sacramento.

I went out to their ranch at Roseville, a beautiful little town about twenty miles out of Sacramento toward Reno. We just stood and looked at each other, Buck and I. Here, thirty years ago we had stepped on the stage together, only he was on horseback. He always said, "I can get away if anything happens, but the audience can get you." Those were great old days, but darn it, any old days are great old days. Even the tough ones, after they are over, you can look back with great memories.

I was married too in 1908. And sometimes the salary wasn't any too big to ship Buck and his wife and Teddy, and my wife and self, to the next town. In fact, I think Buck rode some of the shorter jumps. It was great fun, not a worry. I regret the loss of vaudeville more than any part of it. It was the greatest form of entertainment ever conceived. We was mighty proud to be playing in it. It had class in those days.

Buck looks fine, no older, and of course, I am just practically a babe in arms yet. But lots of old friends and old-timers will want to know about Buck. Roseville, Cal., will catch him. Well, old-timers talk too much, so I must shut up.

Syndicated column, June 2, 1935

Will Rogers Said

I first want to tell the radio audience where I am at. I am broadcasting from Sacramento, California. That's the beautiful state capital, located in the civilized end of the state.

We are up here in Sacramento with a movie company, and the legislature, they are here, and people can't hardly tell which is which.

We are up here making a comedy called *Steamboat*

Round the Bend. We are taking scenes on the river. We could have worked on the Los Angeles River, but they would have had to haul the water too far. Mr. McAdoo, our senator, is going to see if he can't get them to irrigate this Los Angeles River.

Anyhow, we are making a comedy, while the legislature is going to have a little drama. They are going to put a tax on movies—three times bigger than anywhere else. But the joke of it to us in the movies is that it won't hook us as bad, because we don't have to pay on what we are advertised that we get paid. We only have to pay on what we really get. So this legislature, when they collect that new tax, they are going to get a terrible jolt.

You know, in this movie thing, they don't realize that us movie folks, our careers don't last very long. You know, naturally we are just in as long as our looks—well, now take me, I'm going twice a week now for a facial, and I'm liable to have to stretch that out into three times.

But they are doing pretty good, the legislature. The other day they repealed a law where everybody—when you used to get married you used to have to give three days notice in this state to show intention of marrying. Well, they did away with that now. That was longer than most of the marriages in California was lasting. Now you don't have to file any intention of marrying at all. You just pay a small amusement tax—is all.

Anyhow, we are up here, working on this film. It is supposed to be a scene laid on the Ohio River near Paducah, Kentucky, Mr. Cobb's home. We couldn't put it there, because he couldn't go back. In the story, which is from a very popular book called *Steamboat Round the Bend*, we play steamboat captains. Cobb is the captain of the *Pride of Paducah*, and I'm the admiral of the *Claremore Queen*. Mr. Cobb is the author also of our most popular picture, *Judge Priest*, and he is getting another Judge Priest type of story ready for us.

And now I take great pleasure in introducing my very good friend, and one of America's greatest humorists, writers, and an all-around human being, Irvin Cobb. Hullo, Irv.

WR: Well, you're out here, Irvin. How do you like Hollywood?
IC: Asking a man how he likes Hollywood is like asking a man with a wen on his nose how he likes having the wen on his nose. You in time get used to a wen on your nose, but you never really care for it.
WR: What is a wen? You know I'm from Oklahoma. Is it a wart?
IC: You can call it a wart.
WR: I didn't know what it was, honest I didn't. Do you like the movie business?
IC: I didn't know it was a business, I thought it was a racket.
WR: The longer you stay in it the more you realize it is, that's right. What would your advice be to men of your age and looks? Would it be to come to Hollywood?
IC: If there is one that answers to that description, it is a rotten thing to say about both of us, and I would rather he didn't come. I don't want any competition.
WR: What do you do to keep your weight down like it is?
IC: I don't keep my weight down; it is my weight that is keeping me down.
WR: You do, you are looking a little thinner, I believe. Have you ever seen Greta Garbo?
IC: No, I never saw her. I think Garbo must be like Santa Claus. Everybody talks about it, nobody ever sees one. But I'm living in the house she used to live in. She left me a legacy, too. I found a Swedish hot water bottle after she left.
WR: He is at that, living in her house. He bought this place.
IC: Some people who haven't heard the news drive in looking for Greta, and they see me sitting there, and as one old lady from the Middlewest said, "Oh, Lord, how that girl has changed," and rolled right out.
WR: Say, do you feel yourself kind of going Hollywood in any way? You know, we all kind of do, it kind of gets us down here.
IC: Well, I find that I am talking to myself, and worse than that, I am answering back.
WR: And saying your own yesses, eh?
IC: Yes, I'm living in yes-man's-land, which is worse than no-man's-land was during the war.
WR: Say, now listen, who is your favorite male actor?
IC: In affection to you, as a tribute to you, I ought to say my favorite performer is Will Rogers, but since I must be honest before this great audience, I'll admit that my favorite is Stepin Fetchit.

Radio broadcast, May 19, 1935

Interview with Irvin S. Cobb

We went out to make *Steamboat Round the Bend*. The first day of shooting, Will and I were to have a scene together.

"Do either of you two gentlemen by any chance happen to have the faintest idea of what this story is about?" inquired John Ford, with his gentle, Celtic sarcasm, which can be so biting.

"I don't, for one," confessed Rogers, and grinned sheepishly. "Something about a river, ain't it? Well, I was raised in Claremore, Oklahoma, where we don't have any rivers to speak of, so you might say I'm a stranger here, myself."

"I thought so," murmured Ford, who had directed Rogers before. "And I don't suppose, Mr. Rogers, you've gone so far as to glance at the script?"

"Been too busy ropin' calves," admitted Rogers. "Tell you what, John, you sort of generally break the news to us what this sequence is all about and I'll think up a line for Cobb to speak and then Cobb'll think up a line for me to speak, and that way there will be no ill feelings and the feller that can remember after it's all over what the plot is about—if there is any plot by then—gets first prize, which will be a kiss on the forehead from Mister John Ford."

As heaven is my judge, that is how we did the scene with Ford sitting by as solemn as a hoot owl.

Interview with Ben Lucien Burman, May 4, 1977

You see, John Ford bought the book from me. I had been paid a lot of money for the serial rights in the *Pictorial Review*—now let's keep in mind that this is 1933—and my wife, Alice, and I went out to Hollywood. I was a very bad manager in those days. I had a very expensive apartment and spent all my money, and it was the bottom of the depression. Here we are, my wife and I, stuck with this expensive apartment and all my money gone. So Alice had read somewhere that lentils were the most nutritious and cheapest food that you could get, so we had lentils for breakfast, we had lentils for lunch, and lentils for dinner, and I remember our dessert generally consisted of something you could get in the drugstore—an Eskimo Pie, called the Milk Nickel. Very often, if you were lucky, you got a nickel wrapped in waxed paper inside, so it didn't cost you anything. That was our dessert.

Now John Ford offered me ten thousand dollars for the film rights. Five-hundred dollars for an option, and ninety-five hundred dollars on picking up the option—or a percentage. I said: "John, I am tired of living on lentils, I'll take the cash." It was 1933, and nobody had any money at all.

Just as an aside, a friend of mine at Twentieth Century-Fox, I happened to be out on the coast in 1946—now this was before television, and you know they televised this film greatly—so this friend looked up the figures, and I would have made—up to that time—three hundred fifty thousand dollars if I had taken the percentage deal they offered.

Now there is more to the story. Alice's cousin out on the coast was a physician, and after John gave me the option of five hundred dollars, and they paid it, I developed something on my arm that I had never had before. So I went to see Alice's cousin and he diagnosed it as herpes zoster—shingles. He told me: "You got so nervous wondering whether John Ford will take up the option, or not, that you developed this case of shingles." Obviously John picked up the option, and I got the ninety-five hundred dollars and the shingles disappeared—and so did the lentils.

The book had had a lot of publicity and had been a terrific hit, which is probably one of the reasons why they bought it. So the producer, Sol Wurtzel, said to me: "We've done a thing you are going to like. We have changed the time of the story [you see it was con-temporary when I wrote it] back to the nineties. We wanted to give it a faraway feeling."

Well, I didn't like it.

Then he said, in the very next breath, "Then we've done another thing you're going to like. We've changed the name of the boat" from whatever I had it, I think I called it the *Bayou Queen*—that's my recollection, after all, it's been how many years? I wrote this in 1933 and I have written an awful lot of books since then. Well, Sol Wurtzel went on: "We're going to change the name of the *Bayou Queen* to the *Claremore Queen*—that's Will Rogers' hometown and we thought that would be nice." In one gulp they set the story back fifty years, and in the next they named the boat for a living person. So that was typical Hollywood, and that wasn't all.

Having bought the book for publicity, partly, they now decided to change the title, too. They were going to call it *Steamboat Bill*, which made me sick. And Will was furious, he was absolutely furious. I, of course, had no power, I was a young writer, this was only my second film. But Will had quite a lot of power, so he began to work against it.

You know that the film story depends on a missing witness. I wouldn't write that kind of a story today, but I was very young then. The missing witness was called the "New Moses," one of those phony prophets, who had witnessed this murder. Will Rogers' nephew—in the story—had committed this crime in self-defense, but there was only the New Moses who had witnessed it. So you see there is this search for this prophet, the New Moses. So one day, we were on the set—you see, I was stage-struck, I was on the set every day. They were shooting and they had a phony pilothouse, you know, just part of a boat, with the pilothouse going along on rollers, past the camera. Will in the pilothouse was leaning out, calling to the crowd on shore: "Has anyone here seen the New Moses?" And somebody in the crowd on shore would call back: "No, we ain't even seen the Old Moses!"

And they would shoot another scene, the boat would move along, and again Will would lean out the pilothouse and call: "Has anyone here seen that New Moses?" And back would come the reply: "No, we ain't seen him!"

And finally there was a pause, and Will didn't say a word to me, but they started shooting again, and Will called out again: "Anyone here seen the New Moses? If you see him tell him to tell Winnie Sheehan and Sol

Wurtzel that we got the name changed back to *Steamboat Round the Bend!*"

They would see it in the rushes that night, and this was his way of telling them.

The dialogue was often my dialogue, taken directly from the book. I remember saying to John Ford one day: "John, you used three or four pages of my story today." And he said: "That's a mistake, we'll take it right out!"

They also hired me as a writer for the film at one of their fantastic salaries, but they wouldn't let me write a line—authors were something to be avoided in those days. So to my astonishment one day, the music department called me up and said: "That song you have in the book, *Eagle Nest*, is that a folk song?" I told them: "It's a folk song, all I did is flesh it out and put it in good poetic form." And they said: "Where can we get the music for it? We'd like the music."

I told them that I didn't have the faintest idea, but if they sent their scouts around Natchez, Mississippi, they might be able to pick it up. I only heard it once in all my river travels, and it was sung by a literally crazy man, and it was a beautiful thing, and I remembered it—but not the music. Well, a couple of weeks later, they called me up and said: "We can't find any trace of the music, what are we going to do—we want that song."

Well, I was born with Negro music in my ears and I played the mandolin, and so I said, okay, I'll write you the music. I sat down one night and wrote five themes that I thought would capture the feeling that I wanted, very poignant. But I am no professional musician, and here I go to the music department, which was then a tremendous affair, and I forget now the name of the head of it, he had been the assistant conductor of the Philharmonic, and they were really great musicians; and with the worst voice in the world, I started to sing the songs. On the third one they stopped me and said: "This is great, this is terrific, this is going to be the musical hit of 1935!" And they were going to orchestrate it and build the whole film around it. They made me sign a contract for the sheet music and radio rights and the phonograph record rights.

Now by pure coincidence, that night my wife and I happened to see *Unfinished Symphony*, the film about the life of Schubert, and I said to my wife: "Isn't it extraordinary that on the day I start my new career as a composer, that I should see this film?" And my wife said: "You're crazy!" She just thought I was absolutely mad.

Well, time passed; they brought the—which one was it?—the Hal Johnson Choir out to sing, and they spent fifty thousand dollars on this number, and everybody said: "Oh, I hear you have written the great musical hit of the year." And finally they had a preview of the film, and, of course, my great interest was what they had done with my music. Imagine, and you will see it when you watch the movie, in one corner of the marriage scene in prison, you will hear a faint hum, a faint background of the music. That's it! That's the song I wrote! They had decided not to use music in the film! So that was my experience . . . oh! The climax came—now this is what Hollywood was like in those days. Comes the next February, I get a special-delivery letter from the Academy Awards Committee. So I said, eh, this is great; maybe they liked my book, and I opened it, and I memorized that letter—I still remember it: "Dear Mr. Burman, as one of the outstanding composers for the screen, we would like to have you submit what you consider your best musical work of the year." And that is my brief career as a composer.

IN OLD KENTUCKY

A 20th Century Production, Copyright September 6, 1935, LP 6188; renewed August 21, 1963, R 320841; b&w; sound; 9 reels, 7,649 ft. Shooting began April 15, 1935; preview: July 1, 1935; reviewed in Los Angeles, November 22; in Chicago, November 25. Release: Roxy Theatre, NYC. Review in *New York Times*, November 29, 1935. Shooting scripts at AMPAS, UCLA, USC. Extant. Location shots: Santa Anita Racetrack, Carleton Burke's stock ranch.

Production Staff: Producer: Edward Butcher; director: George Marshall; assistant director: Ray Flynn; cameraman: L. W. O'Connell; from play (1894) by Charles T. Dazey; screenplay by Sam Hellman and Gladys Lehman; additional dialogue: Henry Johnson; music director: Arthur Lange; editor: Jack Murray; recording engineer: W. D. Flick; art director: William Darling; wardrobe: William Lambert; unit manager: Percy Ikerd.

Cast   (Fox Movietone Studio, Call Bureau Cast Service, May 31, 1935):

Will Rogers	Steve Tapley	Charles Sellon	Ezra Martingale
Dorothy Wilson	Nancy Martingale	Charles Richman	Pole Shattuck
Russell Hardie	Lee Andrews	Esther Dale	Dolly Breckenridge
Bill Robinson	Wash Jackson	Etienne Girardot	Pluvius J. Aspinwall, the rainmaker
Louise Henry	Arlene Shattuck	John Ince	The sheriff
Alan Dinehart	Slick Doherty		

Bits

Fritz Johannet	Jockey	Dora Clemant	Saleslady
Everett Sullivan	Jailer	Ned Norton	Bookie
G. Raymond (Bill) Nye	Deputy officer	Eddie Tamblyn	Jockey
William J. Worthington	Bit	Allen Caven	Steward
Edward Le Saint	Steward	Stanley Andrews	Steward
Bobby Rose	Jockey		

Synopsis: Steve Tapley trains racehorses for a millionaire's stable, while befriending an aged neighbor, Ezra Martingale. Ezra also raises horses, but on a much smaller scale; however, he carries on a one-man feud against Tapley's employer. Whenever and wherever he can, he will try to best his rival. Nancy Martingale, Ezra's daughter, falls in love with Lee Andrews, the young veterinarian.

An important race is coming up, and naturally, the Martingales have an entry against their neighbor. But Ezra's entry has a chance to win only if the track is muddy. And so Pluvius J. Aspinwall, the famous rainmaker, is hired to make certain that on the day of the race, the track is very muddy.

With Tapley playing Cupid, and with Pluvius plying his trade, the two young lovers are united, and Nancy's horse wins the race.

Reviews: ★ "*In Old Kentucky* has been released throughout the country. The same absence of morbidity which made audience reaction to *Steamboat Round the Bend* so remarkable, when that picture was shown soon after his death early this fall, is apparent now. Audiences in the West and New England are flocking to the film and reacting to it much as though the comedian still were alive."

The Literary Digest, November 30, 1935

★ ". . . so entertaining is it that the spectator is carried along by the cheerful mood of the story, and not until the end is suddenly overcome by the realization that there can be no more such films."

Boston Herald, November 1935

★ "Fast, laughter-laden farce lets Will Rogers leave 'em smiling in the fun-freighted picture which comes as his final gesture to the Roxy Theatre. Will, the well-beloved, was never more entertaining, never in truer form, nor more universally appealing. . . . Carping critics may smile at the obvious hokum of the piece, but any supercilious snickers will be lost in genuine hilarity before the piece gets even well under way. . . ."

New York American, November 30, 1935

★ "Rogers seldom tried harder to bring happiness to his followers than in *In Old Kentucky*. Rogers seems to bring his whole career to a climax in this, his last performance. Heretofore dialogue was Rogers' forte. In *In Old Kentucky* he shows screen audiences how to clown in movie language.

"Rogers has sung, danced and blackened his face for your pleasure in the current film. Dancing obviously was a talent which waited to be discovered by Bill Robinson."

Elsie Finn, in the *Philadelphia Record*

With Esther Dale, *In Old Kentucky*, 1935.

A dance lesson from the master, Bill ("Bojangles") Robinson, from *In Old Kentucky*, 1935.

Will Rogers Said

This is the home of the famous Santa Anita racetrack. We are here shooting some race sences. I can't even pick the winner in a movie race where it's fixed.

Syndicated column, May 6, 1935

★

I been busy on a movie. It's called *In Old Kentucky*. It was one of the most famous old plays of our young days. I never was fortunate enough to see it, but I heard a lot about it. It was written by Mr. Dazey. He has a son, Frank Dazey, that's a fine scenario writer, and also his wife is a dandy scenario writer. She is called Agnes Johnson.

When our youngest kid Jimmy was about twelve, he used to play polo. He had a couple of little old ponies, and he played quite a bit with the women, and Agnes played, and Jimmy had heard all the other women call her "Aggie" so he used to holler, "Leave it Aggie, leave it Aggie!

My wife told him he shouldn't call a lady by her first or nickname. Jim said, "Well, when you are going so fast and you want her to leave the ball, you haven't got time to say a lot of names. I can't holler 'Leave it Mrs. Agnes Johnson Dazey!' The game would be over by then."

Well, I got to get back to *Old Kentucky*. Anyhow, we are working out at a fine stock ranch owned by Mr. Carleton Burke, the head of California's racing commission.

Syndicated column, May 12, 1935

★

I have been working pretty hard (laugh) on some movies. It just happened that I almost had three right in a row. Now, that don't mean that they will be released as fast as we made 'em. They only come out about every four months, but we got a couple ahead, already made, and that means that I will have little time off to do a few things I had been planning on and that I won't look like I am trying to get in front of every camera that is grinding.

Well, after I finish a long siege, I sorter begin to looking up in the air and see what is flying over, and Mrs. Rogers in her wise way will say: "Well, I think you better get on one. You are getting sorter nervous."

Syndicated column, July 14, 1935

Hollywood, August 20, 1935

"Hollywood dates Will Rogers' last gag as of July 30, a few days before he left for Alaska. The comedian heard there was a shortage of office space on the lot for the merged staffs of 20th Century-Fox, so he called up Darryl Zanuck and offered to rent him the fancy studio bungalow Fox had built for him, but which Rogers never occupied."

Variety, August 21, 1935

Will Rogers' contract with Fox called for "no less than three, and no more than four" motion pictures per year. Will liked to work on his films consecutively, in the shortest period of time, which would allow him the maximum time away from the studio afterward. He wanted to complete one picture and then immediately start on the next one.

With Life Begins at Forty, Doubting Thomas, In Old Kentucky, *and* Steamboat Round the Bend, *Will Rogers would have lived up to his contractual obligation in the first half of 1935, and he would have had the second half of the year to himself; however, there had been talk of one additional film.*

AH, WILDERNESS!

The year is 1934. Having appeared in wild west shows, circuses, vaudeville, musical comedies, the Follies, and motion pictures, Will Rogers enters a new arena of show business, the legitimate theater. The play is Eugene O'Neill's Ah, Wilderness!

George M. Cohan had opened in the role of Nat Miller on Broadway to rave reviews, and Will Rogers had been approached by producer Henry Duffy to play the part in a West Coast production. After months of coaxing, Rogers had at last accepted. With his friend Fred Stone as adviser, he had rehearsed the first straight role of his career:

And say, you have to learn lines, not my lines, but Eugene O'Neill's lines. He is that highbrow writer, and I have quite a bit of trouble reading 'em, much less learning 'em. For instance: "So that's where you drive the Tumbril from and piled poor Pierpont on it."

Now that is a sort of saying from Carlyle's French Revolution but that word "Tumbril," what you boys from the forks of the creek going to do with that? I couldn't handle it. I imagine it's sorter like an old buckboard, with the slats out.

Course this play, *Ah, Wilderness!*, is pretty sane outside of a few of those "Tumbrils." It's just a homely old family affair that's laid around New England in 1906.

★

The show opened in San Francisco. This is what News-Week *printed:*

The shrewd, simple philosophy of Nat Miller might have been written for Mr. Rogers, so easily does he slip into the part and make it his own.

And the New York Times *thought the event important enough to cover:*

He [Will Rogers] made Nat Miller a delightful personage, and in the father's scene with his adolescent son, Richard, he played with a simple sincerity that brought out handkerchiefs and made tears and smiles mingle.

Now let Eddie Cantor, Will's friend since 1913, tell the story:

When Eugene O'Neill's play *Ah, Wilderness!* opened in San Francisco, Will played the lead. His performance had the audience throwing their hats in the air and the critics their adjectives even higher. But during the play's run something happened which, I feel sure, indirectly led to his death. Will received a letter from a clergyman: "Relying on you to give the public nothing that could bring the blush of shame to the cheeks of a Christian, I attended your performance with my 14-year-old daughter. But when you did the scene in which the father lectures the son on the subject of his relations with an immoral woman, I took my daughter by the hand and we left the theater. I have not been able to look her in the eye since."

This so disturbed Rogers that he finally withdrew from the play. He also asked to be released from his commitment to do the screen version for Metro-Goldwyn-Mayer, promising to do another film in its place as soon as a suitable script was found. While waiting, Will accepted an invitation from the famous pilot, Wiley Post, to fly around the world—the trip which ended in the death of both men.

Will Rogers opened the limited engagement of Ah, Wilderness! *on April 30, 1934, at the Curran Theatre, in San Francisco. It was understood from the very beginning that there would be a three-week run in San Francisco and that the show would also play three weeks at the El Capitan Theatre in Los Angeles. Advance sales in Los Angeles were extremely heavy, however, and the attendance figures set records for West Coast theater audiences. The El Capitan Theatre had 1,571 seats, with top prices for matinees $1.65 and for evenings $2.00. To accommodate the crowds in Los Angeles during the third week, Will Rogers agreed to an additional matinee show, thus giving nine performances in one week, for a gross revenue*

of $18,500. When approached by the producer, Will agreed to a fourth week; revenue was $22,000 for ten performances, the extra performance being given on Sunday. And still more people wanted to see the show. Will agreed to extend the show's run to a fifth week, with again nine performances. And then there was still another week—the sixth; in all some 72,000 came to the El Capitan Theatre.

It would seem that with three extensions—doubling the length of the planned run—Will Rogers was not exactly anxious to leave the show—unless, of course, the accusing letter mentioned by Eddie Cantor came during the final week, and it was then that Will would not extend the run any further.

Variety *wrote after the closing: "[This show] could have continued indefinitely."*★

Why then did this show close? For the three weeks in San Francisco and the six weeks in Los Angeles, the show grossed $190,000—so said Variety—*a record total. Why did Will not continue?* Variety *offered an explanation: "Engagement was terminated only because of picture work of Rogers' at Fox prevented his continuing doubling for screen and stage." This may have been the official reason issued by the production office, however.* Ah, Wilderness! *closed on Saturday night, June 30, 1934. Ten days later, Will was in Texas, visiting, and by the twenty-second, he was aboard the S.S. Malolo, on his way to Honolulu and a trip around the world. Will Rogers would not return to America until the last week of September 1934.*

So it seems that the story released to the press, that the closing was due to pressing "picture work at Fox," is not quite the true reason. If, however, a letter such as the one quoted by Eddie Cantor was received by Will Rogers, his reaction, as described above, would be perfectly consistent with his character. While he thought it to be "just a homely old family affair," and while millions would see nothing wrong in a scene the New York Times *described as one Will Rogers "played with a simple sincerity that brought out handkerchiefs and made tears and smiles mingle," Will Rogers would never wish to continue in any endeavor once it had been found even slightly objectionable.*

As for the film version of Ah, Wilderness!, *Metro-Goldwyn-Mayer went ahead with its plans for the production. Studio News, M-G-M's in-house publication, reported in large headlines:* BEERY, BARRYMORE IN "AH, WILDERNESS!" *and went on to tell about the company's departure for Massachusetts for the filming of exterior scenes. One of the paragraphs said:*

Based upon Eugene O'Neill's stage play, *Ah, Wilderness!* brings [Lionel] Barrymore to the screen in the role of Dad Miller, made famous by George M. Cohan in the East and by Will Rogers in the Western presentation.

The date of this publication is Thursday, August 8,

★July 3, 1934, p. 63:1/2.

1935. If Will Rogers had been prepared to make this film on loan from Fox, he would have been on his way to New England with the rest of the cast.

Instead, on August 8, 1935, Will Rogers was in Juneau, Alaska, firmly committed to a trip that would end tragically one week later near Barrow.

POSTSCRIPT

No man without a title or office was ever so missed and mourned as was Will Rogers. Women and men, alike, young and old, whether in the cities or in rural areas, they all knew Will Rogers. He was not some impersonal writer or distant movie star; millions who had never met him thought of him as a close member of their family, and loved him well. And now he had died. The shock of the loss stunned the nation, and it grieved.

One hundred fifty thousand walked silently past his bier, guarded by eight fliers from the army post at Marsh Field. Services were held privately in the little chapel at Forest Lawn Memorial Park. At that same moment, a public memorial program was conducted in the Hollywood Bowl, where more than twenty thousand gathered. The NBC and CBS radio networks went off the air for half an hour of silence, beginning at two o'clock, the time of the services. Motion-picture theaters throughout the country darkened their screens for two minutes, in silent tribute. Expressions of sorrow came from President

M-G-M Studio News announces departure of cast for filming of *Ah, Wilderness!* in New England. Note date: August 8, 1935.

This newspaper photograph of Will Rogers and Wiley Post carries the dateline Juneau, August 8, 1935. If Will had been prepared to make the film *Ah, Wilderness!* he would have been on his way to New England instead.

173

Roosevelt and high government officials, from rich and unemployed, from cities and villages.

Congress voted five hundred thousand dollars for a memorial, which was wisely vetoed by President Roosevelt; private donations poured in. The money thus collected was eventually used to establish scholarships—still active today—at universities in Texas, Oklahoma, and California.

With Wiley Post, inspecting equipment to be carried on flight.

The motion-picture industry decided on its own permanent memorial, The Will Rogers Hospital project, then at Saranac Lake, New York, now at White Plains, New York.

Remembrances to Will Rogers are in many places; from Barrow, Alaska, to Fort Worth, Texas, from southern California to the island of Manhattan there are statues and memorials, there are high schools and libraries, sports arenas and hotels, motels, parks, streets, and even churches named after him.

Will Rogers is the only comedian to have two United States postage stamps issued in his memory. Nicaragua issued a set of five stamps bearing his likeness, as an expression of gratitude for being among the first to bring assistance immediately after the 1931 earthquake. Will is the only humorist to have his statue in the nation's Capitol Building, in Washington, D.C. A Polaris-type submarine bears his name, sharing this distinction with George Washington, Thomas Jefferseon, Francis Scott Key, Benjamin Franklin, and Robert E. Lee.

The toll road from the Missouri border to Tulsa, Oklahoma, is the Will Rogers Turnpike; the new government office building in Oklahoma City carries his name. In the West, a strip of the California coast is named in his honor, while in the East, at Newark Airport, the observation deck was dedicated to Will's memory. And almost within sight of the Atlantic Ocean, high above the Hudson River, rotates a beacon on the peak of the eastern support of the George Washington Bridge. Its beam is intended to warn low-flying aircraft of the danger. On all navigational charts it is identified as the Will Rogers–Wiley Post Memorial Beacon.

When the National Cowboy Hall of Fame and Western Heritage Center was founded by seventeen western states, Will Rogers was the first to be unanimously voted into it.

Almost fifty years have passed since his death and still people flock to the memorials in his honor. At Pacific Palisades, California, is Will's last home. The "Ranch," as it is called, is on Sunset Boulevard, about two miles from the Pacific Ocean. Any visitor must make a special trip to drive there; it is not on the way to any other landmark. Last year more visitors came to the Ranch than the entire population of San Francisco, St. Louis, or Washington, D.C.

On the eastern slopes of the Rocky Mountains, at Colorado Springs, Colorado, pointing like a finger toward heaven, stands the Will Rogers Shrine. Over a quarter of a million tourists visit here each year. Every fifteen minutes chimes play and can be heard up to twenty miles away. Will would find the location of this memorial amusing, for the sound of the chimes carries easily to the U.S. Air Force Academy nearby. Will was one of the foremost pioneers in aviation, advocating a strong air force. Stranger still, the shrine is built on the side of Cheyenne Mountain, which contains NORAD (North American Defense Command); Rogers was among the first to warn of attacks from the air in future wars.

Will and Wylie in Alaska with Seppala, famed dogsled racer, and, *far right*, veteran pilot Joe Crosson. (*National Air and Space Museum, Smithsonian Institution*)

Close-up of wrecked plane. (*National Air and Space Museum, Smithsonian Institution*)

Eskimo camp by Walakpa Lagoon.

Wiley Post beside plane while fuel tanks are being topped for departure.

The California ranch house: family bedrooms are upstairs, to the right, over family room; dining room is to the left, with guest rooms overhead.

Living area with artifacts and mementos sent by friends and fans; some of Rogers' substantial Charles M. Russell collection are on display.

Living area with staircase to guest rooms. The calf, a gift from friend, western artist Ed Borein, lost its ears—worn away by Will's constant roping.

Present-day photo of dining area with portraits of Betty and Will.

About two miles from tiny Oologah, Oklahoma, is Will's birthplace. The house still stands, though it had to be moved to higher ground when an engineering project created the Oologah Reservoir. Most of the sixty thousand acres of Clem Rogers' grazing range, where Will rode his first pony, are now underwater.

The memorial at Claremore, Oklahoma, was built by Will's native state for its favorite son. Will had bought the twenty acres on which it stands and had planned to retire there someday. After his death, the family turned the land over to the state, and now Will's final resting place is there; beside him are Betty, his wife, and Fred, their infant son.

There, too, at Claremore, are his films and manuscripts. At a brand-new theater you can see some of the films and learn firsthand what made Will Rogers such a popular performer.

Of all the remarkable things to be seen there—as in California and Colorado—the most surprising is the youth of the visitors. They come by the hundreds of thousands, students, newlyweds, young couples bringing their small children. Obviously there exists no personal bond with this generation as there still does between Will and their parents and grandparents, but it seems as if a legacy of that bond has been passed from age to age.

No one has taken Will Rogers' place. America is still looking for another man like him. Every time a new humorist appears, he is at first dubbed "another Will Rogers." But Will was far more than just a humorist—though he was the best. He was the most widely read columnist of his day; he was the nation's most widely listened to radio commentator, its number-one motion-picture star. He was both cowboy and Indian, philosopher and philanthropist; he was "congressman-at-large," and he was America's "unofficial president."

Perhaps England's foremost theater critic, James Agate, observing Will Rogers in the Charles Cochran Revue, *phrased it most poignantly when he wrote in the* London Times, *Sunday, July 25, 1926: "A superior power had seen fit to fling into the world, for once a truly fine specimen, fine in body, fine in soul, fine in intellect. . . ."*

★

He loved and was loved by the American people. His memory will ever be in benediction with the hosts of his countrymen who felt the spell of that kindly humor which, while seeing facts, could always laugh at fantasy. That was why his message went straight to the heart of his fellow men.

We pay grateful homage to the memory of a man who helped the nation to smile. And, after all, I doubt if there is among us a more useful citizen than the one who holds the secret of banishing gloom, of making tears give way to laughter, of supplanting desolation and despair with hope and courage.

There was something infectious about his humor. His appeal went straight to the heart of the nation. Above all things, in a time grown too solemn and sober he brought his countrymen back to a sense of proportion.

Franklin Delano Roosevelt

INDEX